Microsoft® Official Academic Course

Networking Fundamentals, Exam 98-366

WILEY

VP & PUBLISHER	Barry Pruett
SENIOR EXECUTIVE EDITOR	Jim Minatel
MICROSOFT PRODUCT MANAGER	Microsoft Learning
SENIOR EDITORIAL ASSISTANT	Devon Lewis
TECHNICAL EDITOR	Ron Handlon
CHANNEL MARKETING MANAGER	Michele Szczesniak
CONTENT MANAGEMENT DIRECTOR	Lisa Wojcik
CONTENT MANAGER	Nichole Urban
PRODUCTION COORDINATOR	Nicole Repasky
PRODUCTION EDITOR	Umamaheswari Gnanamani
COVER DESIGNER	Tom Nery

COVER PHOTO: © shutterstock/wavebreakmedia

This book was set in Garamond by SPi Global and printed and bound by Quad/Graphics.
The covers were printed by Quad/Graphics.

ISBN: 9781119428824 (PBK)
ISBN: 9781119428848 (EVAL)

The inside back cover will contain printing identification and country of origin if omitted from this page.
In addition, if the ISBN on the back cover differs from the ISBN on this page, the one on the back cover is correct.
V10004220_091318

Preface

Welcome to the Microsoft Official Academic Course (MOAC) program for Networking Fundamentals. MOAC represents the collaboration between Microsoft Learning and John Wiley & Sons, Inc. publishing company. Microsoft and Wiley teamed up to produce a series of textbooks that deliver compelling and innovative teaching solutions to instructors and superior learning experiences for students. Infused and informed by in-depth knowledge from the creators of Microsoft products, and crafted by a publisher known worldwide for the pedagogical quality of its products, these textbooks maximize skills transfer in minimum time. Students are challenged to reach their potential by using their new technical skills as highly productive members of the workforce.

Because this knowledge base comes directly from Microsoft, creator of the Microsoft Certified IT Professional (MCITP), Microsoft Certified Technology Specialist (MCTS), and Microsoft Certified Professional (MCP) exams (www.microsoft.com/learning/certification), you are sure to receive the topical coverage that is most relevant to students' personal and professional success. Microsoft's direct participation not only assures you that MOAC textbook content is accurate and current; it also means that students will receive the best instruction possible to enable their success on certification exams and in the workplace.

■ The Microsoft Official Academic Course Program

The *Microsoft Official Academic Course* series is a complete program for instructors and institutions to prepare and deliver great courses on Microsoft software technologies. With MOAC, we recognize that, because of the rapid pace of change in the technology and curriculum developed by Microsoft, there is an ongoing set of needs beyond classroom instruction tools for an instructor to be ready to teach the course. The MOAC program endeavors to provide solutions for all these needs in a systematic manner in order to ensure a successful and rewarding course experience for both instructor and student—technical and curriculum training for instructor readiness with new software releases; the software itself for student use at home for building hands-on skills, assessment, and validation of skill development; and a great set of tools for delivering instruction in the classroom and lab. All are important to the smooth delivery of an interesting course on Microsoft software, and all are provided with the MOAC program. We think about the model below as a gauge for ensuring that we completely support you in your goal of teaching a great course. As you evaluate your instructional materials options, you may wish to use the model for comparison purposes with available products.

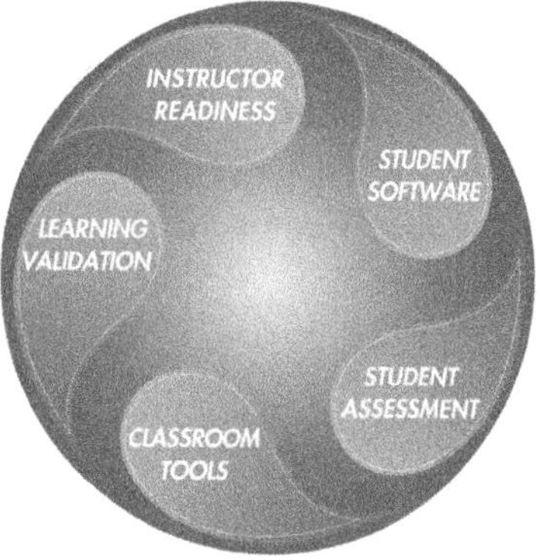

Illustrated Book Tour

Pedagogical Features

The MOAC textbook for Networking Fundamentals is designed to cover all the learning objectives for that MTA exam 98-366, which is referred to as its "objective domain." The Microsoft Technology Associate (MTA) exam objectives are highlighted throughout the textbook. Many pedagogical features have been developed specifically for *Microsoft Official Academic Course* programs.

Presenting the extensive procedural information and technical concepts woven throughout the textbook raises challenges for the student and instructor alike. The Illustrated Book Tour that follows provides a guide to the rich features contributing to *Microsoft Official Academic Course* program's pedagogical plan. Following is a list of key features in each lesson designed to prepare students for success as they continue in their IT education, on the certification exams, and in the workplace:

- Each lesson begins with a **Lesson Skill Matrix**. More than a standard list of learning objectives, the Domain Matrix correlates each software skill covered in the lesson to the specific exam objective domain.
- Concise and frequent **Step-by-Step** instructions teach students new features and provide an opportunity for hands-on practice. Numbered steps give detailed, step-by-step instructions to help students learn software skills.
- **Illustrations:** Screen images provide visual feedback as students work through the exercises. The images reinforce key concepts, provide visual clues about the steps, and allow students to check their progress.
- **Key Terms:** Important technical vocabulary is listed with definitions at the beginning of the lesson. When these terms are used later in the lesson, they appear in bold italic type and are defined. The Glossary contains all of the key terms and their definitions.
- Engaging point-of-use **Reader Aids**, located throughout the lessons, tell students why this topic is relevant (*The Bottom Line*), provide students with helpful hints (*Take Note*). Reader Aids also provide additional relevant or background information that adds value to the lesson.
- **Certification Ready** features throughout the text signal students where a specific certification objective is covered. They provide students with a chance to check their understanding of that particular MTA objective and, if necessary, review the section of the lesson where it is covered. MOAC offers complete preparation for MTA certification.
- **End-of-Lesson Questions:** The Knowledge Assessment section provides a variety of multiple-choice, true-false, matching, and fill-in-the-blank questions.
- **End-of-Lesson Exercises:** Competency Assessment case scenarios, Proficiency Assessment case scenarios, and Workplace Ready exercises are projects that test students' ability to apply what they've learned in the lesson.

Lesson Features

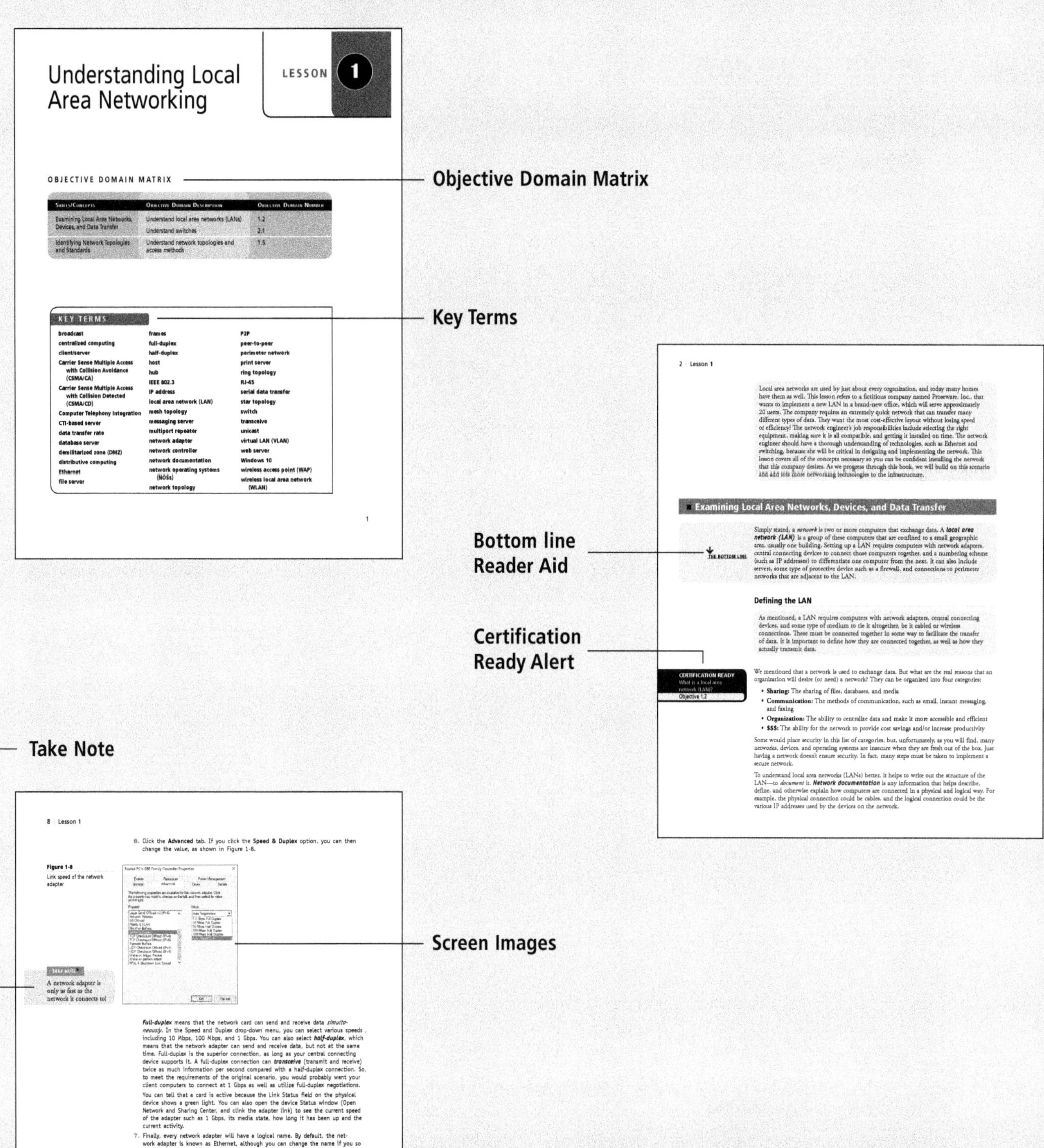

house number and the street you live on, an IP address identifies your computer number and the network it lives on. A common example of an IP address is 192.168.1.1.

Now, every IP address is broken down into two parts: the network portion, in this case 192.168.1, which is the network your computer is a member of, and the host portion, which is the individual number of your computer, differentiating your computer from any others on the network. In this case, it's .1. How do we know this? The subnet mask tells us.

The subnet mask is a group of four numbers that define what IP network the computer is a member of. All of the 255s in a subnet mask collectively refer to the network portion, while the 0s refer to the host portion. This is illustrated in Table 1-1. This table shows a typical Class C IP address and the default corresponding subnet mask. If you were to configure the IP address of a Windows computer as 192.168.1.1, Windows would automatically default to a subnet mask of 255.255.255.0. If any other computers would like to communicate with yours, they need to be configured with the same network number; however, every computer on the same network needs to have a different host number or an IP conflict might ensue. Of course, as a talented administrator, you'll learn how to avoid IP conflicts—and you'll learn some tips on how to do so in Lessons 4 and 5.

Table 1-1

An IP Address and Corresponding Subnet Mask

Type of Address	First Octet	Second Octet	Third Octet	Fourth Octet
IP address	192	168	1	1
Subnet mask	255	255	255	0

Easy to read Tables

IP addresses are actually 32-bit dotted-decimal numbers. If you were to convert an IP address's decimal numbers to binary, you'd have a total of 32 bits. It is considered dotted because each number is separated by a dot. Altogether, they contain four numbers, each of which is a byte or octet. For example, 192 is an octet and its binary equivalent is 11000000, which is 8 bits. 168 is also an octet, its binary equivalent is 10101000, and so on. Adding all four octets together equals 32 bits.

IP addresses are usually applied to your network adapter, but can be applied to other devices, such as switches, routers, and so on. It's the fact that the device or computer has an IP address that makes it a ***host***. Let's configure IP on our Windows 10 host now. Remember that other Windows computers will be configured in a very similar way.

CONFIGURE IP ADDRESSES

GET READY. To configure IP addresses, perform the following steps.

1. Access the Ethernet Properties dialog box.
2. Click **Internet Protocol Version 4** and then click the **Properties** button. The Internet Protocol Version 4 Properties dialog box opens. Write down the current settings (if there are any) so that you can return the computer to these settings at the end of the exercise.
3. By default, the Obtain an IP address automatically and Obtain DNS server address automatically radio buttons are enabled, as shown in Figure 1-11. That means that the network adapter will attempt to get all its IP information from a DHCP server or other device like a SOHO (Small Office/Home Office) four-port router. However, we want to configure the adapter statically, so let's continue on!

Understanding Local Area Networking | 11

house number and the street you live on, an IP address identifies your computer number and the network it lives on. A common example of an IP address is 192.168.1.1.

Now, every IP address is broken down into two parts: the network portion, in this case 192.168.1, which is the network your computer is a member of, and the host portion, which is the individual number of your computer, differentiating your computer from any others on the network. In this case, it's .1. How do we know this? The subnet mask tells us.

The subnet mask is a group of four numbers that define what IP network the computer is a member of. All of the 255s in a subnet mask collectively refer to the network portion, while the 0s refer to the host portion. This is illustrated in Table 1-1. This table shows a typical Class C IP address and the default corresponding subnet mask. If you were to configure the IP address of a Windows computer as 192.168.1.1, Windows would automatically default to a subnet mask of 255.255.255.0. If any other computers would like to communicate with yours, they need to be configured with the same network number; however, every computer on the same network needs to have a different host number or an IP conflict might ensue. Of course, as a talented administrator, you'll learn how to avoid IP conflicts—and you'll learn some tips on how to do so in Lessons 4 and 5.

Table 1-1

An IP Address and Corresponding Subnet Mask

Type of Address	First Octet	Second Octet	Third Octet	Fourth Octet
IP address	192	168	1	1
Subnet mask	255	255	255	0

IP addresses are actually 32-bit dotted-decimal numbers. If you were to convert an IP address's decimal numbers to binary, you'd have a total of 32 bits. It is considered dotted because each number is separated by a dot. Altogether, they contain four numbers, each of which is a byte or octet. For example, 192 is an octet and its binary equivalent is 11000000, which is 8 bits. 168 is also an octet, its binary equivalent is 10101000, and so on. Adding all four octets together equals 32 bits.

IP addresses are usually applied to your network adapter, but can be applied to other devices, such as switches, routers, and so on. It's the fact that the device or computer has an IP address that makes it a ***host***. Let's configure IP on our Windows 10 host now. Remember that other Windows computers will be configured in a very similar way.

Step by Step

CONFIGURE IP ADDRESSES

GET READY. To configure IP addresses, perform the following steps.

1. Access the Ethernet Properties dialog box.
2. Click **Internet Protocol Version 4** and then click the **Properties** button. The Internet Protocol Version 4 Properties dialog box opens. Write down the current settings (if there are any) so that you can return the computer to these settings at the end of the exercise.
3. By default, the Obtain an IP address automatically and Obtain DNS server address automatically radio buttons are enabled, as shown in Figure 1-11. That means that the network adapter will attempt to get all its IP information from a DHCP server or other device like a SOHO (Small Office/Home Office) four-port router. However, we want to configure the adapter statically, so let's continue on!

to increase the speed of torrent downloads. It is estimated that between 20% and 35% of the data transfers on the Internet involve torrents. Another benefit of the BitTorrent client is that you can line up a large number of downloads from one torrent location (or multiple locations), and just let your computer download them while you do other things. A file is seeded (stored) on one or more computers. Then, as clients (peers) download that file (or portions of the file), they are automatically set up to distribute the file (or portions of the file). This way, more and more computers are added to the "swarm," making the availability of the file much greater. Computers are set up to automatically distribute the file; it's the default setting, but you can turn off seeding/distribution in your client. You could also block it at your firewall.

Instead of a server hosting the file, a server simply tracks and coordinates the distribution of files. The actual torrent starts with an initial small file (called a torrent file) that you download, which contains information about the files to be downloaded. The reason the whole process is called a torrent is because it usually begins with a small file that starts the download. One of the differences is that when downloading a torrent, there is more than one TCP connection (could be quite a few) to different machines in the P2P network. Contrast this to a single file download from a web server where only one TCP connection is made. This is controlled in a pseudorandom fashion by the tracking server to ensure availability of data. Another difference is that most web servers will put a cap on the number of concurrent downloads you can do, but not so with the torrent client program. The average person uses a BitTorrent client to download movies, MP3s, and other media. Sometimes, these are distributed with the consent of the owner; other times (and quite often), they are illegally seeded and distributed—as well as downloaded! An example of legitimate usage is the *World of Warcraft* game. The owners of the game use the Blizzard BitTorrent to distribute just about everything involved in the game. Newer games for the PS3 and other consoles are doing the same type of thing. D-Link and other network equipment companies are embracing torrent technology as well.

SKILL SUMMARY

Skill Summary

IN THIS LESSON, YOU LEARNED:

- A network is two or more computers that exchange data. A local area network (LAN) is a group of these computers that are confined to a small geographic area, usually one building.
- The network adapter, also known as a network interface card (NIC), is the device that enables the sending and receiving of data to and from your computer. Today, multiple devices can connect to each other and communicate using a switch.
- Internet Protocol (IP) is the part of TCP/IP that, among other things, governs IP addresses. The IP address is the cornerstone of networking. It defines the computer or host you are working on.
- A wireless local area network (WLAN) has many advantages, the most standout of which is the ability to roam. A person with a laptop, handheld computer or PDA, or other like device can work from anywhere.
- Network topologies define the physical connections of hosts in a computer network. There are several types of physical topologies, including bus, ring, star, mesh, and tree.
- Today's computing is known as distributive computing and is used for both client/server and peer-to-peer networks. This means that every device or workstation has its own processing power.
- The client/server model is an architecture that distributes applications between servers, such as Windows Server 2016, and client computers, such as Windows 8/8.1 or Windows 10.
- Peer-to-peer networking, first and foremost, means that each computer is treated as an equal. This means each computer has the equal ability to serve data and to access data, just like any other computer on the network. Before servers became popular in PC-based computer networks, each PC had the ability to store data.

Case Scenarios

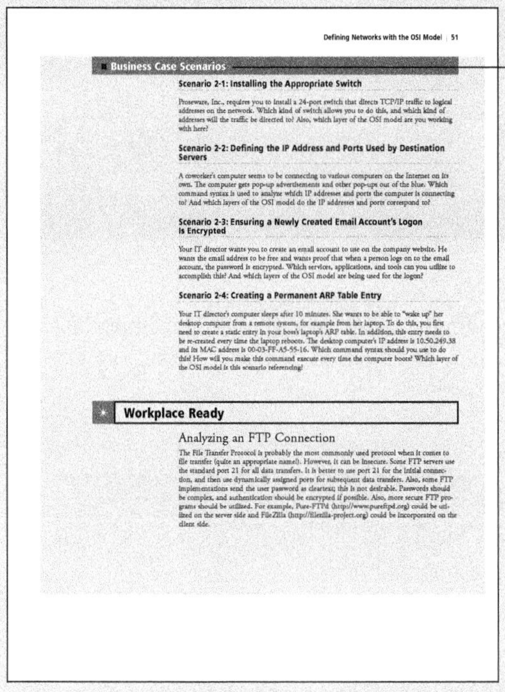

Defining Networks with the OSI Model | 51

Business Case Scenarios

Scenario 2-1: Installing the Appropriate Switch

Proseware, Inc., requires you to install a 24-port switch that directs TCP/IP traffic to logical addresses on the network. Which kind of switch allows you to do this, and which kind of addresses will the traffic be directed to? Also, which layer of the OSI model are you working with here?

Scenario 2-2: Defining the IP Address and Ports Used by Destination Servers

A coworker's computer seems to be connecting to various computers on the Internet on its own. The computer gets pop-up advertisements and other pop-ups out of the blue. Which command syntax is used to analyze which IP addresses and ports the computer is connecting to? And which layers of the OSI model do the IP addresses and ports correspond to?

Scenario 2-3: Ensuring a Newly Created Email Account's Logon Is Encrypted

Your IT director wants you to create an email account to use on the company website. He wants the email address to be free and wants proof that when a person logs on to the email account, the password is encrypted. Which services, applications, and tools can you utilize to accomplish this? And which layers of the OSI model are being used for the logon?

Scenario 2-4: Creating a Permanent ARP Table Entry

Your IT director's computer sleeps after 10 minutes. She wants to be able to "wake up" her desktop computer from a remote system, for example from her laptop. To do this, you first need to create a static entry in your boss's laptop's ARP table. In addition, this entry needs to be re-created every time the laptop reboots. The desktop computer's IP address is 10.50.249.38 and its MAC address is 00-03-FF-A5-55-16. Which command syntax should you use to do this? How will you make this command execute every time the computer boots? Which layer of the OSI model is this scenario referencing?

Workplace Ready

Analyzing an FTP Connection

The File Transfer Protocol is probably the most commonly used protocol when it comes to file transfer (quite an appropriate name!). However, it can be insecure. Some FTP servers use the standard port 21 for all data transfers. It is better to use port 21 for the initial connection, and then use dynamically assigned ports for subsequent data transfers. Also, some FTP implementations send the user password as cleartext; this is not desirable. Passwords should be complex, and authentication should be encrypted if possible. Also, more secure FTP programs should be utilized. For example, Pure-FTPd (http://www.pureftpd.org) could be utilized on the server side and FileZilla (http://filezilla-project.org) could be incorporated on the client side.

Photos

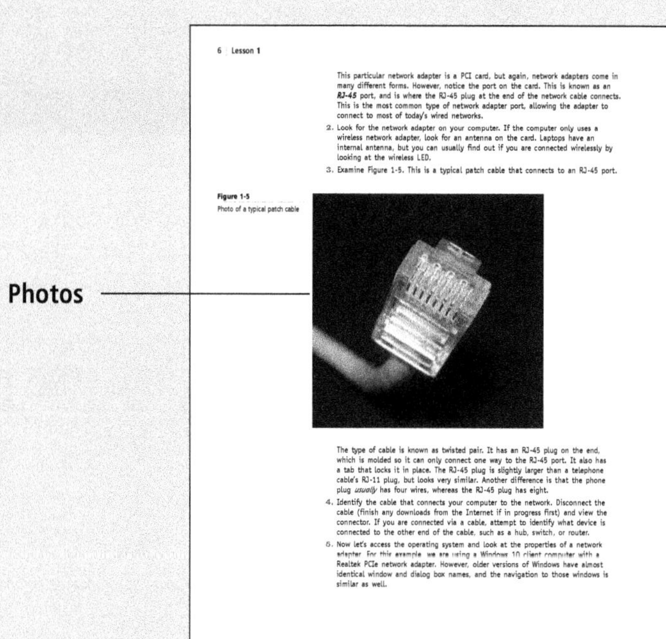

6 | Lesson 1

This particular network adapter is a PCI card, but again, network adapters come in many different forms. However, notice the port on the card. This is known as an ***RJ-45*** port, and is where the RJ-45 plug at the end of the network cable connects. This is the most common type of network adapter port, allowing the adapter to connect to most of today's wired networks.

2. Look for the network adapter on your computer. If the computer only uses a wireless network adapter, look for an antenna on the card. Laptops have an internal antenna, but you can usually find out if you are connected wirelessly by looking at the wireless LED.
3. Examine Figure 1-5. This is a typical patch cable that connects to an RJ-45 port.

Figure 1-5
Photo of a typical patch cable

The type of cable is known as twisted pair. It has an RJ-45 plug on the end, which is molded so it can only connect one way to the RJ-45 port. It also has a tab that locks it in place. The RJ-45 plug is slightly larger than a telephone cable's RJ-11 plug, but looks very similar. Another difference is that the phone plug *usually* has four wires, whereas the RJ-45 plug has eight.

4. Identify the cable that connects your computer to the network. Disconnect the cable (finish any downloads from the Internet if in progress first) and view the connector. If you are connected via a cable, attempt to identify what device is connected to the other end of the cable, such as a hub, switch, or router.
5. Now let's access the operating system and look at the properties of a network adapter. For this example, we are using a Windows 10 client computer with a Realtek PCIe network adapter. However, older versions of Windows have almost identical window and dialog box names, and the navigation to those windows is similar as well.

Knowledge Assessment

Understanding Local Area Networking | 27

Knowledge Assessment

Multiple Choice

Select the correct answer for each of the following questions.

1. Which of the following regenerates the signal and broadcasts the signal to every computer connected to it?
   a. Hub
   b. Switch
   c. Router
   d. Firewall
2. Which of the following is *not* a central connecting device?
   a. Hub
   b. Switch
   c. SOHO router
   d. Windows 10 client
3. When installing a network adapter to a computer so that it can be connected to a network that uses twisted-pair cabling, which type of port must be used by the network adapter?
   a. RJ-11
   b. RJ-45
   c. RG-58
   d. Fiber optic
4. In Windows 10, which of the following should be used to access the properties of a network adapter?
   a. Device Manager
   b. Ping
   c. Advanced Firewall
   d. Task Manager
5. When connecting a computer's network adapter to a switch—with the desire for the connection to be able to send and receive data simultaneously—which type of connection is required?
   a. Half-duplex
   b. Full-duplex
   c. Simplex
   d. 100 Mbps
6. When connecting a computer at a rate of 100,000,000 bits per second, which of the following should be the speed of the network adapter being installed?
   a. 10 Mbps
   b. 100 MB/s
   c. 100 Mbps
   d. 1,000 Mbps
7. When connecting to a router that has the IP address 192.168.1.100 on a standard, default Class C network using the subnet mask 255.255.255.0, which of the following is a valid IP address for the network adapter?
   a. 192.168.0.1
   b. 192.168.1.1
   c. 192.168.100.1
   d. 192.168.1.100

X REF

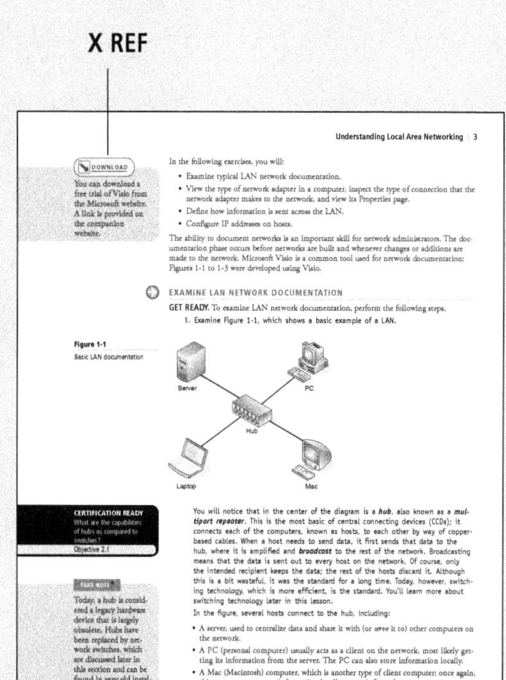

Understanding Local Area Networking | 3

DOWNLOAD
You can download a free trial of Visio from the Microsoft website. A link is provided on the companion website.

In the following exercises, you will:

- Examine typical LAN network documentation.
- View the type of network adapter in a computer, inspect the type of connection that the network adapter makes to the network, and view its Properties page.
- Define how information is sent across the LAN.
- Configure IP addresses on hosts.

The ability to document networks is an important skill for network administrators. The documentation phase occurs before networks are built and whenever changes or additions are made to the network. Microsoft Visio is a common tool used for network documentation; Figures 1-1 to 1-3 were developed using Visio.

EXAMINE LAN NETWORK DOCUMENTATION

GET READY. To examine LAN network documentation, perform the following steps.

1. Examine Figure 1-1, which shows a basic example of a LAN.

Figure 1-1
Basic LAN documentation

CERTIFICATION READY
What are the capabilities of hubs as compared to switches?
Objective 2.1

You will notice that in the center of the diagram is a ***hub***, also known as a ***multiport repeater***. This is the most basic of central connecting devices (CCDs); it connects each of the computers, known as hosts, to each other by way of copper-based cables. When a host needs to send data, it first sends that data to the hub, where it is amplified and ***broadcast*** to the rest of the network. Broadcasting means that the data is sent out to every host on the network. Of course, only the intended recipient keeps the data; the rest of the hosts discard it. Although this is a bit wasteful, it was the standard for a long time. Today, however, switching technology, which is more efficient, is the standard. You'll learn more about switching technology later in this lesson.

TAKE NOTE*
Today, a hub is considered a legacy hardware device that is largely obsolete. Hubs have been replaced by network switches, which are discussed later in this section and can be found in very old installations or specialized applications.

In the figure, several hosts connect to the hub, including:

- A server, used to centralize data and share it with (or *serve* it to) other computers on the network.
- A PC (personal computer) usually acts as a client on the network, most likely getting its information from the server. The PC can also store information locally.
- A Mac (Macintosh) computer, which is another type of client computer; once again, this computer can store information locally, or get it from the server.
- A laptop, which could be a PC or a Mac, is meant for portability. However, it can also store and access data the same way the other computers do.

Conventions and Features Used in This Book

This book uses particular fonts, symbols, and heading conventions to highlight important information or to call your attention to special steps. For more information about the features in each lesson, refer to the Illustrated Book Tour section.

CONVENTION	MEANING
THE BOTTOM LINE	This feature provides a brief summary of the material to be covered in the section that follows.
CLOSE	Words in all capital letters indicate instructions for opening, saving, or closing files or programs. They also point out items you should check or actions you should take.
CERTIFICATION READY	This feature signals the point in the text where a specific certification objective is covered. It provides you with a chance to check your understanding of that particular MTA objective and, if necessary, review the section of the lesson where it is covered.
TAKE NOTE*	Reader aids appear in shaded boxes found in your text. *Take Note* provides helpful hints related to particular tasks or topics.
DOWNLOAD	Download provides information on where to download -useful software.
X REF	These notes provide pointers to information discussed elsewhere in the textbook or describe interesting features of Windows Server that are not directly addressed in the current topic or exercise.
Alt + Tab	A plus sign (+) between two key names means that you must press both keys at the same time. Keys that you are instructed to press in an exercise will appear in the font shown here.
Example	Key terms appear in bold italic.

Instructor Support Program

The *Microsoft Official Academic Course* programs are accompanied by a rich array of resources that incorporate the extensive textbook visuals to form a pedagogically cohesive package. These resources provide all the materials instructors need to deploy and deliver their courses. Resources available online for download include:

- The **Instructor's Guide** contains Solutions to all the textbook exercises and Syllabi for various term lengths. The Instructor's Guide also includes chapter summaries and lecture notes. The Instructor's Guide is available from the Book Companion site (http://www.wiley.com/college/microsoft).
- The **Test Bank** contains hundreds of questions in multiple-choice, true-false, short answer, and essay formats, and is available to download from the Instructor's Book Companion site (www.wiley.com/college/microsoft). A complete answer key is provided.
- A complete set of **PowerPoint presentations and images** are available on the Instructor's Book Companion site (http://www.wiley.com/college/microsoft) to enhance classroom presentations. Approximately 50 PowerPoint slides are provided for each lesson. Tailored to the text's topical coverage and Skills Matrix, these presentations are designed to convey key concepts addressed in the text. All images from the text are on the Instructor's Book Companion site (http://www.wiley.com/college/microsoft). You can incorporate them into your PowerPoint presentations, or create your own overhead transparencies and handouts. By using these visuals in class discussions, you can help focus students' attention on key elements of technologies covered and help them understand how to use it effectively in the workplace.

Student Support Program

■ Additional Resources

Book Companion Web Site (www.wiley.com)

The students' book companion site for the MOAC series includes any resources, exercise files, and Web links that will be used in conjunction with this course.

■ About the Microsoft Technology Associate (MTA) Certification

Preparing Tomorrow's Technology Workforce

Technology plays a role in virtually every business around the world. Possessing the fundamental knowledge of how technology works and understanding its impact on today's academic and workplace environment is increasingly important—particularly for students interested in exploring professions involving technology. That's why Microsoft created the Microsoft Technology Associate (MTA) certification—a new entry-level credential that validates fundamental technology knowledge among students seeking to build a career in technology.

The Microsoft Technology Associate (MTA) certification is the ideal and preferred path to Microsoft's world-renowned technology certification programs, such as Microsoft Certified Technology Specialist (MCTS) and Microsoft Certified IT Professional (MCITP). MTA is positioned to become the premier credential for individuals seeking to explore and pursue a career in technology, or augment related pursuits such as business or any other field where technology is pervasive.

MTA Candidate Profile

The MTA certification program is designed specifically for secondary and post-secondary students interested in exploring academic and career options in a technology field. It offers students a certification in basic IT and development. As the new recommended entry point for Microsoft technology certifications, MTA is designed especially for students new to IT and software development. It is available exclusively in educational settings and easily integrates into the curricula of existing computer classes.

MTA Empowers Educators and Motivates Students

MTA provides a new standard for measuring and validating fundamental technology knowledge right in the classroom while keeping your budget and teaching resources intact. MTA helps institutions stand out as innovative providers of high-demand industry credentials and is easily deployed with a simple, convenient, and affordable suite of entry-level technology certification exams. MTA enables students to explore career paths in technology without requiring a big investment of time and resources, while providing a career foundation and the confidence to succeed in advanced studies and future vocational endeavors.

In addition to giving students an entry-level Microsoft certification, MTA is designed to be a stepping stone to other, more advanced Microsoft technology certifications, like the Microsoft Certified Technology Specialist (MCTS) certification.

Acknowledgments

MOAC MTA Technology Fundamentals Reviewers

We'd like to thank the many reviewers who pored over the manuscript and provided invaluable feedback in the service of quality instructional materials:

Yuke Wang, University of Texas at Dallas
Palaniappan Vairavan, Bellevue College
Harold "Buz" Lamson, ITT Technical Institute
Colin Archibald, Valencia Community College
Catherine Bradfield, DeVry University Online
Robert Nelson, Blinn College
Kalpana Viswanathan, Bellevue College
Bob Becker, Vatterott College
Carol Torkko, Bellevue College
Bharat Kandel, Missouri Tech
Linda Cohen, Forsyth Technical Community College
Candice Lambert, Metro Technology Centers
Susan Mahon, Collin College
Mark Aruda, Hillsborough Community College
Claude Russo, Brevard Community College
David Koppy, Baker College
Sharon Moran, Hillsborough Community College
Keith Hoell, Briarcliffe College and Queens College—CUNY
Mark Hufnagel, Lee County School District
Rachelle Hall, Glendale Community College
Scott Elliott, Christie Digital Systems, Inc.
Gralan Gilliam, Kaplan
Steve Strom, Butler Community College
John Crowley, Bucks County Community College
Margaret Leary, Northern Virginia Community College
Sue Miner, Lehigh Carbon Community College
Gary Rollinson, Cabrillo College
Al Kelly, University of Advancing Technology
Katherine James, Seneca College

Brief Contents

Contents

Lesson 1: Understanding Local Area Networking 1

Lesson 2: Defining Networks with the OSI Model 30

Lesson 3: Understanding Wired and Wireless Networks 53

Lesson 4: Understanding Internet Protocol 72

Lesson 5: Implementing TCP/IP in the Command Line 104

Understanding Local Area Networking

LESSON 1

OBJECTIVE DOMAIN MATRIX

Skills/Concepts	Objective Domain Description	Objective Domain Number
Examining Local Area Networks, Devices, and Data Transfer	Understand local area networks (LANs)	1.2
	Understand switches	2.1
Identifying Network Topologies and Standards	Understand network topologies and access methods	1.5

KEY TERMS

broadcast
centralized computing
client/server
Carrier Sense Multiple Access with Collision Avoidance (CSMA/CA)
Carrier Sense Multiple Access with Collision Detected (CSMA/CD)
Computer Telephony Integration
CTI-based server
data transfer rate
database server
demilitarized zone (DMZ)
distributive computing
Ethernet
file server
frames
full-duplex
half-duplex
host
hub
IEEE 802.3
IP address
local area network (LAN)
mesh topology
messaging server
multiport repeater
network adapter
network controller
network documentation
network operating systems (NOSs)
network topology
P2P
peer-to-peer
perimeter network
print server
ring topology
RJ-45
serial data transfer
star topology
switch
transceive
unicast
virtual LAN (VLAN)
web server
Windows 10
wireless access point (WAP)
wireless local area network (WLAN)

Local area networks are used by just about every organization, and today many homes have them as well. This lesson refers to a fictitious company named Proseware, Inc., that wants to implement a new LAN in a brand-new office, which will serve approximately 20 users. The company requires an extremely quick network that can transfer many different types of data. They want the most cost-effective layout without losing speed or efficiency! The network engineer's job responsibilities include selecting the right equipment, making sure it is all compatible, and getting it installed on time. The network engineer should have a thorough understanding of technologies, such as Ethernet and switching, because she will be critical in designing and implementing the network. This lesson covers all of the concepts necessary so you can be confident installing the network that this company desires. As we progress through this book, we will build on this scenario and add lots more networking technologies to the infrastructure.

■ Examining Local Area Networks, Devices, and Data Transfer

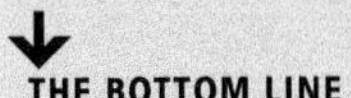

Simply stated, a *network* is two or more computers that exchange data. A ***local area network (LAN)*** is a group of these computers that are confined to a small geographic area, usually one building. Setting up a LAN requires computers with network adapters, central connecting devices to connect those computers together, and a numbering scheme (such as IP addresses) to differentiate one computer from the next. It can also include servers, some type of protective device such as a firewall, and connections to perimeter networks that are adjacent to the LAN.

Defining the LAN

As mentioned, a LAN requires computers with network adapters, central connecting devices, and some type of medium to tie it altogether, be it cabled or wireless connections. These must be connected together in some way to facilitate the transfer of data. It is important to define how they are connected together, as well as how they actually transmit data.

CERTIFICATION READY
What is a local area network (LAN)?
Objective 1.2

We mentioned that a network is used to exchange data. But what are the real reasons that an organization will desire (or need) a network? They can be organized into four categories:

- **Sharing:** The sharing of files, databases, and media
- **Communication:** The methods of communication, such as email, instant messaging, and faxing
- **Organization:** The ability to centralize data and make it more accessible and efficient
- **$$$:** The ability for the network to provide cost savings and/or increase productivity

Some would place security in this list of categories, but, unfortunately, as you will find, many networks, devices, and operating systems are insecure when they are fresh out of the box. Just having a network doesn't ensure security. In fact, many steps must be taken to implement a secure network.

To understand local area networks (LANs) better, it helps to write out the structure of the LAN—to *document* it. ***Network documentation*** is any information that helps describe, define, and otherwise explain how computers are connected in a physical and logical way. For example, the physical connection could be cables, and the logical connection could be the various IP addresses used by the devices on the network.

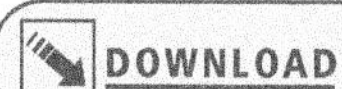

DOWNLOAD

You can download a free trial of Visio from the Microsoft website. A link is provided on the companion website.

In the following exercises, you will:

- Examine typical LAN network documentation.
- View the type of network adapter in a computer, inspect the type of connection that the network adapter makes to the network, and view its Properties page.
- Define how information is sent across the LAN.
- Configure IP addresses on hosts.

The ability to document networks is an important skill for network administrators. The documentation phase occurs before networks are built and whenever changes or additions are made to the network. Microsoft Visio is a common tool used for network documentation; Figures 1-1 to 1-3 were developed using Visio.

EXAMINE LAN NETWORK DOCUMENTATION

GET READY. To examine LAN network documentation, perform the following steps.

1. Examine Figure 1-1, which shows a basic example of a LAN.

Figure 1-1

Basic LAN documentation

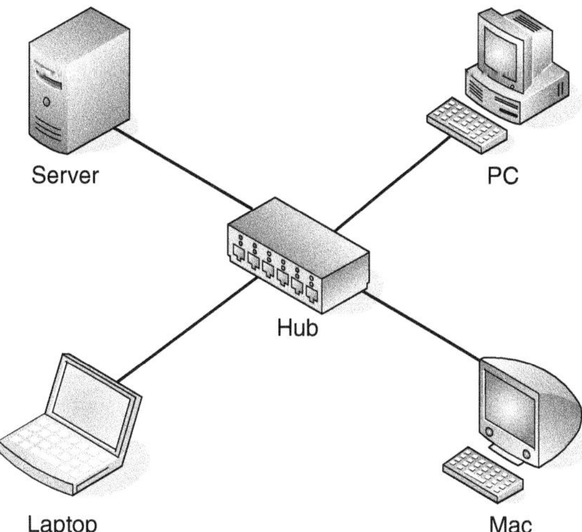

CERTIFICATION READY
What are the capabilities of hubs as compared to switches?
Objective 2.1

You will notice that in the center of the diagram is a ***hub***, also known as a ***multiport repeater***. This is the most basic of central connecting devices (CCDs); it connects each of the computers, known as hosts, to each other by way of copper-based cables. When a host needs to send data, it first sends that data to the hub, where it is amplified and ***broadcast*** to the rest of the network. Broadcasting means that the data is sent out to every host on the network. Of course, only the intended recipient keeps the data; the rest of the hosts discard it. Although this is a bit wasteful, it was the standard for a long time. Today, however, switching technology, which is more efficient, is the standard. You'll learn more about switching technology later in this lesson.

TAKE NOTE*

Today, a hub is considered a legacy hardware device that is largely obsolete. Hubs have been replaced by network switches, which are discussed later in this section and can be found in very old installations or specialized applications.

In the figure, several hosts connect to the hub, including:

- A server, used to centralize data and share it with (or *serve* it to) other computers on the network.
- A PC (personal computer) usually acts as a client on the network, most likely getting its information from the server. The PC can also store information locally.
- A Mac (Macintosh) computer, which is another type of client computer; once again, this computer can store information locally, or get it from the server.
- A laptop, which could be a PC or a Mac, is meant for portability. However, it can also store and access data the same way the other computers do.

TAKE NOTE*

If you are using Microsoft Visio, utilize the Basic Network Diagram template. This can be accessed in the Network section when starting a new document.

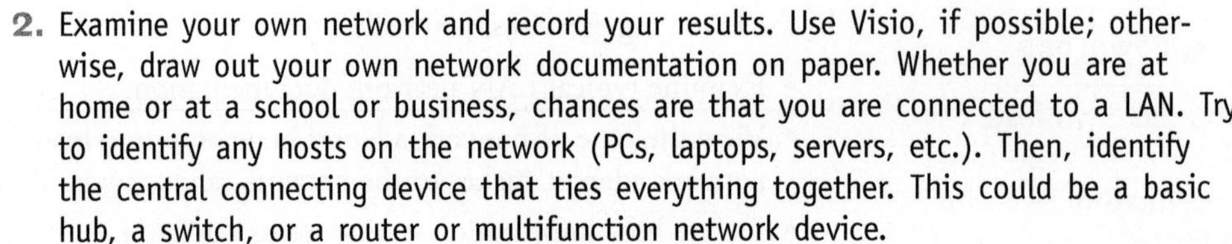

2. Examine your own network and record your results. Use Visio, if possible; otherwise, draw out your own network documentation on paper. Whether you are at home or at a school or business, chances are that you are connected to a LAN. Try to identify any hosts on the network (PCs, laptops, servers, etc.). Then, identify the central connecting device that ties everything together. This could be a basic hub, a switch, or a router or multifunction network device.
3. Examine Figure 1-2. This is an intermediate example of a LAN.

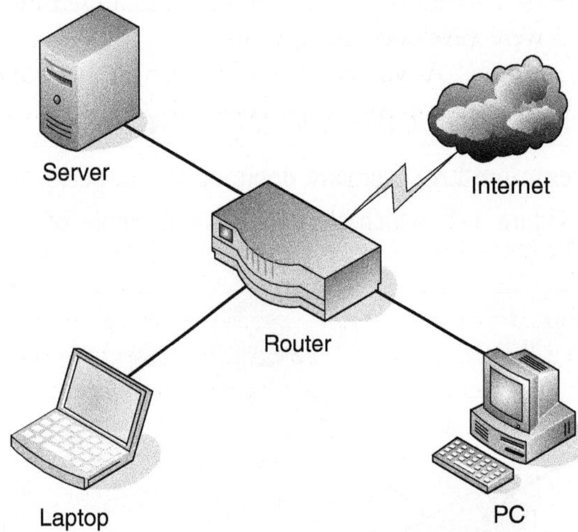

Figure 1-2
Intermediate LAN documentation

In Figure 1-2, the hub is replaced with a basic four-port router; these are also referred to as SOHO (Small Office/Home Office) routers. The router acts as a central connecting device, connecting the hosts together, but also has a special communications link to the Internet, allowing the hosts to send and receive data to and from computers on the Internet. That communications link between the router and the Internet is where the LAN ends. So, the PC, laptop, server, and router are part of the LAN. Anything else beyond the router is considered to be outside of the LAN.

4. Examine your own LAN again. If possible, identify any routers and connections to the Internet (or other networks). Add these to your written, or Visio, documentation.
5. Examine Figure 1-3. This is a slightly more advanced example of a LAN.

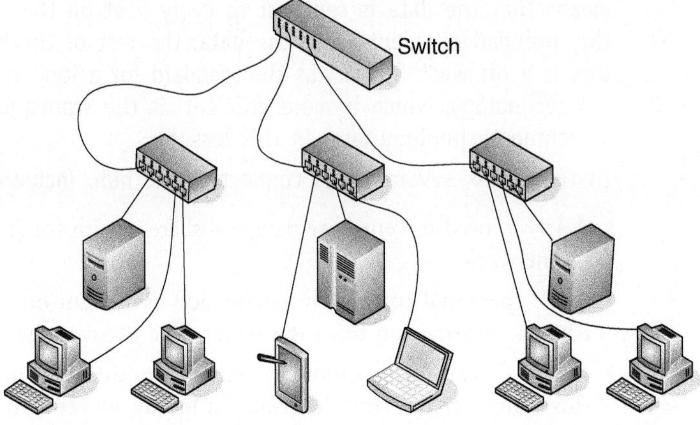

Figure 1-3
Advanced LAN documentation

In Figure 1-3, more central connecting devices are added. Instead of connecting hundreds of devices to a single central connecting device, you can break up the network in a hierarchical fashion. For example, on the left side of the figure are two PCs and one server connected to a hub. Let's say that these represent 24 computers, and that each other group of computers connected to a hub also represents 24 computers. Instead of connecting all the computers to a single, central connecting device, which might not be able to physically support all of the hosts, the groups of 24 hosts are connected to their own hub. Then, the hubs are all daisy-chained to a ***switch*** at the top of the figure. The switch will most likely be a powerful (and expensive) device, in order to support all of the computers that ultimately connect to it. You can regard the individual hubs as devices that allow connectivity for single departments in a company, or individual classrooms in a school. The master switch at the top of the hierarchical tree connects everything together; however, it also acts as a single point of failure, which is addressed in Chapter 2. As you can guess, this type of network architecture is the kind we will need to use to accomplish the goals laid out in the scenario at the beginning of this lesson.

The ***network adapter***, also known as a network interface card (NIC), is the device that enables the sending and receiving of data to and from your computer. It might be integrated into the motherboard or it might act as a separate device that connects to a PCI slot, or perhaps connects to a PC Card slot or USB port. It connects to the network by way of cable (wired) or by air (wireless). It has its own basic CPU to process transmitted data and a ROM chip to store information about itself. Network adapters also have a software component known as a driver, defining how the card will interact with the operating system; this usually includes a Properties page that can be accessed in the operating system, enabling the user to configure the adapter as he sees fit.

VIEW THE NETWORK ADAPTER

GET READY. To view the network adapter, perform the following steps.

1. Examine Figure 1-4, which shows a typical network adapter.

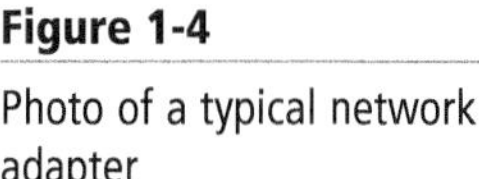

Figure 1-4

Photo of a typical network adapter

This particular network adapter is a PCI card, but again, network adapters come in many different forms. However, notice the port on the card. This is known as an ***RJ-45*** port, and is where the RJ-45 plug at the end of the network cable connects. This is the most common type of network adapter port, allowing the adapter to connect to most of today's wired networks.

2. Look for the network adapter on your computer. If the computer only uses a wireless network adapter, look for an antenna on the card. Laptops have an internal antenna, but you can usually find out if you are connected wirelessly by looking at the wireless LED.
3. Examine Figure 1-5. This is a typical patch cable that connects to an RJ-45 port.

Figure 1-5

Photo of a typical patch cable

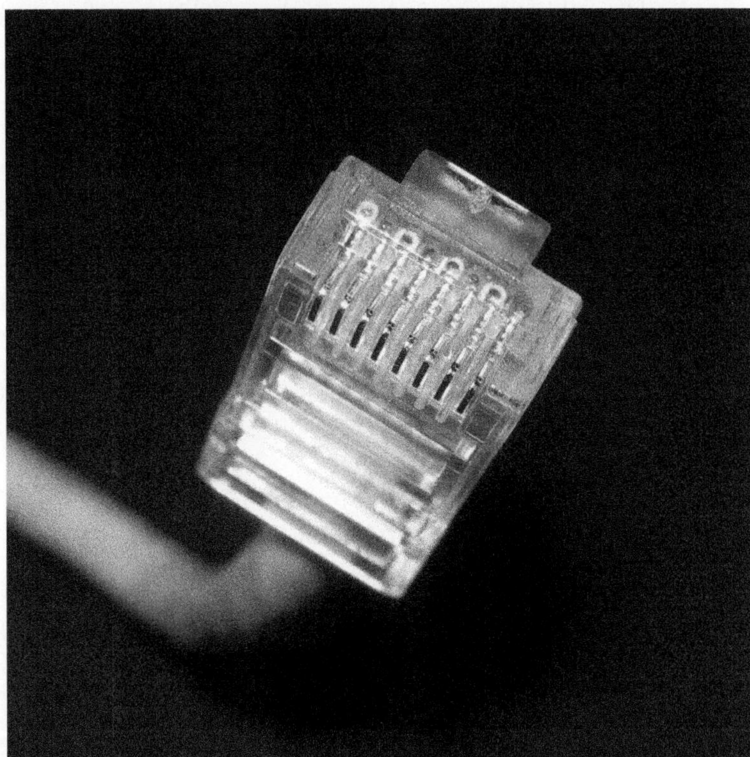

The type of cable is known as twisted pair. It has an RJ-45 plug on the end, which is molded so it can only connect one way to the RJ-45 port. It also has a tab that locks it in place. The RJ-45 plug is slightly larger than a telephone cable's RJ-11 plug, but looks very similar. Another difference is that the phone plug *usually* has four wires, whereas the RJ-45 plug has eight.

4. Identify the cable that connects your computer to the network. Disconnect the cable (finish any downloads from the Internet if in progress first) and view the connector. If you are connected via a cable, attempt to identify what device is connected to the other end of the cable, such as a hub, switch, or router.
5. Now let's access the operating system and look at the properties of a network adapter. For this example, we are using a Windows 10 client computer with a Realtek PCIe network adapter. However, older versions of Windows have almost identical window and dialog box names, and the navigation to those windows is similar as well.

a. Right-click **Start** and choose **Computer Management.** Alternatively for Windows 10, and for Windows Server 2016, click **Start**, type **Computer Management**, and then press **Enter.**

b. Click **Device Manager.**

c. Click the **>** sign to expand the **Network adapters** category, as shown in Figure 1-6.

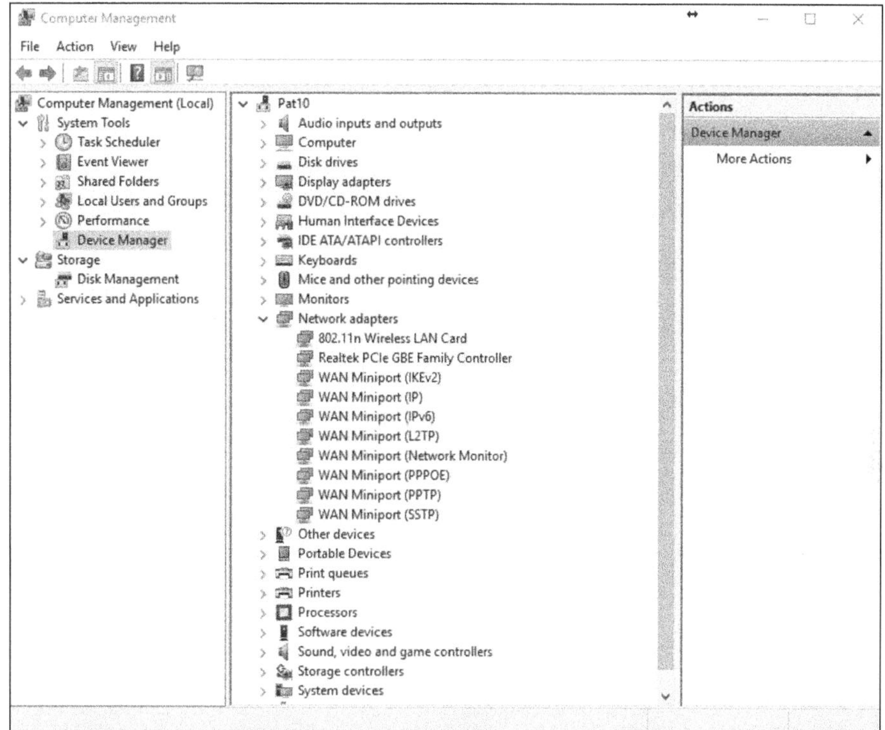

Figure 1-6

Device Manager with the Network adapters category expanded

d. Right-click the network adapter and choose **Properties.** A dialog box similar to the one shown in Figure 1-7 opens.

Figure 1-7

Properties dialog box of a Realtec network adapter

6. Click the **Advanced** tab. If you click the **Speed & Duplex** option, you can then change the value, as shown in Figure 1-8.

Figure 1-8

Link speed of the network adapter

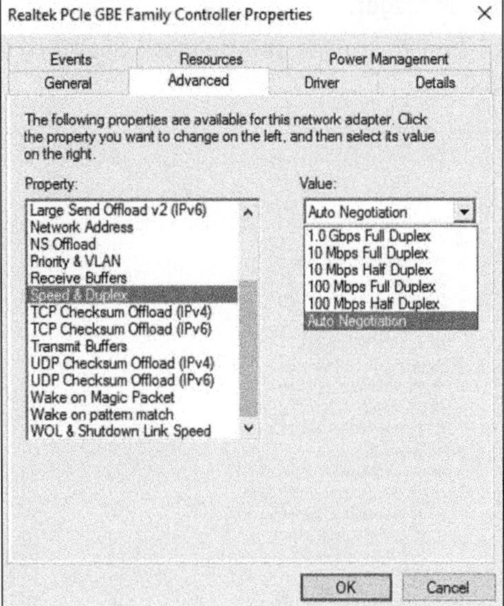

TAKE NOTE*

A network adapter is only as fast as the network it connects to!

Full-duplex means that the network card can send and receive data *simultaneously*. In the Speed and Duplex drop-down menu, you can select various speeds, including 10 Mbps, 100 Mbps, and 1 Gbps. You can also select ***half-duplex***, which means that the network adapter can send and receive data, but not at the same time. Full-duplex is the superior connection, as long as your central connecting device supports it. A full-duplex connection can ***transceive*** (transmit and receive) twice as much information per second compared with a half-duplex connection. So, to meet the requirements of the original scenario, you would probably want your client computers to connect at 1 Gbps as well as utilize full-duplex negotiations.

You can tell that a card is active because the Link Status field on the physical device shows a green light. You can also open the device Status window (Open Network and Sharing Center, and clink the adapter link) to see the current speed of the adapter such as 1 Gbps, its media state, how long it has been up and the current activity.

7. Finally, every network adapter will have a logical name. By default, the network adapter is known as Ethernet, although you can change the name if you so desire. Ethernet will have its own Properties page and a status page. Let's view these now:

    a. Right-click the **Network** icon on the far right of the taskbar and choose **Open Network and Sharing Center**. The Network and Sharing Center window opens. An alternate way to access the Network and Sharing Center is to right-click **Start** and choose **Control Panel**. Then, navigate to **Network and Internet > Network and Sharing Center.**

    b. Click the **Change adapter settings** link. The Network Connections window opens. (Navigation to this window is slightly different in other versions of Windows.)

    c. In this window, right-click the **Ethernet** icon and choose **Properties**. The Ethernet Properties dialog box opens, as shown in Figure 1-9.

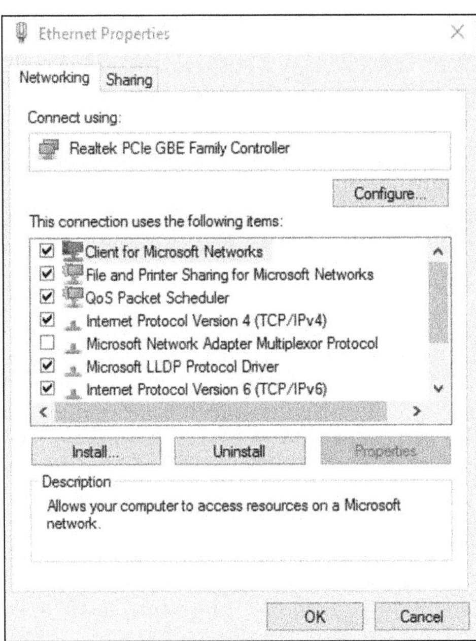

Figure 1-9

The Ethernet Properties dialog box

From here, you can configure Internet Protocol (IP), bind new protocols to the network adapter, and so on. You'll access this dialog box frequently during the course of this book.

d. Click **Cancel** to close the dialog box. This should return you to the Network Connections window.

e. Now, double-click the **Ethernet** icon. The Ethernet Status dialog box opens, as shown in Figure 1-10. This dialog box displays the type of connectivity, speed, and how long the adapter has been connected; it also shows the total bytes sent and received. In addition, from this dialog box, you can access the Properties dialog box and diagnose the network adapter, if necessary.

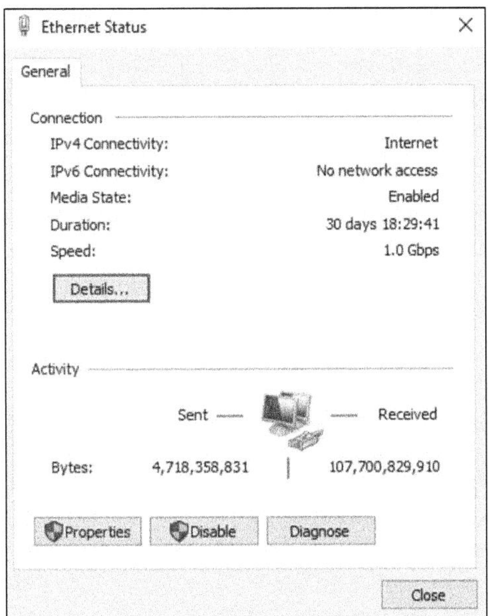

Figure 1-10

The Ethernet Status dialog box

DEFINING DATA TRANSFER ON THE LAN

Generally, when data is transferred on the LAN, it is sent in a serial fashion over twisted-pair cabling. ***Serial data transfer*** means the transfer of one bit at a time—a single bit stream. This is usually the format that information is sent from one network adapter to another. Let's discuss this in a little more depth. Suppose one user wants to send a small text file (100 bytes in size) to another user on the network. There are many ways to do this; one way is to map a network drive to the other user's computer and simply copy and paste the text file to the other computer's hard drive. When this is done, a few things happen:

1. First, the text file is packaged by the operating system into what is known as a packet. This packet is slightly larger than the original file. That packet is then sent to the network adapter.
2. Next, the network adapter takes that packet and places it inside of a frame, which is slightly larger than a packet. Usually, this is an Ethernet frame.
3. Now, the frame of information needs to be sent on to the physical media—the cabling. To do this, the network adapter breaks down the frame of information into a serial bit stream to be sent one bit at a time across the cables to the other computer.
4. The receiving computer takes the serial bit stream and re-creates the frame of data. After analyzing the frame and verifying that it is indeed the intended recipient, it strips the frame information so that only the packet remains.
5. The packet is sent to the operating system, and, ultimately, the text file shows up on the computer's hard drive, available to the other user through Windows Explorer. This is a very basic example of data transfer, which is expanded on in Lesson 2.

Usually, local area networks utilize one of several Ethernet standards. *Ethernet* is a set of rules that govern the transmission of data between network adapters and various central connecting devices. All network adapters and central connecting devices must be compatible with Ethernet in order to communicate with each other. A very common type of Ethernet is known as 802.3u or Fast Ethernet that runs at 100 Mbps. Another common one is 802.3ab or Gigabit Ethernet.

In this type of network, when a computer wants to send data, that data is broadcast to every other host on the network by default. The problem with this is that usually there is only one recipient of the data. The rest of the computers simply drop the data packets. This, in turn, wastes network bandwidth. To alleviate this, about 15 years ago, Ethernet switching was developed, and it is used in most networks today. Switching has many advantages, one of which is that the switch only sends unicast traffic. ***Unicast*** is when information is sent to one host only. This reduces network traffic greatly, and helps with packet loss and duplicates.

We have mentioned network speed a few times already. A more accurate term is ***data transfer rate***, otherwise known as bit rate. This is defined as the maximum bits per second (bps) that can be transmitted over the network. As mentioned, it is rated in bits and is signified with a lowercase *b*, for example, 10 Mbps. The lowercase b helps to differentiate from data that is stored on a hard drive, which uses an uppercase *B* that stands for bytes, for example 10 MB.

Of course, all this means nothing without an addressing system in place. The most common type of network address is the Internet Protocol address, or IP address.

CONFIGURING INTERNET PROTOCOL

Internet Protocol, or IP, is the part of TCP/IP that, among other things, governs IP addresses. The ***IP address*** is the cornerstone of networking. It defines the computer or host you are working on. Today, every computer and many other devices have one. An IP address allows each computer to send and receive information back and forth in an orderly and efficient manner. IP addresses are like your home address. Just like your home address identifies your house number and the street you live on, an IP address identifies your computer number and the network it lives on. A common example of an IP address is 192.168.1.1.

Now, every IP address is broken down into two parts: the network portion, in this case 192.168.1, which is the network your computer is a member of, and the host portion, which is the individual number of your computer, differentiating your computer from any others on the network. In this case, it's .1. How do we know this? The subnet mask tells us.

The subnet mask is a group of four numbers that define what IP network the computer is a member of. All of the 255s in a subnet mask collectively refer to the network portion, while the 0s refer to the host portion. This is illustrated in Table 1-1. This table shows a typical Class C IP address and the default corresponding subnet mask. If you were to configure the IP address of a Windows computer as 192.168.1.1, Windows would automatically default to a subnet mask of 255.255.255.0. If any other computers would like to communicate with yours, they need to be configured with the same network number; however, every computer on the same network needs to have a different host number or an IP conflict might ensue. Of course, as a talented administrator, you'll learn how to avoid IP conflicts—and you'll learn some tips on how to do so in Lessons 4 and 5.

Table 1-1

An IP Address and Corresponding Subnet Mask

Type of Address	First Octet	Second Octet	Third Octet	Fourth Octet
IP address	192	168	1	1
Subnet mask	255	255	255	0

IP addresses are actually 32-bit dotted-decimal numbers. If you were to convert an IP address's decimal numbers to binary, you'd have a total of 32 bits. It is considered dotted because each number is separated by a dot. Altogether, they contain four numbers, each of which is a byte or octet. For example, 192 is an octet and its binary equivalent is 11000000, which is 8 bits. 168 is also an octet, its binary equivalent is 10101000, and so on. Adding all four octets together equals 32 bits.

IP addresses are usually applied to your network adapter, but can be applied to other devices, such as switches, routers, and so on. It's the fact that the device or computer has an IP address that makes it a ***host.*** Let's configure IP on our Windows 10 host now. Remember that other Windows computers will be configured in a very similar way.

CONFIGURE IP ADDRESSES

GET READY. To configure IP addresses, perform the following steps.

1. Access the Ethernet Properties dialog box.
2. Click **Internet Protocol Version 4** and then click the **Properties** button. The Internet Protocol Version 4 Properties dialog box opens. Write down the current settings (if there are any) so that you can return the computer to these settings at the end of the exercise.
3. By default, the Obtain an IP address automatically and Obtain DNS server address automatically radio buttons are enabled, as shown in Figure 1-11. That means that the network adapter will attempt to get all its IP information from a DHCP server or other device like a SOHO (Small Office/Home Office) four-port router. However, we want to configure the adapter statically, so let's continue on!

Figure 1-11

The Internet Protocol Version 4 Properties dialog box

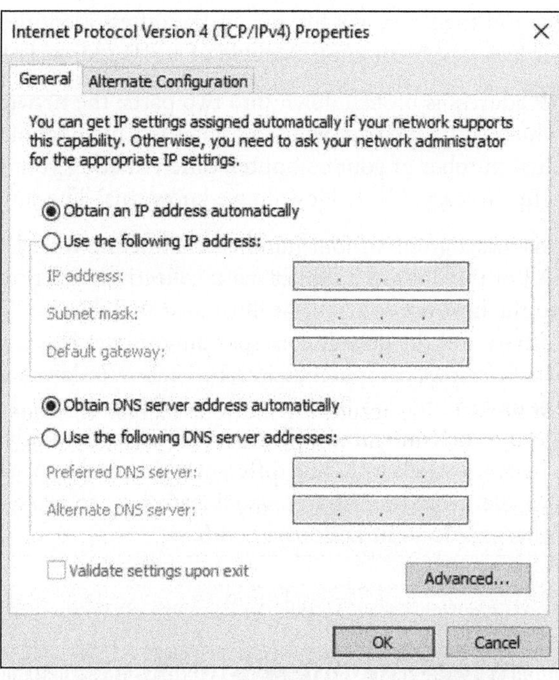

4. Click the **Use the following IP address** radio button. This enables the other fields so you can type in the IP information. Enter the following:
   - For the IP address, enter **192.168.1.1**.
   - For the Subnet mask, enter **255.255.255.0**.
   - Leave the Default gateway and the Preferred DNS server fields blank. The Default gateway is needed if you need to communicate with remote computers. The DNS is needed if you need to perform name resolution (names to IP addresses).
   - When you are finished, it should look like Figure 1-12.
   - If you have other computers, try configuring their IP addresses as well; the host portion of the IP should ascend once for each computer: .1, .2, .3, and so on.

Figure 1-12

The Internet Protocol Version 4 Properties dialog box configured statically

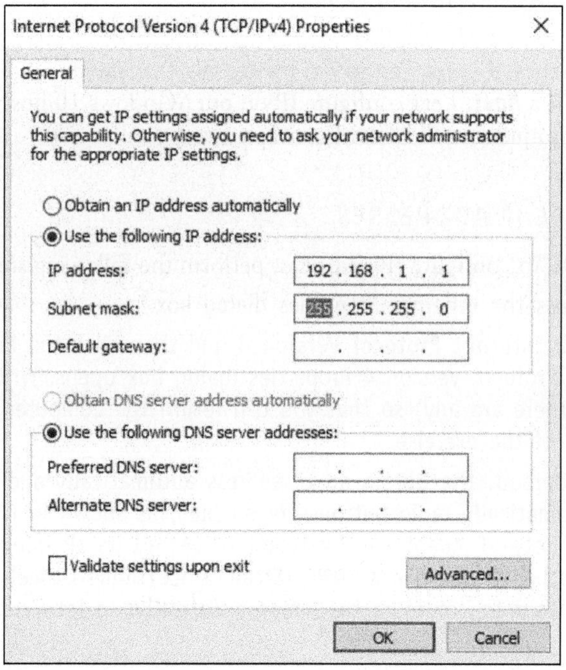

TAKE NOTE* If you are working with others as you complete this exercise, each person should enter a different IP address. For example, the first person should enter 192.168.1.1, the second person should enter 192.168.1.2, and so on. This avoids any possible IP conflicts.

5. Click **OK**. Then, in the Ethernet Properties dialog box, click **OK**. This completes and binds the configuration to the network adapter.
6. Test your configuration. We will do this in two ways, first with the `ipconfig` command, and second with the `ping` command:
   a. Open the Command Prompt window. Do this by pressing the **Windows+R** keys and typing **cmd** in the Open field. In the Command Prompt window, type **`ipconfig`**. The results should look similar to Figure 1-13. Notice the IPv4 Address field in the results and the IP address that is listed. It should be the IP address you configured previously. If not, go back and check your Internet Protocol Properties dialog box.

Figure 1-13

`Ipconfig` results in the Command Prompt window

```
Administrator: Command Prompt
C:\>ipconfig

Windows IP Configuration


Ethernet adapter Ethernet:

   Connection-specific DNS Suffix  . :
   IPv6 Address. . . . . . . . . . . : 2001:db8:1::1060
   Link-local IPv6 Address . . . . . : fe80::ec90:5993:7dc6:c53%11
   IPv4 Address. . . . . . . . . . . : 192.168.1.1
   Subnet Mask . . . . . . . . . . . : 255.255.255.0
   Default Gateway . . . . . . . . . :
```

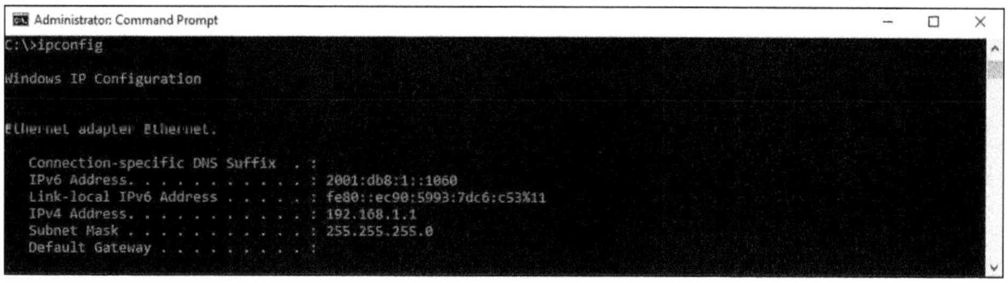

   b. Ping a computer on the same 192.168.1 network. If there are no other computers, ping your own IP address. For example, type the following command:

   `ping 192.168.1.1`

   This command sends requests out to the other IP address. If the other computer is running and configured properly, it should reply back. A positive ping would look similar to Figure 1-14, where four replies are received by the pinging computer.

Figure 1-14

`Ping` results in the Command Prompt window

```
Administrator: Command Prompt
C:\>ping 192.168.1.1

Pinging 192.168.1.1 with 32 bytes of data:
Reply from 192.168.1.1: bytes=32 time<1ms TTL=128
Reply from 192.168.1.1: bytes=32 time<1ms TTL=128
Reply from 192.168.1.1: bytes=32 time<1ms TTL=128
Reply from 192.168.1.1: bytes=32 time<1ms TTL=128

Ping statistics for 192.168.1.1:
    Packets: Sent = 4, Received = 4, Lost = 0 (0% loss),
Approximate round trip times in milli-seconds:
    Minimum = 0ms, Maximum = 0ms, Average = 0ms

C:\>_
```

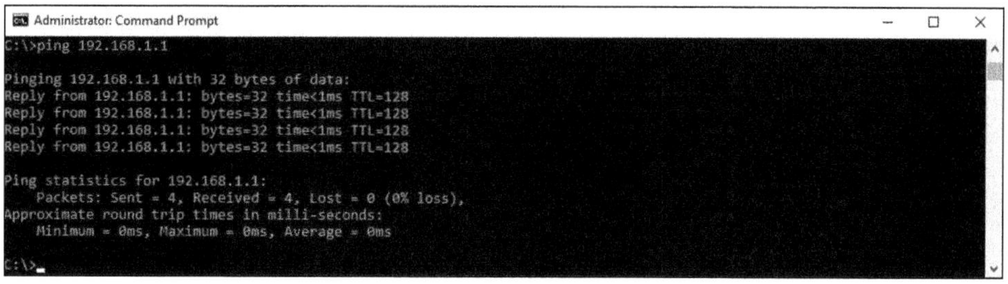

If you do not receive replies, but do receive another message, for example, "request timed out," check the IP configuration again, and check to ensure that the computer you are trying to ping is configured properly. In addition, make sure that the computers are wired to the network.

TAKE NOTE* Always test your network configurations!

You can also ping your own computer by way of the loopback address, also known as the local loopback. Every Windows computer automatically gets this address; it is 127.0.0.1. This is in addition to the logical address that you assigned earlier. Try the command `ping loopback` and check out the results you get. You can also try `ping localhost` and `ping 127.0.0.1`.

Regardless, you should get results from 127.0.0.1. When pinging this address, no network traffic is incurred because the network adapter is really just looping the ping back to the OS; it never places any packets on to the network, so this is a solid way to test if TCP/IP is installed correctly to a network adapter, even if you aren't physically connected to the network!

When you are finished, return your computer back to its regular IP settings. You'll learn more about the Internet Protocol in Lesson 4.

Identifying Types of LANs

There are several types of local area networks that a computer can connect to. An organization must make a choice as to whether it will have wired connections, wireless connections, or a mix of the two. In addition, it is also possible to have virtual LANs. You should know these types of LANs for the exam.

CERTIFICATION READY
What is the difference between a wired LAN and a wireless LAN?
Objective 1.2

The first and most common type of LAN is the wired LAN. Computers and other devices are wired together by way of copper-based, twisted-pair cables. These cables have RJ-45 plugs on each end, making the actual connection to RJ-45 ports that reside on the computer's network adapter, and on hubs, switches, or routers. (Of course, there will probably be some other cabling equipment in between each of these, but this equipment is covered in more depth in Lesson 3.)

Figure 1-15 gives yet another diagram, but this time it's three LANs connected together by a router. Some new devices appear in this figure: a firewall, which protects the LAN (or LANs) from the Internet, and a supercomputer, which occupies its own little LAN.

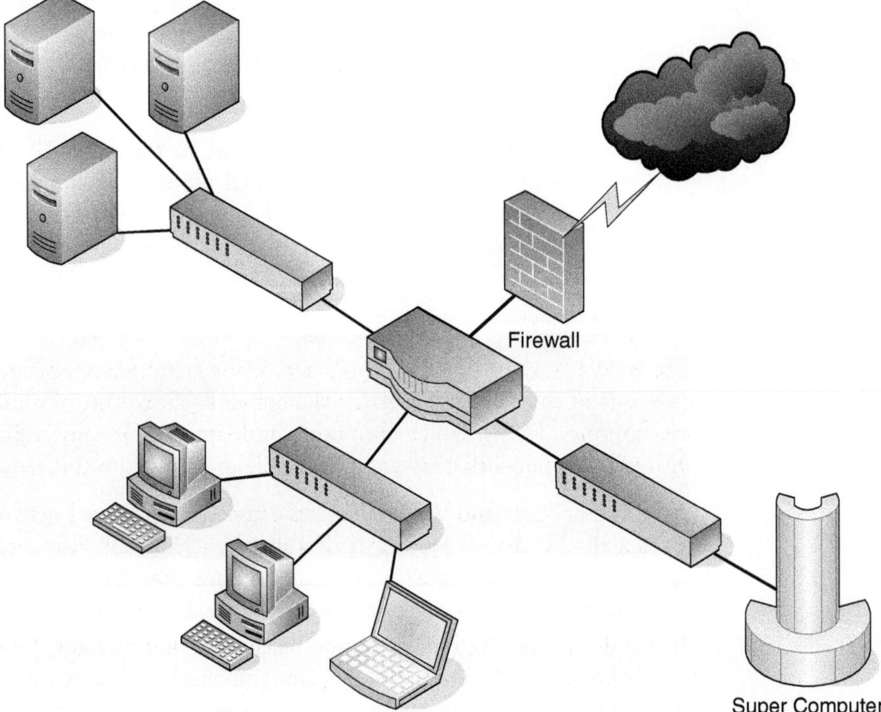

Figure 1-15
Wired LAN diagram

Generally, the connection from the PCs to their switch will be either 100 Mbps or 1 Gbps. Whatever speed you decide to use must be supported by each port of the switch and by each of the computers. In this diagram, they are wired to the switch. To accomplish gigabit network speeds, the cables used would have to be Category 5e or greater (more details on the types of cabling are covered in Lesson 3).

However, the connection from the server farm to the switch in the upper left of the figure and the supercomputer to its switch should be faster than your average PC connection. So, if the PCs on the LAN are connecting at 100 Mbps, the servers might be better off connecting at 1 Gbps; or, if the PCs are connecting at 1 Gbps, the servers would connect at 10 Gbps. High-speed connections should also be made between the three switches and the router. Now we are looking at a more accurate representation of a network setup our fictitious company needs from the original scenario! But just wait, the network documentation is going to get much more detailed. After all, we are only in Lesson 1!

Historically, wired networks are much faster than wireless networks. But now, it is by a much smaller margin due to the fact that wireless networking technology has made giant leaps and bounds over the past decade or so. A ***wireless local area network (WLAN)*** has many advantages, the most standout of which is the ability to roam. A person with a laptop, handheld computer or PDA, or another like device can work from anywhere. However, because wireless LANs can pose additional security problems, some companies have opted not to use them in their main offices. But with advancements in security, including developments in encryption, wireless is now more popular than ever. Figure 1-16 illustrates some wireless devices.

Figure 1-16
Wireless LAN diagram

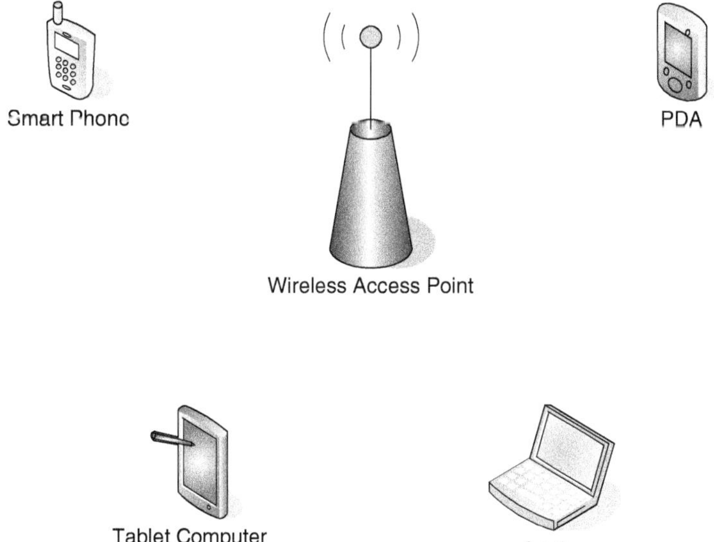

The ***wireless access point (WAP)*** acts as the central connecting device for the network. But now, one of the advantages is that the network can consist of more types of devices, including smartphones, PDAs, tablet computers, and laptops. Of course, PCs and laptops equipped with wireless network adapters will be able to connect to this network as well.

Wireless networks and wired networks can coexist. In small networks, a single device can act as a wireless access point, switch, router, and firewall! However, larger networks usually have one or more separate wireless access points that connect in a wired fashion to a network switch. And wireless access points have a limited range. Therefore, you might need to implement multiple WAPs depending on the size of the building and the area you want to cover.

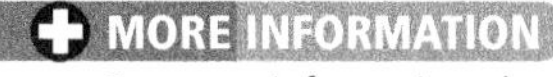

For more information about wired and wireless networks, refer to Lesson 3.

CERTIFICATION READY
What is a VLAN?
Objective 1.2

There is another type of LAN, the virtual LAN. A ***virtual LAN (VLAN)*** is a group of hosts with a common set of requirements that communicate as if they were connected together in a normal fashion on one switch, regardless of their physical location.

A VLAN is implemented to segment the network, reduce collisions, organize the network, boost performance, and increase security. Usually, switches control the VLAN. Like subnetting, a VLAN compartmentalizes the network and can isolate traffic. But unlike subnetting, a VLAN can be set up in a physical manner; an example of this is the port-based VLAN, as is shown in Figure 1-17. In this example, each set of computers, such as Classroom 2, has its own VLAN (which is dedicated to the 192.168.2.0 network in this case); however, computers in that VLAN can be located anywhere on the *physical* network. As another example, computers within the VLAN "Staff" could be located in several physical areas in the building, but regardless of where they are located, they are associated with the Staff VLAN because of the physical port they connect to.

Figure 1-17

Example of a VLAN

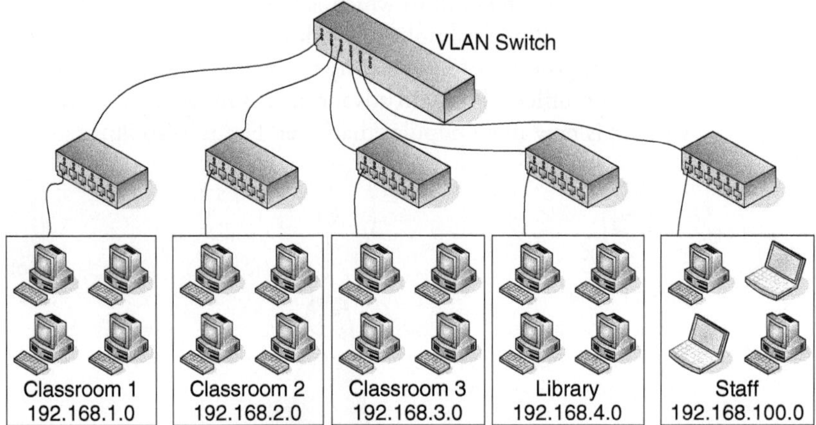

There are also logical types of VLANs like the protocol-based VLAN and the MAC address-based VLAN, but by far the most common is the port-based VLAN. The most common standard associated with VLANs is IEEE 802.1Q, which modifies Ethernet frames by "tagging" them with the appropriate VLAN information, based on which VLAN the Ethernet frame should be directed to.

Getting to Know Perimeter Networks

Perimeter networks are small networks that usually consist of only a few servers, which have some form of access to the Internet. Generally, the term perimeter network is synonymous with DMZ. You should be able to identify a DMZ and its purpose in an organization, as well as know how to implement a basic DMZ.

CERTIFICATION READY
Can you describe the various security zones?
Objective 1.2

A ***perimeter network*** (also known as a ***demilitarized zone [DMZ]***) is a small network that is set up separately from a company's private local area network and the Internet. It is called a perimeter network because it is usually on the edge of the LAN, but DMZ has become a much more popular term. The DMZ allows users outside of the company LAN to access specific services located on the DMZ. However, when set up properly, those users are blocked from gaining access to the company LAN. Users on the LAN will quite often connect to the DMZ as well, but without having to worry about outside attackers gaining access to their private LAN. The DMZ might house a switch with servers connected to it that offer web, email, and other services. Two common configurations of a DMZ include:

- **Back-to-back configuration:** This configuration has a DMZ situated in between two firewall devices, which could be black box appliances. An illustration of this is shown in Figure 1-18. In this configuration, an attacker would have to get through two firewalls in order to gain access to the LAN.

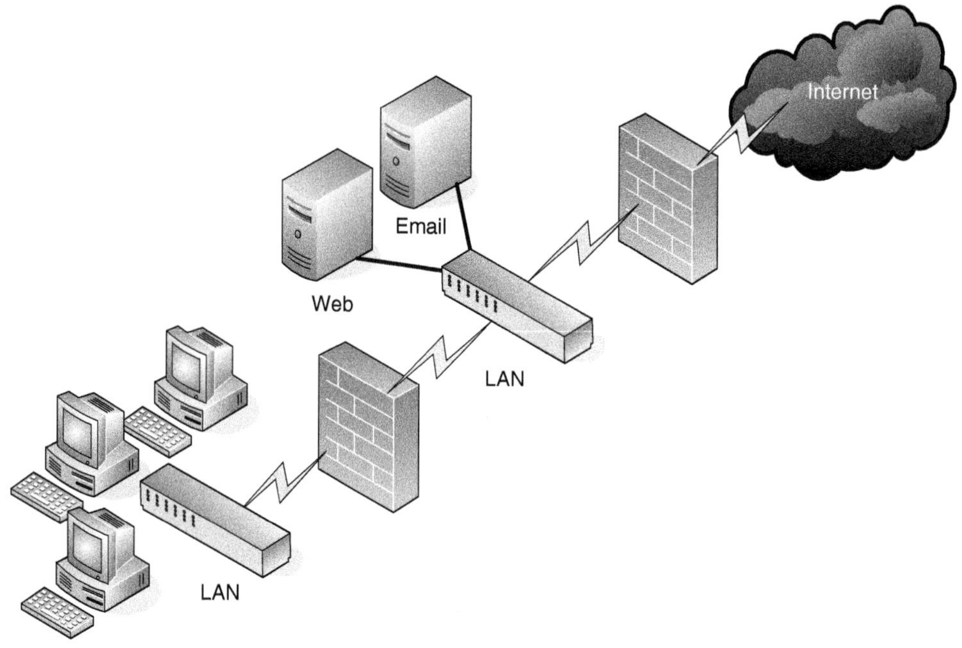

Figure 1-18

A back-to-back DMZ configuration

- **3-leg perimeter configuration:** In this scenario, the DMZ is usually attached to a separate connection of the company firewall. So, the firewall would have three connections: one to the company LAN, one to the DMZ, and one to the Internet, as shown in Figure 1-19. Once again, this could be done with a firewall appliance or server. In this configuration, an attacker would only need to break through one firewall to gain access to the LAN. Although this is a disadvantage, technologies like network intrusion detection/prevention systems can help alleviate most security issues. Also, one firewall means less administration.

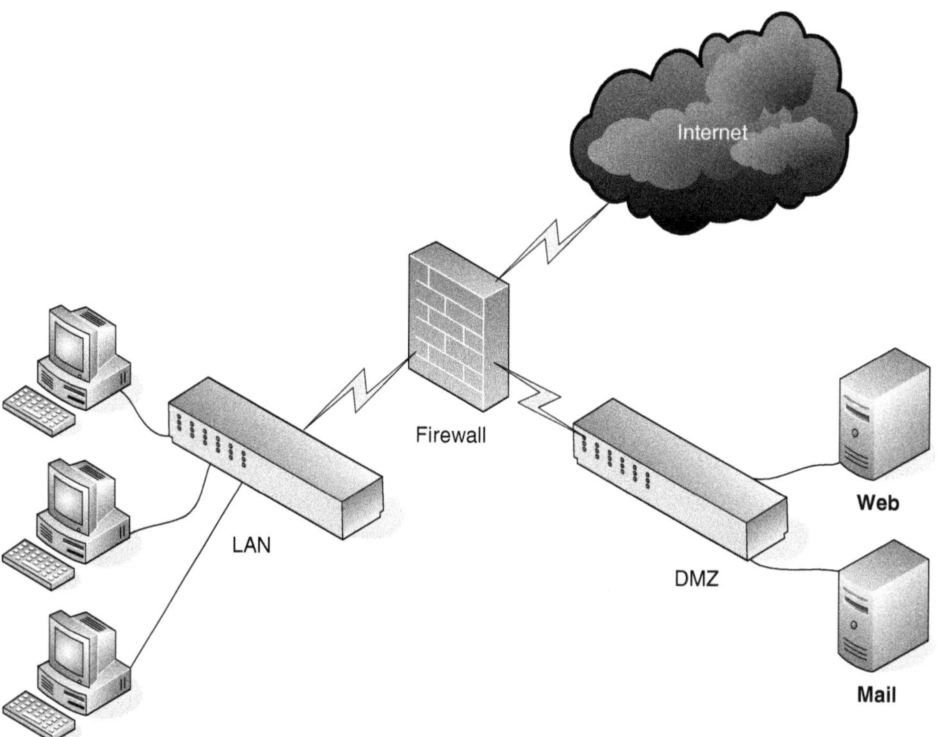

Figure 1-19

A 3-leg perimeter DMZ configuration

Identifying Network Topologies and Standards

THE BOTTOM LINE

Networks need to be situated in some way to facilitate the transfer of data. Topologies are the physical orientations of computers in a LAN. Access methods are ways that the computer will send data; the most common of these is the client/server-based Ethernet configuration, although there are others. In order to build a LAN, you must first plan out what topology (or topologies) will be used and what type of access method will be implemented. Access methods tend to be not so clear and definite, so let's begin with discussing network topologies.

Identifying Network Topologies

CERTIFICATION READY
Can you describe network topologies and access methods?
Objective 1.5

Network topologies define the physical connections of hosts in a computer network. There are several types of physical topologies, including bus, ring, star, mesh, and tree. For the exam, you should know the star, ring, and mesh technologies. We'll throw in the tree topology, known as hierarchical star, for good measure as well because it is considered by many as an extension of the star topology. We will also identify logical topologies because they are characterized differently than physical topologies.

In this exercise, you examine the following *physical* topologies:

- Star
- Mesh
- Ring

By far, the most common topology is the ***star topology***. When a star topology is used, each computer is individually wired to a central connecting device with twisted-pair cabling. The central connecting device could be a hub, a switch, or a SOHO router. This is the type of topology you will usually use when implementing networks.

IDENTIFY TOPOLOGIES

GET READY. To identify topologies, perform the following steps.

1. Examine Figure 1-20. This illustrates a simple star topology. Notice that it is like Figures 1-1 and 1-2 earlier in this lesson. Indeed, those other figures also illustrate star topologies. Note that the hub in the center of the figure connects each computer by a single cable. This way, if one cable is disconnected, the rest of the network can still function. This is the standard physical topology for an Ethernet network.

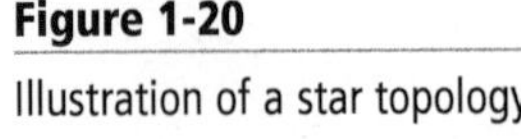

Figure 1-20
Illustration of a star topology

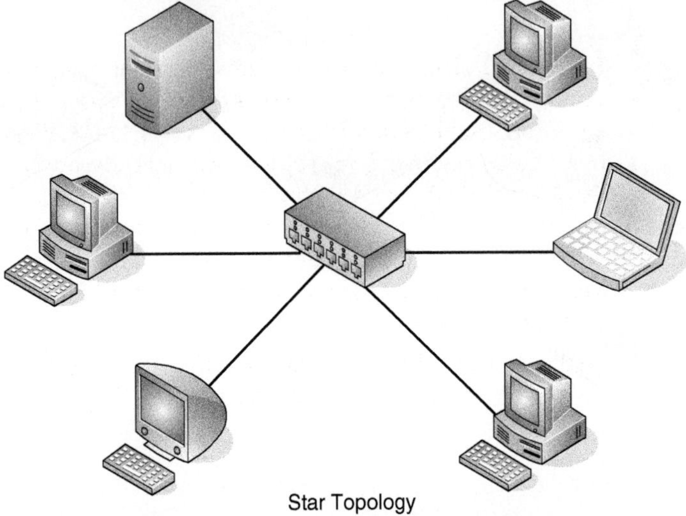

2. Examine your own computer network. Check to see if it meets the characteristics of the star; namely, is each computer connected to a central connecting device? Are they individually cabled to that device? Add to your network documentation the fact that it is a star if you identify it as such.

   In the old days, we had what was known as the bus topology. This is now deprecated because all computers were connected to a single bus cable; if one computer failed, the whole network went down! However, part of this idea was passed on to the star topology. For example, two individual star networks can be connected (by the central connecting devices) to create a star-bus topology. This is done by daisy-chaining (or stacking) one or more hubs or switches, usually by a special medium dependent interface (MDI) port; this is where the "bus" part of a star-bus topology comes in.

MORE INFORMATION

You will learn more about MDI ports in Lesson 3.

   The problem with the star-bus topology is that it is based on the stacking concept. This can pose organizational problems, and is not the best use of bandwidth. A better solution in most scenarios is to use the hierarchical star shown in Figure 1-3 earlier in this lesson.

3. In a ***mesh topology***, every computer connects to every other computer; no central connecting device is needed. As you can guess, a true, or "full" mesh, requires a lot of connections, as is illustrated in Figure 1-21. Examine the figure, and calculate how many connections would be needed at each computer to ensure a full mesh configuration.

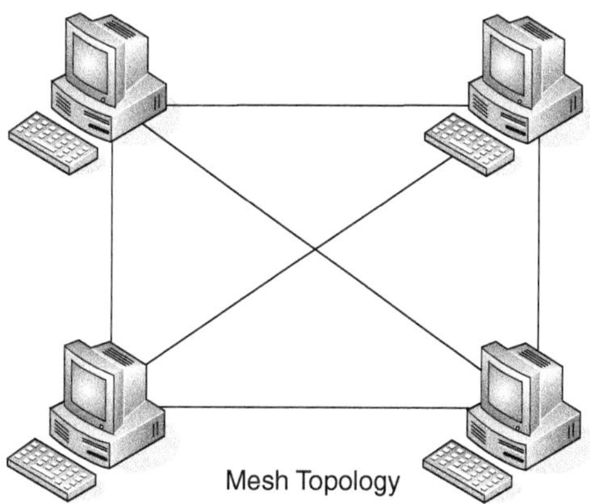

Figure 1-21

Illustration of a mesh topology

   The number of network connections that each computer will need is the total number of computers minus one. As you can guess, this type of topology is rare, but is necessary in some lab situations and fault-tolerant scenarios (where data needs to be replicated to multiple machines). A lesser version of this topology is the "partial mesh," where only one or a couple of the computers on the network have a second network connection, for example, if a computer needs to replicate a database to another computer but doesn't want the connection to be bothered by any other traffic. A computer with two or more network connections is known as a multihomed computer.

4. Lastly, we have the ***ring topology***. Examine Figure 1-22, which illustrates how computers are connected in a ring fashion.

Figure 1-22

Illustration of a ring topology

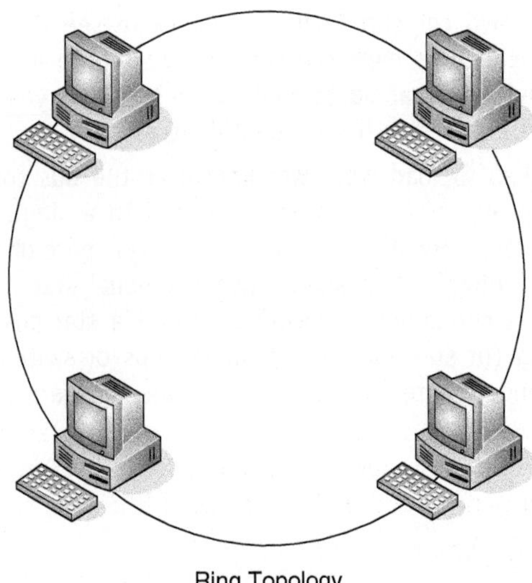

In a LAN environment, each computer is connected to the network by way of a closed loop, which was historically done with coaxial cable. When it comes to today's LANs, the use of coaxial cable has been deprecated; however, when applied to other types of networks like Token Ring, or Fiber Distributed Data Interface (FDDI), it takes on a different meaning—that of a logical topology.

A logical topology describes how the data is actually sent from one computer to the next. Token Ring and FDDI utilize a token-passing system. Instead of computers broadcasting their information to all other computers on an Ethernet network using a star topology, Token Ring and FDDI computers wait to obtain a token. The token is passed from computer to computer, picking up data and dropping it off as needed. Most of these networks have one token, but it is possible to have two in larger networks. The biggest advantage of Token Ring is that collisions become a nonfactor. A collision is when two computers attempt to send information simultaneously. The result is signal overlap, creating a collision of data, making both pieces of data unrecoverable. In Ethernet networks, data collisions are common due to the whole idea of broadcasting. But in token-based systems, there is only one item flying around the network at high speeds; it has nothing to collide with! Disadvantages include cost and maintenance, plus the fact that Ethernet switching and other Ethernet technologies have done away with a lot of the collisions that were the banes of network engineers until 15 or 20 years ago. Although FDDI networks also utilize ring topology logically as well as physically, they differ from Token Ring networks. A Token Ring network sends data logically in a ring fashion, meaning that a token goes to each computer, one at a time, and continues in cycles. However, the Token Ring computers are physically connected in a star fashion. All computers in a Token Ring network are connected to a central connecting device known as a Multistation Access Unit (MAU or MSAU). You'll learn more about Token Ring in Lesson 2.

Defining Ethernet Standards

Ethernet is far and away the most common type of LAN standard used by today's organizations. It is a scalable technology, but to get the most out of Ethernet, devices, computers, and other hosts should be compatible. This means knowing the various Ethernet standards is very important.

CERTIFICATION READY
Can you identify and describe Ethernet standards?
Objective 1.5

Ethernet is a group of networking technologies that define how information is sent and received between network adapters, hubs, switches, and other devices. An open standard, Ethernet is the de facto standard and has the largest share of networks in place today, with Token Ring and FDDI filling in the small gaps where Ethernet does not exist. It is standardized by the Institute of Electrical and Electronics Engineers (IEEE) as 802.3. Developed originally by Xerox, it was later championed by DEC, Intel, as well as Xerox. Now, Ethernet products are offered by hundreds of companies, such as D-Link, Linksys, 3Com, HP, and so on.

Computers on Ethernet networks communicate by sending Ethernet ***frames***. The frame is a group of bytes packaged by a network adapter for transmission across the network; these frames are created and reside on Layer 2 of the OSI model, which is covered in more depth in the next lesson. By default, computers on Ethernet networks all share a single channel. Because of this, only one computer can transmit at a time. However, newer networks with more advanced switches transcend this limitation of Ethernet, and is covered in more depth in Lesson 2.

IEEE 802.3 defines carrier sense multiple access with collision detection or ***Carrier Sense Multiple Access with Collision Detected (CSMA/CD)***. Because computers on a default Ethernet LAN all share the same channel, CSMA/CD governs the way that computers coexist with limited collisions. The basic steps for CSMA/CD are as follows:

1. The network adapter builds and readies a frame for transmission across the network.
2. The network adapter checks if the medium (for example, twisted-pair cable) is idle. If the medium is not idle, it waits for approximately 10 microseconds (10 μs). This delay is known as the interframe gap.
3. The frame is transmitted across the network.
4. The network adapter checks if any collisions occurred. If so, it moves on to the *collision detected* procedure.
5. The network adapter resets any retransmission counters (if necessary) and ends the transmission of the frame.

If a collision was detected in Step 4, another procedure called the collision detected procedure is employed:

1. The network adapter continues transmission until the minimum packet time is reached (known as a jam signal). This ensures that all receivers have detected the collision.
2. The network adapter increments the retransmission counter.
3. The network adapter checks if the maximum number of transmission attempts was reached. If it was, the network adapter aborts its transmission.
4. The network adapter calculates and waits a random back off period based on the number of collisions detected.
5. Finally, the network adapter starts the original procedure at Step 1 of the CSMA phase of the CSMA/CD process.

If an organization utilizes wireless Ethernet, ***Carrier Sense Multiple Access with Collision Avoidance (CSMA/CA)*** is employed. CSMA/CA is a network multiple access method in which carrier sensing is used, but nodes attempt to avoid collisions by transmitting only when the channel is identified as idle. When nodes do transmit, they transmit their packet data in its entirety. CSMA/CA is particularly important for wireless networks, where the collision detection of CSMA/CD is unreliable due to the hidden node problem

Devices on an Ethernet network must be compatible to a certain extent. If you are using an Ethernet switch, a computer's network adapter must also be of an Ethernet type in order to communicate with it. However, unlike some other networking technologies, different speeds can be negotiated. For example, suppose your switch had a maximum data transfer rate of

100 Mbps, but your network adapter only connected at 10 Mbps. The network adapter would still be able to communicate with the switch, but at the lesser rate. The various speeds of Ethernet and the cable media they use are defined by the various 802.3 standards listed in Table 1-2. Although 802.3 by itself is generally thought of as 10 Mbps, it is further broken up into various subgroups, as shown in the table.

Table 1-2

802.3 Ethernet Standards

802.3 Version	Data Transfer Rate	Cable Standard	Cabling Used
802.3	10 Mbps	10BASE5	Thick coaxial
802.3a	10 Mbps	10BASE2	Thin coaxial
802.3i	10 Mbps	10BASE-T	Twisted pair (TP)
802.3j	10 Mbps	10BASE-F	Fiber optic
802.3u	100 Mbps	100BASE-TX (most common) 100BASE-T4 100BASE-FX	TP using two pairs TP using four pairs Fiber optic
802.3ab	1,000 Mbps or 1 Gbps	1000BASE-T	Twisted pair
802.3z	1,000 Mbps or 1 Gbps	1000BASE-X	Fiber optic
802.3ae	10 Gbps	10GBASE-SR, 10GBASE-LR, 10GBASE-ER, and so on. . .	Fiber optic
802.3an	10 Gbps	10GBASE-T	Twisted pair
802.3ba	40 Gbps and 100 Gbps	40GBASE-T	Twisted pair

All of the 10-Mbps standards listed are a bit slow for today's network applications, but you might find them in some organizations and in other countries outside the United States. Of course, a good network administrator can make even 10-Mbps networks run quickly and efficiently. In fact, an efficient 10-Mbps network can easily outperform a poorly designed 100-Mbps network.

The 10-Gbps standards are much newer as of the writing of this book, and, therefore, are much more expensive. Currently, 1-Gbps connections for clients and 10-Gbps connections for network backbones are common. The most common cabling standards used today are 100BASE-TX and 1000BASE-T. Keep in mind that new standards are constantly being released by the IEEE.

10 Mbps is typically referred to as Ethernet, 100 Mbps is known as Fast Ethernet, and 1 Gbps is known as Gigabit Ethernet.

Identifying the Differences Between Client/Server and Peer-to-Peer

Most of today's networks are distributed. This means that CPU power and applications are not centralized, but instead, every host has a CPU, and every host can run programs that connect to other computers. The most common types of distributed networks are client/server and peer-to-peer. It is important to know the differences between these so you can decide which technology is best for any given customer scenario.

The older type of computing was known as ***centralized computing***. This was the case during the days of the mainframe, where there was one supercomputer, and the rest of the devices that connected to the supercomputer were known as terminals (or dumb terminals). They were strictly a keyboard and display with no processing power. Today's computing is known as ***distributive computing*** and is used for both client/server and peer-to-peer networks. This means that every device or workstation has its own processing power. However, in a way, the idea of centralized computing has made a comeback of sorts. Terminal services and remote sessions to computers are based on the centralized computing model. Also, thin-client computing has been slowly gaining in market share for the past decade or so. Thin-client computers do not have a hard drive. Instead, they store an operating system in RAM, which is loaded up every time the device is turned on. All other applications and data are stored centrally. So, in a way, this is sort of blending some centralized computing in with today's distributive computing.

DEFINING THE CLIENT/SERVER MODEL

The ***client/server*** model is an architecture that distributes applications between servers, such as Windows Server 2016, and client computers, such as Windows 8/8.1 or Windows 10. It also distributes the necessary processing power. It is extremely common in today's LANs, as with most applications that an average user would utilize when connecting to the Internet. For example, when users first come into work, they typically log on to the network. Chances are this is a client/server network. They might be using Windows 10 as the client computer to log on to a Microsoft domain, which is controlled by a Windows server. A simpler example would be a user at home connecting to the Internet. When a user wants to go to a website such as Bing, the user opens a web browser and types http://www.bing.com/ (or one of many shortcuts). The web browser is the client application. Bing's web server is obviously the "server." It serves the web pages filled with highly functional HTML code. The client computer's web browser decodes the HTML code and fills the web browser display with data for both on-the-job and personal use from the Internet from useful resources, such as Microsoft Outlook. Outlook is the client application; it connects to a mail server, most likely an SMTP server, perhaps run by Microsoft Exchange Server. The examples are endless, but client/server is not the end all when it comes to networking. Sometimes, it is more efficient to not use a server, particularly with a very small number of users.

Here are some examples of usages for servers:

- ***File server***: A file server stores files for computers to share. The connection to a file server could be made by browsing, by mapping a network drive, by connecting in the command line, or by connecting with an FTP client. The latter would require special FTP server software to be installed and configured on the file server. By default, Windows Server 2008 and newer can be file servers right out of the box.
- ***Print server***: A print server controls printers that can be connected directly to the server or (and more commonly) are connected to the network. The print server can control the starting and stopping of documents, as well as concepts such as spooling, printer pooling, ports, and much more. By default, Windows Server 2008 and newer can also be print servers right out of the box.

- ***Database server*:** A database server houses a relational database, one that is made up of one or more files. SQL databases fall into this category. They would require special software such as Microsoft SQL Server. Access databases (which are just one file) would not necessarily require a database server; they would usually be stored on a regular file server.
- ***Network controller*:** A network controller is a server, such as a Microsoft domain controller that oversees user accounts, computer accounts, network time, and the general well-being of the entire domain of computers and users. Windows Server 2016 servers can be domain controllers, but they need to be promoted to that status. By default, a Windows Server operating system is not a controller. Network controller operating systems are also referred to as ***network operating systems (NOSs)***.
- ***Messaging server*:** This server category is enormous. Providing simple services alone would make this a full-time job, but you have to add in fax servers, instant messaging, collaborative, and other types of messaging servers. For a Windows Server to control email, special software known as Exchange Server needs to be loaded in addition to the operating system.
- ***Web server*:** Web servers are important to share data and give information about a company. Windows servers can be web servers, but Internet Information Services (IIS) must be installed and configured in order to do so.
- ***CTI-based server*:** CTI is short for ***Computer Telephony Integration***. This occurs when a company's telephone system meets the computer system. Special PBXs that used to control phones as a separate entity can now be controlled by servers with powerful software.

UNDERSTANDING NEWER OPERATING SYSTEMS

The client version of Windows is the version that is purchased and installed on personal computers that include desktop computers, laptops, workstations, and tablets. Windows Server operating systems are purchased and installed on stand-alone physical servers, blades, and virtual machines.

Windows XP unified the consumer-oriented Windows 9x series with Windows NT/2000, while introducing a redesigned user interface, including the Start menu, Internet Explorer 6, and Remote Assistance functionality. As a result, Windows XP became one of the most popular client operating systems in history.

Later, Microsoft attempted to replace Windows XP with Windows Vista, which had an updated graphical user interface and improved security. Unfortunately, Windows Vista was not well received, and it failed to overtake Windows XP. To overcome the shortcomings of Windows Vista, Microsoft released Windows 7, which gave increased performance, a more intuitive interface, and fewer User Account Control pop-ups.

The next version of Windows was Windows 8, which was upgraded to support desktop computers, mobile computers, and tablets, while optimized for touch screens. It replaced the Start button and menu with the Start screen, a new platform for developing apps, and the Windows Store. Unfortunately, the new interface made it confusing and difficult to learn. To address some of these problems, Windows released Windows 8.1, which improved the Start screen.

Windows 10 is the newest client operating system. After the failure of Windows 8, Microsoft listened to customer complaints to develop Windows 10. To distance the new version of Windows from Windows 8/8.1, Microsoft skipped Windows 9 and went to Windows 10. Different from previous versions of windows, Windows 10 is released as an "operating system as a service," which means that it will receive ongoing updates to its features and functionality.

As client operating systems are developed and released, Microsoft also develops and releases server operating systems, as shown in Table 1-3. Until Windows 10, the client operating system and server operating system were introduced together. Although client and server operating systems can provide and request services, server operating systems can provide additional services and can service many more clients simultaneously.

Table 1-3

Client and Server Operating Systems

Client Operating Systems	Server Operating Systems	Version Number
Windows 10	Windows Server 2016	10.0
Windows 8.1	Windows Server 2012 R2	6.3
Windows 8	Windows Server 2012	6.2
Windows 7	Windows Server 2008 R2	6.1
Windows Vista	Windows Server 2008	6.0
Windows XP	Windows Server 2003/Windows Server 2003 R2	5.1/5.2
Windows 2000 Professional	Windows 2000 Server	5.0
Windows NT 4.0 Workstation	Windows NT 4.0 Server	4.0

DEFINING THE PEER-TO-PEER MODEL

Peer-to-peer networking, first and foremost, means that each computer is treated as an equal. This means that each computer has the equal ability to serve data, and to access data, just like any other computer on the network. Before servers became popular in PC-based computer networks, each PC had and still has the ability to store data. Even after the client/server model became king, peer-to-peer networks still had their place, especially in smaller networks with 10 computers or less. Today, peer computers can serve data; the only difference is that they can only serve it to a small number of computers at the same time.

In these small networks, the cost, administration, and maintenance of a server are too much for a small organization to consider viable. A Microsoft peer-to-peer network might consist of a couple Windows 7, 8/8.1, and/or Windows 10 computers. These are each client operating systems, and as such are known as peers because there is no controlling server in the network. This usually works well enough for smaller organizations. The beauty of Microsoft client operating systems is that up to 20 PCs can concurrently access an individual peer's shared resource. So, in these environments, one peer usually acts as a sort of pseudoserver, so to speak. But additional resources, such as files, databases, printers, and so on, could be added to any other computer on the network. The main disadvantage of this network model is that there is no centralized user database. User names and passwords are individually stored per computer. To implement a centralized user database, you would need to have a Windows-based server, which would mean that a client/server model would be employed.

Peer-to-peer has taken on a second meaning over the past decade or so. Now, it refers to file sharing networks, and in this case is referred to as ***P2P***. Examples of file sharing networks include Napster, Gnutella, and G2, but other technologies also take advantage of P2P file sharing, such as Skype, VoIP, and cloud computing. In a P2P network, hosts are added in an ad hoc manner. They can leave the network at any time without impacting the download of files. Many peers can contribute to the availability of files and resources. A person downloading information from a P2P network might get little bits of information from many different computers; afterwards, the downloading computer might help to share the file as well. Most file sharing peer-to-peer networks use special software to download files, such as BitTorrent. BitTorrent is a protocol as well as a program. The program (and others like it) is used to download large files from P2P networks. Instead of the files being stored on a single server, the file is distributed among multiple computers (could be a few, could be many). The possible benefits are availability of data and speed (although some torrent transfers will be slow). A computer, its BitTorrent client, and the router you are connected to can all be optimized to increase the speed of torrent downloads. It is estimated that between 20% and 35% of the data transfers on the Internet involve torrents. Another benefit of the BitTorrent client is that you can line up a large number of downloads from one torrent location (or multiple locations), and just let your computer download them while you do other things. A file is seeded (stored) on one or more computers. Then, as clients (peers) download that file (or portions of the file), they are automatically set up to distribute the file (or portions of the file). This way, more and more computers are added to the "swarm," making the availability of the file much greater. Computers are set up to automatically distribute the file; it's the default setting, but you can turn off seeding/distribution in your client. You could also block it at your firewall.

Instead of a server hosting the file, a server simply tracks and coordinates the distribution of files. The actual torrent starts with an initial small file (called a torrent file) that you download, which contains information about the files to be downloaded. The reason the whole process is called a torrent is because it usually begins with a small file that starts the download. One of the differences is that when downloading a torrent, there is more than one TCP connection (could be quite a few) to different machines in the P2P network. Contrast this to a single file download from a web server where only one TCP connection is made. This is controlled in a pseudorandom fashion by the tracking server to ensure availability of data. Another difference is that most web servers will put a cap on the number of concurrent downloads you can do, but not so with the torrent client program. The average person uses a BitTorrent client to download movies, MP3s, and other media. Sometimes, these are distributed with the consent of the owner; other times (and quite often), they are illegally seeded and distributed—as well as downloaded! An example of legitimate usage is the *World of Warcraft* game. The owners of the game use the Blizzard BitTorrent to distribute just about everything involved in the game. Newer games for the PS3 and other consoles are doing the same type of thing. D-Link and other network equipment companies are embracing torrent technology as well.

SKILL SUMMARY

IN THIS LESSON, YOU LEARNED:

- A network is two or more computers that exchange data. A local area network (LAN) is a group of these computers that are confined to a small geographic area, usually one building.
- The network adapter, also known as a network interface card (NIC), is the device that enables the sending and receiving of data to and from your computer. Today, multiple devices can connect to each other and communicate using a switch.
- Internet Protocol (IP) is the part of TCP/IP that, among other things, governs IP addresses. The IP address is the cornerstone of networking. It defines the computer or host you are working on.
- A wireless local area network (WLAN) has many advantages, the most standout of which is the ability to roam. A person with a laptop, handheld computer or PDA, or other like device can work from anywhere.
- Network topologies define the physical connections of hosts in a computer network. There are several types of physical topologies, including bus, ring, star, mesh, and tree.
- Today's computing is known as distributive computing and is used for both client/server and peer-to-peer networks. This means that every device or workstation has its own processing power.
- The client/server model is an architecture that distributes applications between servers, such as Windows Server 2016, and client computers, such as Windows 8/8.1 or Windows 10.
- Peer-to-peer networking, first and foremost, means that each computer is treated as an equal. This means each computer has the equal ability to serve data and to access data, just like any other computer on the network. Before servers became popular in PC-based computer networks, each PC had the ability to store data.

■ Knowledge Assessment

Multiple Choice

Select the correct answer for each of the following questions.

1. Which of the following regenerates the signal and broadcasts the signal to every computer connected to it?
   a. Hub
   b. Switch
   c. Router
   d. Firewall
2. Which of the following is *not* a central connecting device?
   a. Hub
   b. Switch
   c. SOHO router
   d. Windows 10 client
3. When installing a network adapter to a computer so that it can be connected to a network that uses twisted-pair cabling, which type of port must be used by the network adapter?
   a. RJ-11
   b. RJ-45
   c. RG-58
   d. Fiber optic
4. In Windows 10, which of the following should be used to access the properties of a network adapter?
   a. Device Manager
   b. `Ping`
   c. Advanced Firewall
   d. Task Manager
5. When connecting a computer's network adapter to a switch—with the desire for the connection to be able to send and receive data simultaneously—which type of connection is required?
   a. Half-duplex
   b. Full-duplex
   c. Simplex
   d. 100 Mbps
6. When connecting a computer at a rate of 100,000,000 bits per second, which of the following should be the speed of the network adapter being installed?
   a. 10 Mbps
   b. 100 MB/s
   c. 100 Mbps
   d. 1,000 Mbps
7. When connecting to a router that has the IP address 192.168.1.100 on a standard, default Class C network using the subnet mask 255.255.255.0, which of the following is a valid IP address for the network adapter?
   a. 192.168.0.1
   b. 192.168.1.1
   c. 192.168.100.1
   d. 192.168.1.100

8. After installing a network adapter and configuring an IP address and subnet mask, which command can be used to verify that the IP address is configured and listed properly?
   a. `Ping`
   b. `Tracert`
   c. `CMD`
   d. `Ipconfig`

9. Which of the following commands enables pinging your own computer to see if it is operational?
   a. `ping localclient`
   b. `ping 128.0.0.1`
   c. `ping loopback`
   d. `ping network adapter`

10. Which of the following types of networks should be used to connect a computer to a group of hosts that have been segmented from the regular network?
    a. LAN
    b. WLAN
    c. WAN
    d. VLAN

Fill in the Blank

Fill in the correct answer in the blank space provided.

1. The manager of IT asks you to connect a perimeter network to the firewall, which will be separate from the LAN. This type of network is known as a _____.
2. A _____ topology can be defined by connecting several hubs to a switch.
3. 802.3u Ethernet networks run at _____ Mbps.
4. A _____ is a program used to download files quickly from a P2P network.
5. The _____ network architecture is physically a star and logically a ring.
6. 802.3ab Ethernet networks run at _____ Mbps.
7. A _____ connection is when data can be sent and received, but not at the same time.
8. A _____ topology can be defined as connecting several computers together in a circle, without the use of a hub or a switch.
9. When several computers are connected in a small geographic area, it is known as a _____.
10. A _____ acts as a central connecting device and allows laptops, PDAs, and handheld computers to communicate with each other.

■ Business Case Scenarios

Scenario 1-1: Planning and Documenting a Basic LAN

Proseware, Inc., requires you to implement a 20-computer local area network. Fifteen of these computers will be Windows 10 clients, and five will be Windows Server 2016 computers. They also require a 24-port switch, router, DSL Internet connection, DMZ with web server, and a laptop for the CEO. Create a diagram of the network documentation for this in Microsoft Visio or on paper. Refer to Figures 1-1 through 1-3 for types of devices in the Visio networking stencils.

Scenario 1-2: Selecting the Correct Networking Model

The ABC Company requires a network that can support 50 users. Describe the correct type of networking model to use and explain why.

Scenario 1-3: Selecting Network Adapters for Your LAN Computers

You are consulting for a company that asks you to install five new computers. The network adapter in each computer should be able to communicate at 1,000 Mbps over the preexisting twisted-pair cabling and should be able to send and receive data simultaneously. Which Ethernet standard should be selected and which technology should be utilized?

Scenario 1-4: Configuring the Correct Subnet Mask

A computer is not connecting to certain network devices properly. The IP address information is as follows:

IP address: 192.168.1.210
Subnet mask: 255.254.0.0

Describe how to configure the subnet mask so that the computer can communicate properly with all networking devices and other hosts on the network.

Workplace Ready

Utilizing Full-Duplex Connections

Many network cards have the ability to run in full-duplex mode, but sometimes, it is overlooked. Or, the central connecting device in the network might not have the ability to run in full-duplex, thus reducing the network capability to half-duplex.

When you think about it, that is effectively reducing your network throughput by half. By using full-duplex connections on the central connecting devices, and all of the network adapters, 100 Mbps effectively becomes 200 Mbps, because now the devices can send *and* receive at the same time.

Network devices are usually rated at their half-duplex data transfer rate. So, if you see a network adapter being sold as a 1-Gbps device, look a little further. See if it is full-duplex capable, and if so, you could see a maximum data transfer rate of 2 Gbps.

Remember to set this in the Properties page of the network adapter, which can be found within Device Manager.

For this exercise, access the Internet and locate three different 1-Gbps network adapters that can operate in full-duplex mode. Try manufacturers such as D-Link, Linksys, Intel, and so on. You will need to view the specifications of each device and note the link to those pages as proof of your discovery. Another great source for different equipment is www.pricewatch.com. Access this site to view various networking equipment from different vendors.

2 LESSON

Defining Networks with the OSI Model

OBJECTIVE DOMAIN MATRIX

Skills/Concepts	Objective Domain Description	Objective Domain Number
Understanding OSI Basics Defining the Upper OSI Layers	Understand the Open Systems Interconnection (OSI) model	3.1
Defining the Communications Subnetwork	Understand switches	2.1

KEY TERMS

Address Resolution Protocol
Application layer
ARP table
baseband
broadband
CAM table
communications subnetwork
Data Link layer
encapsulated
encoded
inbound ports
Internet Assigned Numbers Authority (IANA)
Internet Control Message Protocol (ICMP)
Internet Engineering Task Force (IETF)
Internet Protocol (IP)
Layer 2 switch
Layer 3 switch
MAC flood
media access control (MAC) address
Network layer
Open Systems Interconnection reference model (OSI model)
outbound ports
overhead
Physical layer
ports
Presentation layer
protocol stack
Session layer
Transmission Control Protocol (TCP)
Transport layer
User Datagram Protocol (UDP)

The Open Systems Interconnection reference model (OSI model) helps network engineers, network administrators, and systems engineers to define how data networking actually works from one computer to another, regardless of where the computer is or what software it runs. It is composed of seven layers, each of which corresponds to devices, protocols, standards, and applications in the real world. A computer network specialist uses the OSI model to help in designing, maintaining, and troubleshooting networks. This lesson defines each of the OSI model layers using hands-on labs and theory. As we discuss each layer, imagine devices and applications that would be supported by that layer, as you might see in a small office or home office. Using the concepts from Lesson 1, plug them into each of the layers as we go through this lesson.

Understanding OSI Basics

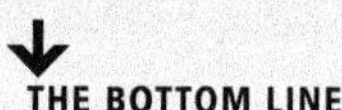

The ***Open Systems Interconnection reference model (OSI model)*** is a reference model used to define how data communications occur on computer networks. It is divided into layers that provide services to the layers above and below. These layers are associated with protocols and devices.

The OSI model was created and ratified by the International Organization for Standardization (ISO), and is represented in the United States by the American National Standards Institute (ANSI). This model was created to do the following:

- Explain network communications between hosts on the LAN or WAN.
- Present a categorization system for communication protocol suites.
- Show how different protocol suites can communicate with each other.

When we say "different protocol suites," keep in mind that TCP/IP is not the only player in town. However, it is by far the most common. If TCP/IP devices need to communicate with other devices using other communication protocols, the OSI model can help to describe how translation between the two will take place. In addition to being described by the OSI model, TCP/IP has its own model—the TCP model, which is discussed toward the end of this lesson.

Know that network communications existed before the model was created. This model is an abstract way of categorizing the communications that already exist. The model was created to help engineers understand what is happening with communication protocols behind the scenes. Let's go ahead and break down the OSI into its distinct layers and functions.

Defining the OSI Model Layers

The OSI model was created as a set of seven layers, or levels, each of which houses different protocols within one of several protocol suites, the most common of which is TCP/IP. The OSI model categorizes how TCP/IP transactions occur. It is invaluable when it comes to installing, configuring, maintaining, and, especially, troubleshooting networks.

CERTIFICATION READY
Can you define the OSI model?
Objective 3.1

Sometimes, a protocol suite such as TCP/IP is referred to as a ***protocol stack***. The OSI model shows how a protocol stack works on different levels of transmission (that is, how it stacks up against the model). Because it is the most tangible, let's start with the Physical layer. Later, when you view the model, it will be from the seventh layer on top to the first layer on bottom. As mentioned previously, a LAN requires computers with network adapters. These must be connected in some way to facilitate the transfer of data. It is important to define how they are connected, as well as how they transmit the data. The OSI model layers do just that. The following list gives a brief description of each of the layers:

- **Layer 1: *Physical layer*:** This is the physical and electrical medium for data transfer. It includes but is not limited to cables, jacks, patch panels, punch blocks, hubs, and multistation access units (MAUs). It is also known as the physical plant. Concepts related to the Physical layer include topologies, analog versus digital/encoding, bit synchronization, baseband versus broadband, multiplexing, and serial (5-volt logic) data transfer. If you can touch it, it is part of the Physical layer, making this layer one of the easiest to understand.

  The unit of measurement used on this layer is *bits*.
- **Layer 2: *Data Link layer*:** This layer establishes, maintains, and decides how transfer is accomplished over the Physical layer. Devices that exist on the DLL are network interface cards and bridges. This layer also ensures error-free transmission over the Physical layer under LAN transmissions. It does this through the use of physical addresses (the hexadecimal address that is burned into the ROM of the NIC), otherwise known as the MAC address (to be discussed more later in this lesson). Just about any device that makes a physical connection to the network and can move data is on the Data Link layer.

  The unit of measurement used on this layer is *frames*.
- **Layer 3: *Network layer*:** The Network layer is dedicated to routing and switching information between different networks, LANs, or internetworks. This can be on the LAN or WAN (wide area network). Devices that exist on the Network layer are routers and IP switches. Now we are getting into the logical addressing of hosts. Instead of physical addresses, the addressing system of the computer is stored in the operating system—for example, IP addresses.

  Now you can see that a typical computer really has *two* addresses: a physical or hardware-based address, such as a MAC address, and a logical or software-based address, such as an IP address. Part of the trick in networking is to make sure the two get along together!

  The unit of measurement used on this layer is *packets*.
- **Layer 4: *Transport layer*:** This layer ensures error-free transmission between hosts through logical addressing. Therefore, it manages the transmission of messages through Layers 1 through 3. The protocols that are categorized by this layer break up messages, send them through the subnet, and ensure correct reassembly at the receiving end, making sure there are no duplicates or lost messages. This layer contains both connection-oriented and connectionless systems, which are covered later in this lesson, in the Defining the Transport Layer section. Inbound and outbound ports are controlled by this layer. When you think *ports*, think the Trans*port* layer.

  The unit of measurement used on this layer is sometimes referred to as segments, or messages. All layers above this use the terms *data* and *messages*.
- **Layer 5: *Session layer*:** This layer governs the establishment, termination, and synchronization of sessions within the OS over the network and between hosts—for example, when you log on and log off. It is the layer that controls the name and address database for the OS or NOS. NetBIOS (Network Basic Input/Output System) works on this layer.
- **Layer 6: *Presentation layer*:** This layer translates the data format from sender to receiver in the various operating systems that may be used. Concepts include code conversion, data compression, and file encryption. Redirectors work on this layer, for example, mapped network drives that enable a computer to access file shares on a remote computer.
- **Layer 7: *Application layer*:** This is where message creation—and, therefore, packet creation—begins. DB access is on this level. End-user protocols, such as FTP, SMTP, Telnet, and RAS, work at this layer. For example, suppose you are using Outlook Express. You type a message and click Send. This initiates SMTP (Simple Mail Transfer Protocol) and other protocols, which send the mail message down through the other layers, breaking it down into packets at the Network layer and so on. This layer is not the application itself, but the protocols that are initiated by this layer.

Sound like a lot of information? Well, it is, but you need to get into the habit of picturing the model whenever you are doing data transfer, and more important, while you are troubleshooting networking issues. That is one of the main reasons a network administrator utilizes the OSI model. An example is illustrated in Figure 2-1. The more you imagine the data transfer through the levels, the more readily you will be able to memorize and understand how the OSI model works. In addition, it will be invaluable to you in the future when troubleshooting network problems. To help memorize the layers, some people use mnemonic devices, such as associating the first letter of each layer name with a different word—for example, *All People Seem To Need Data Processing.* That was from Layer 7 to Layer 1. Or, how about the opposite direction? *Please Do Not Throw Sausage Pizza Away.* Or just memorize the real names! It's up to you. In Figure 2-1, you can imagine a message being created in Outlook Express. The Send button is clicked, and the message goes down the layers of the OSI model to the physical medium. It then crosses the medium (probably cables) and climbs the OSI model at the receiving machine. This happens every time two computers communicate; in fact, it happens every time a packet is sent from one computer to another. Although the OSI model is always in place, all of the levels might not be involved with every communication. For example, if you were to ping another computer, only Layers 1 through 3 would be utilized. It all depends on the type of communication and the number of protocols being used for that specific transmission.

TAKE NOTE*

Use a mnemonic device such as *All People Seem To Need Data Processing* to help memorize the OSI layers.

Figure 2-1

A basic illustration of the OSI model

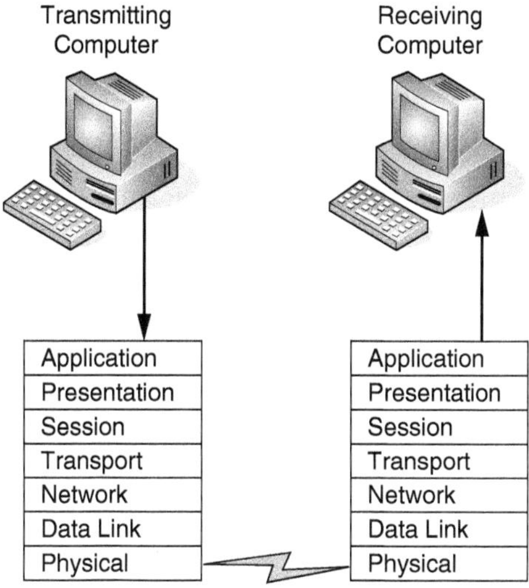

■ Defining the Communications Subnetwork

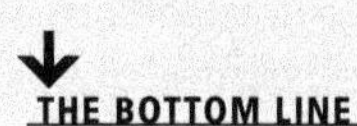

The ***communications subnetwork*** is the core of OSI model transmissions. It comprises Layers 1 through 3. Regardless of what data transmission occurs in a computer network, the communications subnetwork is employed.

CERTIFICATION READY
What are some examples of devices?
Objective 3.1

In the following exercises, you will:

- Define the Physical layer by showing a data transfer.
- Define the Data Link layer by showing the MAC address of a network adapter.
- Define the Network Layer by using ipconfig, ping, and protocol analyzers.
- Define Layer 2 and Layer 3 switches.

Remember that the Physical layer deals with the tangible—the physical—and that it transmits bits of information. In the first exercise, you will test the "speed," or data transfer rate, of a computer's Internet connection.

DEFINE THE PHYSICAL LAYER

GET READY. To define the Physical layer, perform the following steps.

1. Open a web browser and go to SpeedTest.net.
2. Locate a server in your area and click it (make sure that it has availability for testing), and click **BEGIN TEST**.
3. Watch as the web app tests your download and upload speed. In a minute or so, you should see results similar to Figure 2-2.

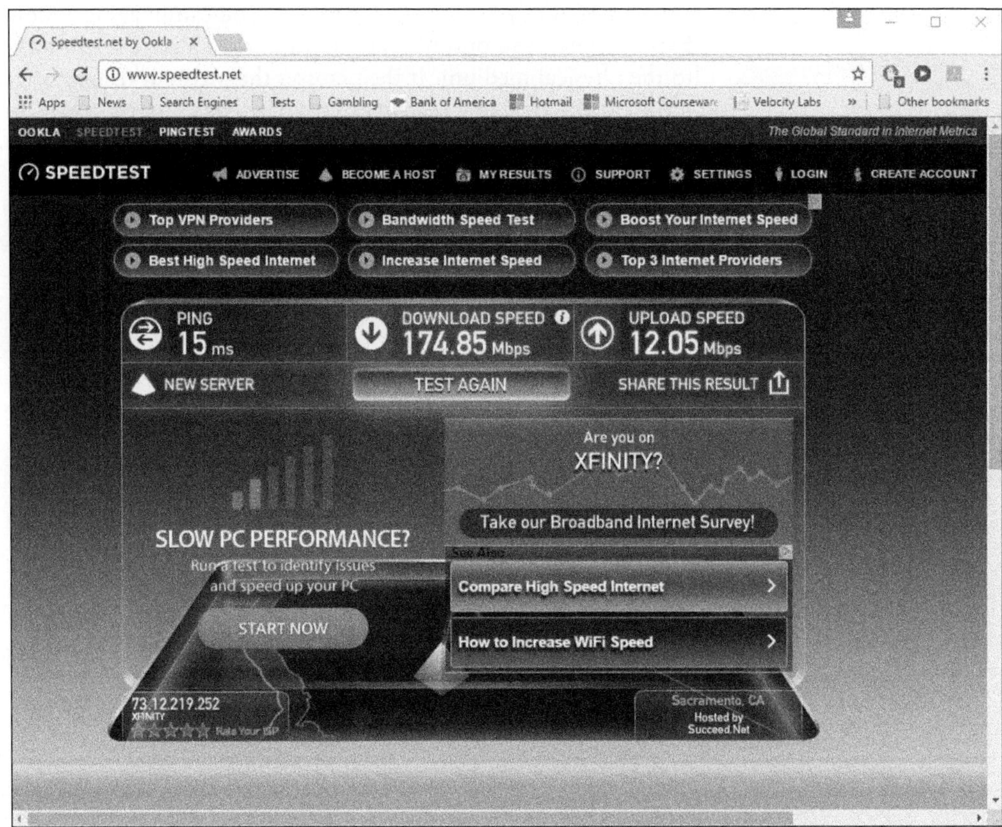

Figure 2-2

Results of a SpeedTest.com speed test

Notice in Figure 2-2 that the results are displayed in bits. The download data transfer rate in the figure is 174.85 Mbps. That is how fast bits were delivered to the tested computer through the Internet connection. These bits are transferred on the Physical layer, and so, this is a test of the Physical layer data transfer rate. Although there are other factors involved, such as your Internet service provider's speed, and so on, this gives a basic example of bps (bits per second) on the Physical layer.

> **TAKE NOTE***
>
> Over time, SpeedTest .net might change its navigation slightly. Just remember that you are looking for the Flash speed test.

To get an accurate representation of your data transfer rate, run this test three times, once every few minutes. Then, average your results to get a more reliable number for your data transfer rate.

Take a look at the local area connection's Status dialog box on a Windows computer. It should look similar to Figure 2-3. Note the Speed is measured in bits as well. In the figure, it is 1.0 Gbps. Either Gbps or Gb/s is acceptable, but generally in this book, when bits are referred to, they are shown as bps.

Networking standards such as 100BASE-T are based on the Physical layer. The 100 in 100BASE-T stands for 100 Mbps, the BASE means ***baseband***, and the T stands for twisted-pair cabling. Baseband refers to the fact that all computers on the LAN share the same channel or frequency to transmit data, in this case 100 MHz. Conversely, ***broadband*** means that there are multiple channels to be utilized by the communications system. Although most LANs are baseband, examples of broadband services include cable TV and FM radio stations.

Figure 2-3

A Windows local area connection Status dialog box

Remember that the Data Link layer governs devices like network adapters. The network adapters must comply with a Data Link layer networking standard such as Ethernet. In an Ethernet network, every network adapter must have a unique ***media access control (MAC) address***. The MAC address is a unique identifier assigned to network adapters by the manufacturer. This address is 6 octets in length and is written in hexadecimal. The following exercise shows this in the command line.

DEFINE THE DATA LINK LAYER

GET READY. To define the Data Link layer, perform the following steps.

1. On a Windows computer, access the Command Prompt window. The easiest way is to press the **Windows+R** keys and at the Run prompt, type **cmd**, and then press **Enter**.
2. Type the **ipconfig/all** command and press **Enter**. (The /all is necessary; otherwise, the MAC address will not be displayed.) The results should look similar to Figure 2-4. Note that the MAC address is listed as a physical address in the results. This is because it is a physical address—it is burned into the ROM chip of the network adapter.
3. Display MAC addresses of other hosts that your computer has recently connected to by executing the **arp -a** command. This shows the IP address and the corresponding MAC address of the remote computers.

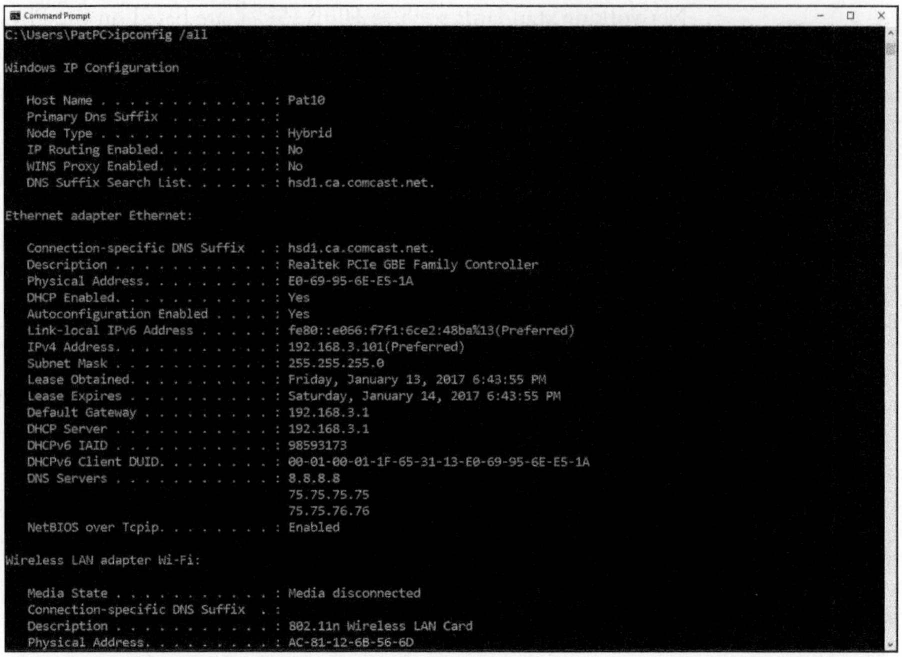

Figure 2-4

A MAC address as shown in the Command Prompt window

```
Command Prompt
C:\Users\PatPC>ipconfig /all

Windows IP Configuration

   Host Name . . . . . . . . . . . . : Pat10
   Primary Dns Suffix  . . . . . . . :
   Node Type . . . . . . . . . . . . : Hybrid
   IP Routing Enabled. . . . . . . . : No
   WINS Proxy Enabled. . . . . . . . : No
   DNS Suffix Search List. . . . . . : hsd1.ca.comcast.net.

Ethernet adapter Ethernet:

   Connection-specific DNS Suffix  . : hsd1.ca.comcast.net.
   Description . . . . . . . . . . . : Realtek PCIe GBE Family Controller
   Physical Address. . . . . . . . . : E0-69-95-6E-E5-1A
   DHCP Enabled. . . . . . . . . . . : Yes
   Autoconfiguration Enabled . . . . : Yes
   Link-local IPv6 Address . . . . . : fe80::e066:f7f1:6ce2:48ba%13(Preferred)
   IPv4 Address. . . . . . . . . . . : 192.168.3.101(Preferred)
   Subnet Mask . . . . . . . . . . . : 255.255.255.0
   Lease Obtained. . . . . . . . . . : Friday, January 13, 2017 6:43:55 PM
   Lease Expires . . . . . . . . . . : Saturday, January 14, 2017 6:43:55 PM
   Default Gateway . . . . . . . . . : 192.168.3.1
   DHCP Server . . . . . . . . . . . : 192.168.3.1
   DHCPv6 IAID . . . . . . . . . . . : 98593173
   DHCPv6 Client DUID. . . . . . . . : 00-01-00-01-1F-65-31-13-E0-69-95-6E-E5-1A
   DNS Servers . . . . . . . . . . . : 8.8.8.8
                                       75.75.75.75
                                       75.75.76.76
   NetBIOS over Tcpip. . . . . . . . : Enabled

Wireless LAN adapter Wi-Fi:

   Media State . . . . . . . . . . . : Media disconnected
   Connection-specific DNS Suffix  . :
   Description . . . . . . . . . . . : 802.11n Wireless LAN Card
   Physical Address. . . . . . . . . : AC-81-12-6B-56-6D
```

The Data Link layer is where networking standards such as Ethernet (802.3) and Token Ring (802.5) reside. You can look up the various IEEE 802 standards at http://standards.ieee.org/getieee802/portfolio.html

Understanding Layer 2 Switching

The Data Link layer is also where Layer 2 switches reside. A ***Layer 2 switch*** is the most common type of switch that is used on a LAN. They are hardware based and they use the MAC address of each host computer's network adapter when deciding where to direct frames of data; every port on the switch is mapped to the specific MAC address of the computer that physically connects to it. Layer 2 switches do not normally modify frames as they pass through the switch on their way from one computer to another. Each port on a switch is its own segment. This means that every computer connected to a Layer 2 switch has its own usable bandwidth—whatever the switch is rated at: 10 Mbps, 100 Mbps, 1 Gbps, and so on.

CERTIFICATION READY
What are Layer 2 switches and MAC tables?
Objective 2.1

Security is a concern with Layer 2 switches. Switches have memory that is set aside to store the MAC address to a port translation table, known as the MAC table or Content Addressable Memory table (***CAM table***). This table can be compromised with a ***MAC flood*** attack. This sends numerous packets to the switch, each of which has a different source MAC address, in an attempt to fill up the memory space on the switch. If this is successful, the switch changes state to what is known as *failopen mode*. At this point, the switch broadcasts data on all ports the way a hub does. This means two things: First, the network bandwidth is dramatically reduced, and second, a mischievous person could now use a protocol analyzer, running in promiscuous mode, to capture data from any other computer on the network.

Layer 2 switching can also allow for a virtual LAN (VLAN) to be implemented. A VLAN is implemented to segment the network, reduce collisions, organize the network, boost performance, and, hopefully, increase security. It is important to place physical network jacks in secure locations, when it comes to VLANs that have access to confidential data. There are also logical types of VLANs, such as the protocol-based VLAN and the MAC address-based VLAN, which have a separate set of security precautions. The most common standard associated with VLANs is IEEE 802.1Q, which modifies Ethernet frames by "tagging" them with the appropriate VLAN information, based on which VLAN the Ethernet frame should be directed to. VLANs are used to restrict access to network resources, but this can be bypassed using VLAN hopping. VLAN hopping can be avoided by upgrading firmware or software, picking an unused VLAN as the default VLAN for all trunks, and redesigning the VLAN if multiple 802.1Q switches are being used.

Wireless access points, bridges, Layer 2 switches, and network adapters all reside on the Data Link layer.

The Network layer governs IP addresses, routers/Layer 3 switches, and the core communications of TCP/IP. In the following exercise, you'll see the Network layer in action by analyzing IP addresses, pinging other computers, and capturing Network layer data with a protocol analyzer. Afterward, we'll define a Layer 3 switch.

DEFINE THE NETWORK LAYER

TAKE NOTE*

Hardware-based and personal firewalls can possibly block some of the following tests and exercises. You might need to disable one or more firewalls for the exercises to complete properly.

GET READY. To define the Network layer, perform the following steps.

1. Open the Command Prompt window.
2. Execute **ipconfig**. This displays your IP address, for example, 192.168.1.1. The IP address is developed from the ***Internet Protocol (IP)***, which resides on Layer 3 of the OSI model. Jot down your IP address and another IP address of a different computer on the network.
3. Ping the other computer's IP address by executing the **ping [ip address]** command (for example, ping 192.168.1.2). Make sure you can get replies from the other computer. Ping utilizes the ***Internet Control Message Protocol (ICMP)*** to send test packets to other computers; this is also a Network layer protocol. Notice the size of the replies you receive; by default, they should be 32 bytes each.
4. Execute **arp - a** to view the IP address to MAC address table. This table should now show the IP address you just pinged. This table is known as the Address Resolution Protocol table, or ***ARP table***. The ***Address Resolution Protocol*** is another Layer 3 protocol that resolves or translates IP addresses to MAC addresses, allowing the connectivity between the Layer 3 IP system and the Layer 2 Ethernet system.
5. Use Wireshark to capture and analyze ICMP packets:
   a. Download and install the Wireshark protocol analyzer (previously known as Ethereal) from: http://www.wireshark.org/. At the time writing, the latest stable version is 1.2.8. Install WinPCap as part of the Wireshark installation.
   b. Go back to the Command Prompt window and run a continuous ping to another computer (for example, ping -t 192.168.1.2). Verify that you get replies, and leave the Command Prompt window open and pinging the other computer while you complete the packet capture.
   c. In the Wireshark utility, from the Interface List, select the interface that serves as your main network adapter. This starts the capture of data from that network adapter.
   d. After a minute, stop the capture by clicking **Capture** on the menu bar and then clicking **Stop**.
   e. View the list of captured packets in the top half of the screen. In the Protocol column, you should see many ICMP packets. Select one that says "reply" in the Info column. When you do so, its information should show up in the middle window pane similar to Figure 2-5. The dark blue packet numbered 98 in the figure is the selected packet. Now let's drill down to see the details of the packet.

Figure 2-5

Wireshark packet capture

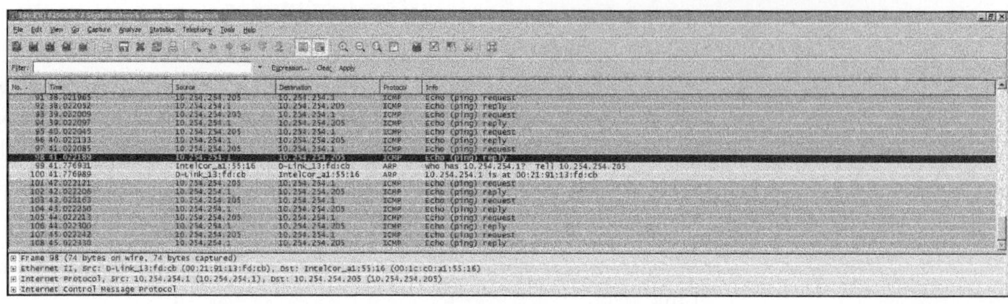

f. Click the + sign next to Internet Control Message Protocol to expand it and display the contents. This should display information about the ICMP packet: the fact that it is a reply packet, the checksum, the sequence number, and so on.

g. Click the + sign next to Internet Protocol. This shows you the version of IP used (IPv4), the size of the packet, and the source and destination IP addresses for the embedded ICMP packet. Both the ICMP and IP pieces of information correspond to the Network layer of the OSI model.

h. Now click the + sign next to Ethernet. This is the network architecture used on the Data Link layer. This field of information tells you the source and destination MAC addresses of the computers involved in the ping transaction.

i. Now click the + sign next to Frame. (There will be a frame number next to the word *Frame*.) This tells you the size of the frame captured and when it was captured. It is these frames of information that the Wireshark application is capturing directly from the network adapter.

Notice that the Ethernet frame is larger than the IP packet. That is because the IP packet is ***encapsulated*** into the frame. That is another difference between frames and packets. It all started with the command prompt sending a 32-byte ping (ICMP packet). This was then placed inside an IP packet with a total size of 60 bytes. The additional 28 bytes is known as Layer 3 ***overhead***, broken down between 20 bytes for the header (includes the IP source and destination addresses) and 8 bytes for additional overhead information (for example, a trailer or checksum). Then, the IP packet is sent to the network adapter where it is placed inside a frame. The frame adds its own Layer 2 overhead, an additional 14 bytes, including the source and destination MAC address. This brings the grand total to 74 bytes—more than double what we started with. The frame is then sent out from the other computer's network adapter (to reply to the pinging computer) as a serial bit stream across the network medium on the Physical layer. This is what happens with every single communication, and the OSI model, particularly the communications subnetwork Layers 1–3, helps us to define what is happening behind the scenes by categorizing each step with a different layer.

TAKE NOTE*

There are many protocol analyzers available. Microsoft incorporates one called Network Monitor into its Windows Server products.

Routers also reside on the Network layer. Routers make connections between one or more IP networks. They are known as the gateway to another IP network, and you would utilize their IP address in the Gateway address field of a computer's IP Properties window, to allow the computer access through to other networks. Don't confuse this definition of a gateway with an Application layer gateway, which we define in the Defining the Application Layer section later in this lesson. Routers use protocols such as Routing Information Protocol (RIP) and Open Shortest Path First (OSPF) to direct packets to other routers and networks.

Understanding Layer 3 Switching

CERTIFICATION READY
What are the differences between Layer 2 switches and Layer 3 switches?
Objective 2.1

Switches also reside on the Network layer. A ***Layer 3 switch*** differs from a Layer 2 switch in that it determines paths for data using logical addressing (IP addresses) instead of physical addressing (MAC addresses). Layer 3 switches are very similar to routers; it's how a network engineer implements the switch that makes them different.

Layer 3 switches forward packets, whereas Layer 2 switches forward frames. Layer 3 switches are usually managed switches; they can be managed via the network engineer by utilizing the Simple Network Management Protocol (SNMP), among other tools. This allows the network engineer to analyze all the packets that pass through the switch, which can't be done with a Layer 2 switch. A Layer 2 switch is more like an advanced version of a bridge, whereas a Layer 3 switch is more like a router. Layer 3 switches are used in busy environments where multiple IP networks need to be connected together.

Understanding Characteristics of Switches

CERTIFICATION READY
Which features are included with expensive switches (as compared with inexpensive switches)?
Objective 2.1

When selecting the type of switches, you should consider the following:

- Number and types of ports and their transmission speed
- Number and speed of uplink ports
- Expandability capabilities
- Managed or unmanaged
- VLAN capabilities
- Hardware redundancy
- Security options
- Routing/Layer 3 capabilities

Larger networks have larger switches, which allow for many more devices to be connected to the switch. As packets traverse the switch, the switch must process the packet and determine which port the packet must be sent to. The more devices that you have, the faster backplane and processing required to handle the traffic and process the packets.

Some switches have uplink ports. Uplink ports are used to connect different types of Ethernet devices to each other, such as connecting a small switch to a larger switch, or a switch to a router.

Switches can also be fixed, modular, and stackable. Fixed configuration switches are low-end switches with a set number of ports. Modular switches have a chassis, where you slide in modular line cards with various ports. The larger the chassis, the more modules it can support. Stackable switches are switches that can be connected together using a special back cable that provides high bandwidth between the switches.

Switches can be divided into unmanaged and managed switches. Unmanaged switches are the least expensive and are used in homes and Small Office/Home Office environments. With unmanaged switches, you just connect AC power to the switch and connect your network devices.

Smart switches are more advanced switches that include a command-line interface or web interface to configure the switch. Managed switches include more advanced features, including supporting Spanning Tree Protocol, port mirroring, setting port bandwidth, and creating and modifying virtual LANs.

The Spanning Tree Protocol (STP) is a network protocol that prevents bridge loops when connecting multiple switches. If a loop is created and the switches do not use STP, looping traffic can take a local area network down. STP also allows you to use redundant links between switches without causing a loop.

Defining the Upper OSI Layers

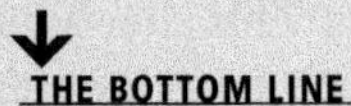

The upper OSI layers are Layers 4-7—the Transport, Session, Presentation, and Application layers. It is this portion of the OSI model that deals with protocols such as HTTP, FTP, and mail protocols. Compression, encryption, and session creation are also performed by these layers.

CERTIFICATION READY
Can you define the upper layers of the OSI model?
Objective 3.1

In the following exercises, you will:

- Define the Transport layer by showing connections in the Command Prompt window and describing ports.
- Define the Session layer by logging into websites and other servers, as well as logging on and off of Microsoft networks and email programs.
- Define the Presentation layer by showing encryption in Windows and within websites.
- Define the Application layer by capturing web server packets and analyzing them.

Defining the Transport Layer

Layer 4 governs the transmission of messages through the communications subnetwork by providing a connection-oriented data stream support, reliability, flow control, and multiplexing. Two common TCP/IP protocols that are utilized on this layer include the ***Transmission Control Protocol (TCP)***, which is a connection-oriented protocol, and the ***User Datagram Protocol (UDP)***, which is connectionless.

An example of an application that uses TCP is a web browser, and an example of an application that uses UDP is streaming media. When you download a web page, you don't want to lose any packets of information. If you did, graphics would be broken, certain text wouldn't read correctly, and so on. Using TCP ensures that data gets to its final destination. If a packet is lost along the way, it is resent until the destination computer acknowledges delivery or ends the session. But with streaming media, we are either watching or listening in real time. So, if a packet is lost, we don't really care because that time frame of the video or music has already passed. Once the packet is lost, we really don't want it back. Of course, if the packet loss becomes too severe, the streaming media becomes incomprehensible.

Connection-oriented communications require that both devices or computers establish an end-to-end logical connection before data can be sent between the two. These connection-oriented systems are often considered to be reliable network services. Connection-oriented communication is also known as CO mode. If an individual packet is not delivered in a timely manner, it is re-sent; this can be done because the sending computer established the connection at the beginning of the session, and it knows where to resend the packet.

In connectionless communications (CL mode), no end-to-end connection is necessary before data is sent. Every packet sent has the destination address located in its header. This is sufficient to move independent packets, for example, in the aforementioned streaming media. But if a packet is lost, it cannot be re-sent because the sending computer never established a logical connection, and it doesn't know which logical connection to use to send the failed packet.

Layer 4 also takes care of the ports that a computer uses for the transmission of data. ***Ports*** act as logical communications endpoints for computers. There are 65,536 ports altogether, numbered between 0 and 65,535. They are defined by the ***Internet Assigned Numbers Authority (IANA)***. The ports are divided into categories, as shown in Table 2-1.

Table 2-1

IANA Port Categories

Port Range	Category Type	Description
0–1023	Well-Known Ports	This range defines commonly used protocols; for example, FTP utilizes port 21 to accept client connections.
1024–49,151	Registered Ports	These ports are used by vendors for proprietary applications. These must be registered with IANA. For example, Microsoft registered port 3389 is used with the Remote Desktop Protocol.
49,152–65,535	Dynamic and Private Ports	These ports can be used by applications, but cannot be registered by vendors.

Port numbers correspond to specific applications; for example, port 80 is used by web browsers via the HTTP protocol. It is important to understand the difference between inbound and outbound ports as described in the following list:

- ***Inbound ports***: These are used when another computer wants to connect to a service or application running on your computer. Servers primarily use inbound ports so that they can accept incoming connections and serve data. IP addresses and port numbers are combined; for example, a server's IP/port 66.249.91.104:80 is the IP address 66.249.91.104 with port number 80 open in order to accept incoming web page requests.
- ***Outbound ports***: These are used when your computer wants to connect to a service or application running on another computer. Client computers primarily use outbound ports, and these are assigned dynamically by the operating system.

There are a lot of ports and corresponding protocols you should know. Although you don't need to know all 65,536, Table 2-2 gives you some of the basic ones that you should memorize.

Table 2-2

Ports and Associated Protocols

Port Number	Associated Protocol	Full Name
21	FTP	File Transfer Protocol
22	SSH	Secure Shell
23	Telnet	TErminaL NETwork
25	SMTP	Simple Mail Transfer Protocol
53	DNS	Domain Name System
80	HTTP	Hypertext Transfer Protocol

Table 2-2 (Continued)

Port Number	Associated Protocol	Full Name
88	Kerberos	Kerberos
110	POP3	Post Office Protocol Version 3
119	NNTP	Network News Transfer Protocol
137–139	NetBIOS	NetBIOS Name, Datagram, and Session Services, respectively
143	IMAP	Internet Message Access Protocol
161	SNMP	Simple Network Management Protocol
389	LDAP	Lightweight Directory Access Protocol
443	HTTPS	Hypertext Transfer Protocol Secure (uses TLS or SSL)
445	SMB	Server Message Block
1701	L2TP	Layer 2 Tunneling Protocol
1723	PPTP	Point-to-Point Tunneling Protocol
3389	RDP	Remote Desktop Protocol (Microsoft Terminal Server)

DEFINE THE TRANSPORT LAYER

GET READY. To define the Transport layer, perform the following steps.

1. Open a web browser and go to www.microsoft.com.
2. Open the Command Prompt window and execute **netstat -a**. This displays a list of all the connections to and from your computer in numeric format, as shown in Figure 2-6.

   Note the multiple Microsoft connections. If you perform an `nslookup` of the 131.253.34.247 and 131.253.34.244 sites, you will find that these addresses are assigned to systems in the wns.windows.com domain. The two connections were initialized by the local computer on outbound ports 54,385 and 58,278. Microsoft is accepting these connections on its web server's inbound port 443. Note that the leftmost column named "Proto" has these connections marked as TCP. So, as we mentioned before, HTTP connections utilize TCP on the Transport layer and are, therefore, connection-oriented.

Figure 2-6

The `netstat` command

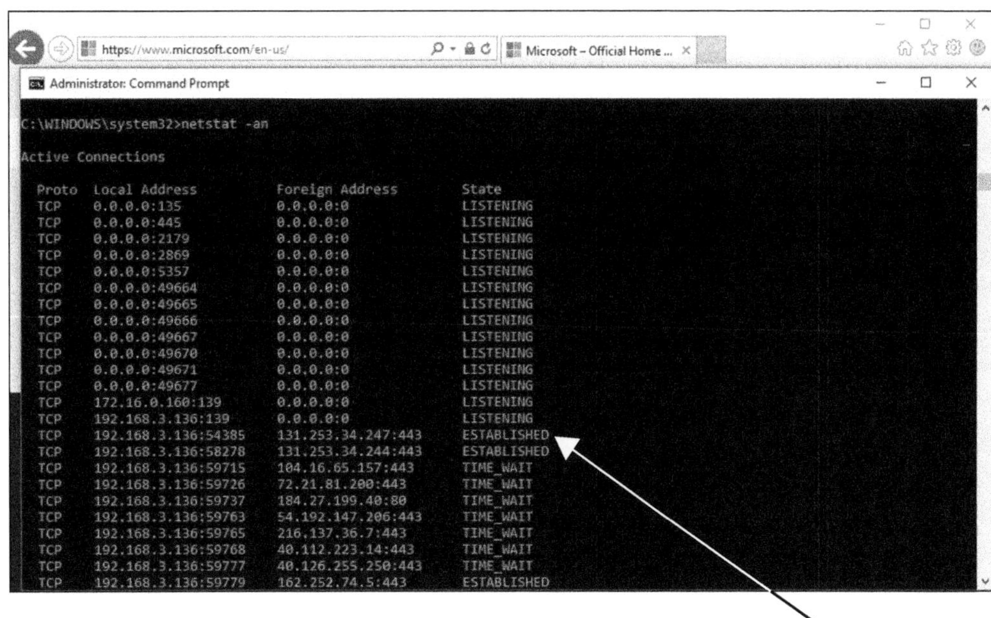

3. Execute a few more commands:

   netstat (the original command, shows basic connections)

   netstat -a (shows in-depth TCP *and* UDP connections)

   netstat -an (shows TCP and UDP connections numerically)

Defining the Session Layer

Every time you connect to a website, a mail server, or any other computer on your network or another network, your computer is starting a session with that remote computer. Every time you log on or log off a network, the Session layer is involved.

The following exercise shows a couple basic examples of the Session layer.

DEFINE THE SESSION LAYER

GET READY. To define the Session layer, perform the following steps.

1. Make several connections to other computers. For example:
   a. www.microsoft.com
   b. A mail account that you have with MSN, Gmail, Yahoo!, or others
   c. A network share (if available)
   d. An FTP server (if available)
2. Go back to the Command Prompt window and execute **netstat -a**; then, in a second Command Prompt window, execute **netstat -an**. Analyze the various sessions that you have created. Compare the results of both commands. See if you can catch the names in one Command Prompt window and their corresponding IP addresses in the other Command Prompt window. Note the "State" of the connections or sessions: Established, Close_wait, and so on.

3. Log on and log off of networks:
   a. Log off/log on your Microsoft network if you are connected to one.
   b. Log on to a website for which you have a membership, such as Amazon.

All of these steps are completed as part of the Session layer. The Session layer also is in charge of the termination of sessions. Notice that after a certain time period of no activity, web sessions change their state from Established to either Time wait, or closed, or something similar. Log off all of your sessions now, and close any connections to any websites or other computers you have connected to. Finally, log off the computer and log back on.

Defining the Presentation Layer

The Presentation layer changes how the data is presented. This could include code conversion from one computer system to another (that both run TCP/IP), or it could be encryption or compression. It also comes into play when you connect to a mapped network drive (known as a redirector).

The following exercise shows a couple of examples of how information is modified before being sent across the network.

DEFINE THE PRESENTATION LAYER

GET READY. To define the Presentation layer, perform the following steps.

1. Access File Explorer on a Windows client computer.
2. Create a simple text file with some basic text and save it to a test folder.
3. Right-click the text file and choose **Properties.**
4. In the Properties window, click the **Advanced** button.
5. Select the **Encrypt contents to secure data** check box.
6. Click **OK.** The file should now be displayed in blue. From now on, if the file is sent across the network, the Presentation layer comes into effect due to the encryption.
7. Open a web browser and go to https://www.microsoft.com.

TAKE NOTE*

Note the HTTPS, which is short for Hypertext Transfer Protocol Secure. This is a secure, encrypted connection to the Microsoft website. Many websites offer this, not only when actual transactions are made, but also as a courtesy to customers, giving them peace of mind in the fact that their entire session with the website is encrypted and somewhat secure. This type of encryption protocol works on port 443, and the actual transmission of encrypted data is governed by the Presentation layer. The most common example as of the writing of this book is Transport Layer Security (TLS), but you might also see Secure Sockets Layer (SSL). Data that is transferred over the web is usually compressed, or ***encoded***, as well. For example, many web browsers accept gzip encoding.

Defining the Application Layer

Layer 7 is where protocols like HTTP, FTP, and POP3 reside. The Application layer is not the applications themselves (Internet Explorer or Outlook), but the network services and protocols that the applications initiate, such as HTTP or POP3. For example, when you open Internet Explorer, you are opening an application. When you type http://www.microsoft.com in the URL field and press Enter, the HTTP protocol is initiated, starting the transfer of data over the OSI model, beginning with the Application layer.

In the following exercise, you will capture some data as you connect to a website.

DEFINE THE APPLICATION LAYER

GET READY. To define the Application layer, perform the following steps.

1. Open Wireshark and begin a packet capture.
2. Open your browser and go to www.microsoft.com.
3. Stop the capture and view the information.
4. Look for the first HTTP packet in the Protocol column. This should be called GET/HTTP/1.1 in the Info column.
5. Click the packet and drill down through the various layers in the middle window pane. Not only will you see Layers 2 and 3 as defined in the Defining the Communications Subnetwork section, but you will also see the upper layers in action. Your results should be similar to Figure 2-7.

Figure 2-7

Wireshark capture of an HTTP packet

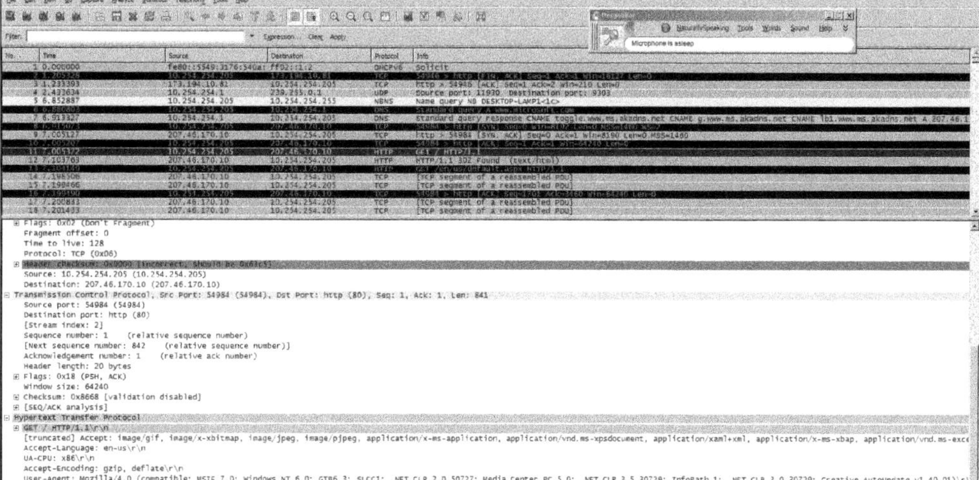

6. Click the + sign next to Hypertext Transfer Protocol. Here, you will see the host that you connected to: www.microsoft.com. You will also notice the gzip and deflate encoding/decoding schemes we alluded to earlier.
7. Click the + sign next to Transmission Control Protocol. Here, you will see the outbound port used by your computer to connect to the web server (known as a source port) and the inbound port (80) that the web server uses (known as a Dst or destination port).
8. Spend some time analyzing the information listed, and match it to the appropriate layer of the OSI model.

Devices known as *gateways* reside on the Application layer. These are not to be confused with gateway devices like routers on the Network layer. An Application layer gateway is a computer that translates from one protocol suite to another, for example from TCP/IP to IPX/SPX. An example, albeit a deprecated one, would be Client Services for NetWare when loaded on a Windows client computer.

Reviewing the OSI Layers

The OSI model contains seven layers, each of which work collectively to define the transmission of data from one computer to another. The mnemonic device *All People Seem To Need Data Processing* can help you to memorize the layer order.

CERTIFICATION READY
Which OSI layer is assigned to hubs, switches, routers, and firewalls?
Objective 3.1

Although we defined each of the layers starting with the bottom, the Physical layer, and moved up from there, quite often, you will see the layers listed from the top down with the Application layer at the top and the Physical layer at the bottom, as shown in Figure 2-8. However, in Wireshark and other protocol analyzers, the Physical layer is displayed at the top. It all depends on what application or technical document you are looking at, so be ready for both orientations.

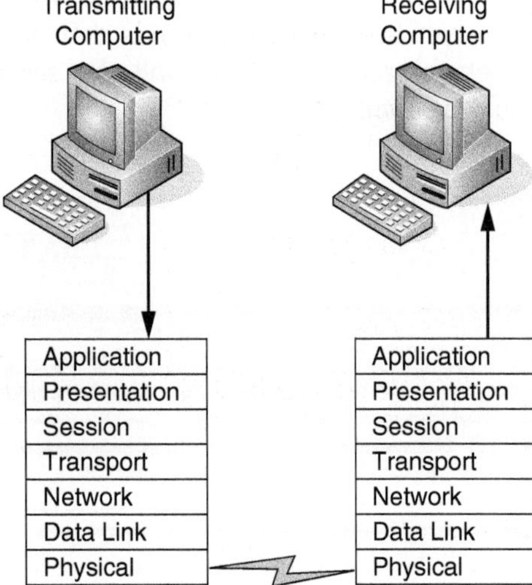

Figure 2-8
The OSI layers revisited

In general, data transactions start at the sending computer, travel down the OSI layers starting with the Application layer and ending with the Physical layer, are transmitted across the physical medium be it wired or wireless, and travel back up the layers of the OSI model at the receiving computer. For example, if you want to connect to a website, type the name of the website in the web browser's address field. When you press Enter, the HTTP protocol takes effect at the Application layer. The packets of data are compressed (with gzip) and possibly encrypted (HTTPS by way of SSL or TLS) at the Presentation layer. The web server acknowledges the session with the client web browser at the Session layer. The information is then transmitted as TCP information on the Transport layer where ports are also selected. The TCP information is broken up into easy-to-send packets on the Network layer and IP addressing information is added. The packets are sent to the Data Link layer where the network adapter encapsulates them into frames of data. Then, at the Physical layer, the network adapter breaks the frames up into a serial bit stream to be sent over the cable media.

When the serial bit stream arrives at the destination client computer with a web browser, it is reconfigured by the client's network adapter as frames of information. The header information of the frames is checked for authenticity and is stripped, leaving the packets to be sent to the operating system. The operating system puts these packets together to form the web page that is displayed on the client's computer screen. Of course, this all happens 10,000 times faster than explained here, and it happens many times every second. If your computer has a 100-Mbps connection, it means that it can take in a maximum of about 12 MB of data per second. Packets of information are variable in size, and can be between approximately 60 and 1,500 bytes. Let's say that you are downloading a large file. This file will be broken down into the largest packet size possible, around 1,500 bytes. We can therefore calculate that an average computer can take in 8,000 packets of data per second. By the way, most client computers will probably not take advantage of this maximum data throughput, but servers and power workstations will.

Table 2-3 reviews the OSI layers and shows the corresponding devices, protocols, and network standards that apply to each layer.

Table 2-3

The OSI Model Layers and Correspondinq Components

LAYER	PROTOCOL	DEVICE
7. Application	FTP, HTTP, POP3, SMTP	Gateway
6. Presentation	Compression, Encryption	
5. Session	Logon/Logoff	
4. Transport	TCP, UDP	
3. Network	IP, ICMP, ARP, RIP	Routers
2. Data Link	802.3, 802.5	NICs, switches, bridges, WAPs
1. Physical	100BASE-T, 1000BASE-X	Hubs, patch panels, RJ-45 jacks

Defining the TCP/IP Model

The TCP/IP (or TCP) model is similar to the OSI model. It is often used by software manufacturers who are not as concerned with how information is sent over physical media, or how the data link is actually made. It is composed of four layers only.

CERTIFICATION READY
Can you define the TCP model?
Objective 3.1

Whereas the OSI model is a reference model, the TCP/IP model (also known as the DoD model or Internet model) is more descriptive, defining principles such as *end-to-end* and *robustness*, which describe strong endpoint connections and conservative transmission of data. It is maintained by the ***Internet Engineering Task Force (IETF)***. The four layers are:

- **Layer 1:** Data Link layer (also simply known as the Link layer)
- **Layer 2:** Network layer (also known as the Internet layer)
- **Layer 3:** Transport layer
- **Layer 4:** Application layer

The OSI Physical layer is skipped altogether, and the Application layer comprises the OSI Application, Presentation, and Session layers.

Programmers utilize this model more often than the OSI model, whereas network administrators usually benefit from the OSI model to a higher degree. Programmers are generally interested in the interfaces made to the Application and Transport layers. Anything below the Transport layer is taken care of by the TCP/IP stack within the operating system, which is set in stone. Programs can be made to utilize the TCP stack, but not to modify it. Again, as a networking person, you will most often refer to the OSI model, but you should know the layers of the TCP model in case you need to interface with programmers and developers, especially when dealing with Microsoft products.

SKILL SUMMARY

IN THIS LESSON, YOU LEARNED:

- The Open Systems Interconnection reference model (OSI model) is a reference model used to define how data communications occur on computer networks. It is divided into layers that provide services to the layers above and below. These layers are associated with protocols and devices.
- The OSI model was created as a set of seven layers, or levels, each of which houses different protocols within one of several protocol suites, the most common of which is TCP/IP. The OSI model categorizes how TCP/IP transactions occur. It is invaluable when it comes to installing, configuring, maintaining, and, especially, troubleshooting networks.
- In an Ethernet network, every network adapter must have a unique media access control (MAC) address. The MAC address is a unique identifier assigned to network adapters by the manufacturer. This address is 6 octets in length and is written in hexadecimal.
- Switches have memory that is set aside to store the MAC address to a port translation table, known as the MAC table or Content Addressable Memory table (or CAM table).
- The Ethernet frame is larger than the IP packet. That is because the IP packet is encapsulated into the frame.
- Two common TCP/IP protocols that are utilized on this layer include the Transmission Control Protocol (TCP), which is a connection-oriented protocol, and the User Datagram Protocol (UDP), which is connectionless.
- Layer 4 also takes care of the ports that a computer uses for the transmission of data. Ports act as logical communications endpoints for computers. There are 65,536 ports altogether, numbered between 0 and 65,535.
- Layer 7 is where protocols like HTTP, FTP, and POP3 reside. The Application layer is not the applications themselves (Internet Explorer or Outlook), but the network services and protocols that the applications initiate, such as HTTP or POP3.
- The TCP/IP (or TCP) model is similar to the OSI model. It is often used by software manufacturers who are not as concerned with how information is sent over physical media, or how the data link is actually made. It is composed of four layers only.

■ Knowledge Assessment

Multiple Choice

Select the correct answer for each of the following questions.

1. How many layers are incorporated in the OSI model communications subnetwork?
   - **a.** 2
   - **b.** 7
   - **c.** 3
   - **d.** 4
2. Which of the following layers deals with the serial transfer of data?
   - **a.** Physical
   - **b.** Data Link
   - **c.** Network
   - **d.** Session
3. When installing a router on a company's network that will allow access to the Internet, the device will reside on which layer of the OSI model?
   - **a.** Physical
   - **b.** Data Link
   - **c.** Network
   - **d.** Transport
4. When executing the `netstat -an` command in the Command Prompt window, many connections are made that say TCP in the leftmost column. Which layer of the OSI model is TCP referring to?
   - **a.** Layer 1
   - **b.** Layer 2
   - **c.** Layer 3
   - **d.** Layer 4
5. A problem is suspected with a computer's network adapter and its ability to send the correct frames of data that correspond with the network architecture used by the rest of the computers. Which layer should be used as a troubleshooting starting point?
   - **a.** Physical
   - **b.** Data Link
   - **c.** Network
   - **d.** Transport
6. A standard such as 100BASE-T refers to which OSI layer?
   - **a.** Physical
   - **b.** Data Link
   - **c.** Network
   - **d.** Transport
7. At an organization, almost all users connect to websites with Internet Explorer. They usually type domain names such as www.microsoft.com. Which protocol is initiated by default when they press Enter after typing the domain name?
   - **a.** FTP
   - **b.** HTTPS
   - **c.** HTTP
   - **d.** HTP

8. A director has given permission to access his computer. To find out the MAC address of the director's computer, the Command Prompt application is accessed. Which command should be used to see the MAC address?
   a. `ipconfig`
   b. `ipconfig/all`
   c. `arp`
   d. `netstat -an`

9. Which of the following commands should be used to view all of the MAC addresses of computers that a particular user's computer has connected to in the recent past?
   a. `ping 127.0.0.1`
   b. `netstat -a`
   c. `arp -a`
   d. `arp -s`

10. Which of the following tools should be used to capture and analyze packets on a server? (Choose the two best answers.)
   a. Protocol analyzer
   b. Command Prompt
   c. `netstat -an`
   d. Wireshark

Fill in the Blank

Fill in the correct answer in the blank space provided.

1. The manager of IT wants to ping his laptop to see if other computers can find it on the network. In this scenario, the _____ protocol is being implemented.
2. A _____ switch is one that uses logical addressing to determine data paths.
3. Ports 1024–49,151 are ports used by vendors for proprietary applications. They are known as _____ ports.
4. Port _____ is used by the File Transfer Protocol.
5. A manager wants to allow HTTP and HTTPS connections to the company web server. To do this, inbound ports _____ and _____ should be open.
6. A company hosts a DNS server that resolves domain names to IP addresses. This server must have _____ open to service those requests for name resolution.
7. As the administrator for a company, you need to find out the Internet connections a particular computer has made in the recent past. You also need to see numeric information so that you know the IP address and port numbers of the destination computers. You should execute the _____ command in the Command Prompt window.
8. The IT director wants to connect a client computer to an 802.3ab network. This network uses the _____ standard.
9. A user has connected to a website. The information that is sent to her computer is in an encrypted, encoded format. This change to the data occurs at the _____ layer.
10. As an administrator delves into a packet of data with his protocol analyzer, he notices that the frame size is bigger than the packet size. This is because the packet is _____ inside the frame.

■ Business Case Scenarios

Scenario 2-1: Installing the Appropriate Switch

Proseware, Inc., requires you to install a 24-port switch that directs TCP/IP traffic to logical addresses on the network. Which kind of switch allows you to do this, and which kind of addresses will the traffic be directed to? Also, which layer of the OSI model are you working with here?

Scenario 2-2: Defining the IP Address and Ports Used by Destination Servers

A coworker's computer seems to be connecting to various computers on the Internet on its own. The computer gets pop-up advertisements and other pop-ups out of the blue. Which command syntax is used to analyze which IP addresses and ports the computer is connecting to? And which layers of the OSI model do the IP addresses and ports correspond to?

Scenario 2-3: Ensuring a Newly Created Email Account's Logon Is Encrypted

Your IT director wants you to create an email account to use on the company website. He wants the email address to be free and wants proof that when a person logs on to the email account, the password is encrypted. Which services, applications, and tools can you utilize to accomplish this? And which layers of the OSI model are being used for the logon?

Scenario 2-4: Creating a Permanent ARP Table Entry

Your IT director's computer sleeps after 10 minutes. She wants to be able to "wake up" her desktop computer from a remote system, for example from her laptop. To do this, you first need to create a static entry in your boss's laptop's ARP table. In addition, this entry needs to be re-created every time the laptop reboots. The desktop computer's IP address is 10.50.249.38 and its MAC address is 00-03-FF-A5-55-16. Which command syntax should you use to do this? How will you make this command execute every time the computer boots? Which layer of the OSI model is this scenario referencing?

Workplace Ready

Analyzing an FTP Connection

The File Transfer Protocol is probably the most commonly used protocol when it comes to file transfer (quite an appropriate name!). However, it can be insecure. Some FTP servers use the standard port 21 for all data transfers. It is better to use port 21 for the initial connection, and then use dynamically assigned ports for subsequent data transfers. Also, some FTP implementations send the user password as cleartext; this is not desirable. Passwords should be complex, and authentication should be encrypted if possible. Also, more secure FTP programs should be utilized. For example, Pure-FTPd (http://www.pureftpd.org) could be utilized on the server side and FileZilla (http://filezilla-project.org) could be incorporated on the client side.

Research exactly what Pure-FTPd is and what it offers. Then, download and install the free FileZilla program. Next, run the Wireshark program and start a capture. Then, open FileZilla and make a connection to ftp.ipswitch.com (no user name or password is necessary). Note the fact that anonymous connections can be made to this server. Look at a few of the folders in the FTP server. Stop the capture and analyze the FTP packets. See if you can find the packets that relate to the initial connection and to the anonymous logon. Document exactly what happened on the OSI layers: Application, Transport, Network, and Data Link.

Understanding Wired and Wireless Networks

LESSON 3

OBJECTIVE DOMAIN MATRIX

Skills/Concepts	Objective Domain Description	Objective Domain Number
Recognizing Wired Networks and Media Types	Understand media types	2.3
Understanding Wireless Networks	Understand wired LAN	1.2
	Understand wireless LAN Understand wireless networking	1.4

KEY TERMS

568A
568B
ad hoc mode
Advanced Encryption Standard
attenuation
BOGB
bridge mode
Category 5e
Category 6
channel bonding
continuity tester
crossover cable
crosstalk
data emanation
electromagnetic interference (EMI)
far end crosstalk (FEXT)
Faraday cage
fiber-optic cable
frame aggregation
IEEE 802.11
IEEE 802.1X
infrastructure mode
interference
MDI
MDI-X
Multiple-Input Multiple-Output (MIMO)
multi-mode
near end crosstalk (NEXT)
plenum-rated
Port-based Network Access Control (PNAC)
punch down tool
radio frequency interference
service set identifier (SSID)
shielded twisted pair (STP)
single-mode
straight-through cable
TIA/EIA
twisted-pair cable
Wi-Fi
Wi-Fi Protected Access
Wired Equivalent Privacy
wireless bridge
wireless network adapter
wireless repeater

Properly installed cabling and wireless networks are the keys to an efficient physical plant; it's the physical wired and wireless connections that are the core of a speedy network. This lesson refers back to the fictitious company, Proseware, Inc., and discusses all the technologies and standards that are needed for Proseware to have a properly installed wired/wireless network. For the client to be happy, twisted-pair cabling and fiber-optic cabling will be necessary, as well as shielded cabling and the latest in wireless equipment. It will also be necessary to verify that signals are not being interfered with and are not being intercepted by undesirable parties. All of this will require tools, plenty of cabling and additional equipment, wireless equipment, testing equipment, and plenty of know-how. Be prepared during this lesson to learn how to cable an entire network and how to set up a wireless network as well!

Recognizing Wired Networks and Media Types

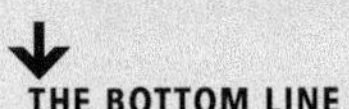

THE BOTTOM LINE

Wired networks are still the most common type of physical connection that computers make. Although wireless networks have made many inroads into many organizations, the wired connection is still king. And twisted-pair cabling is the most common connection that the bulk of computers will make.

Identifying and Working with Twisted-Pair Cables

As mentioned, ***twisted-pair cable*** is the most common cable used in local area networks. It's relatively easy to work with, flexible, efficient, and fast. As a network administrator, you should know how to identify the different types of twisted-pair cabling, as well as how to install twisted-pair cabling in a permanent fashion and as a temporary solution. It's also important to know how to test twisted-pair cables in the event one fails or as a way of proving that new installations work properly.

CERTIFICATION READY
What is the most common type of cable used in wired networks and what are the characteristics of that cable?

Objective 2.3

Twisted-pair cables are the most common of all copper-based cables. A single twisted-pair cable has eight wires; they are insulation-covered copper conductors that transmit electric signals. This is just one type of copper media, but it is the most common. These eight wires are grouped into four pairs: blue, orange, green, and brown. Each pair of wires is twisted along the entire length of the cable. And all of the pairs are twisted together as well. The reason the wires are twisted together is to reduce crosstalk and interference, which you'll learn more about later in this lesson.

EXAMINE TWISTED-PAIR PATCH CABLES

GET READY. To examine a patch cable connected to your computer, or to the central connecting device for your network, perform the following steps.

1. Examine the back of your computer and locate the network adapter. There should be a twisted-pair patch cable that connects the network adapter to the network. If not, and you use a wireless connection, examine the back of your central connecting device, whether it's a router, a switch, or a hub. Identify the patch cable that connects to that device. If you decide to disconnect the cable, keep in mind that the Internet connection will be temporarily lost, and any downloads will be stopped. The cable should look similar to the one shown in Figure 3-1. The cable in the figure is being shown from the side of the RJ-45 plug. You can see where the cable itself enters the plug and where the plastic sheath is cut, exposing the individual wires. Also notice the teeth that bite into the plastic jacket (they are called out with a black rectangle). Once the plug is crimped onto the cable, these teeth ensure that the cable does not slip out of the plug.

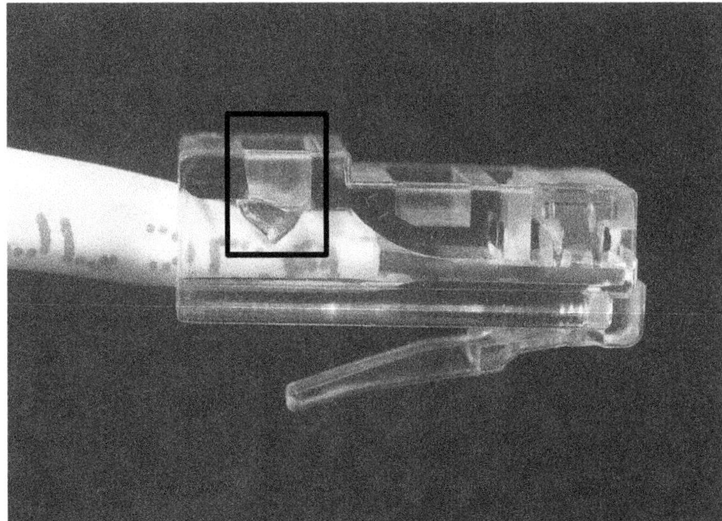

Figure 3-1

Example of a twisted-pair patch cable

2. If you have some extra twisted-pair cable lying around, cut a 6-foot piece with a sharp cutting tool. Then, strip away about 2 inches of the plastic jacket to expose the wires. (The plastic jacket is also known as a plastic or PVC sheath.) You should see something similar to Figure 3-2. The figure illustrates the four twisted pairs of wires. Once again, these four pairs are blue, orange, green, and brown. This is known as the ***BOGB*** colors. Each letter represents a color. B = blue, O = orange, and so on.

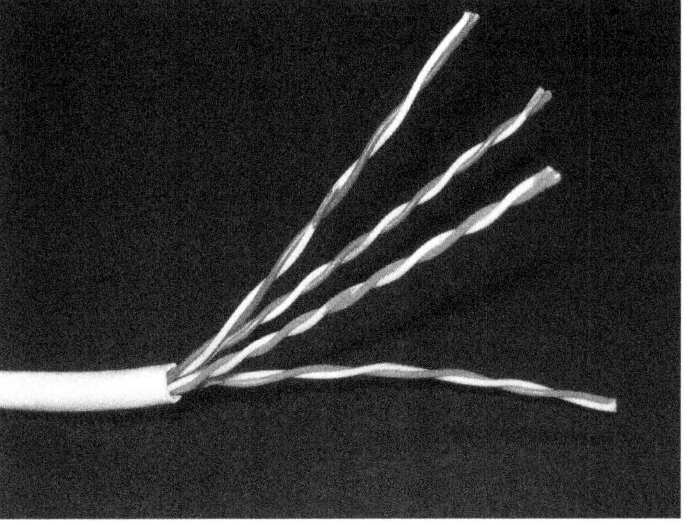

Figure 3-2

Twisted-pair cable with the wires exposed

3. Untwist each of the wires so that they are all separated. This should look similar to Figure 3-3. In the figure, the wires are in the proper order for most of today's twisted-pair networks. Table 3-1 summarizes the cabling standards when it comes to wire (or pin) orientation. Whereas the BOGB standard is where everything originates from, ***568B*** is the most common, and ***568A*** is an older standard. The proper name for 568B is TIA/EIA-568-B; the standard was developed by the Telecommunications Industry Association/Electronics Industries Alliance or ***TIA/EIA***. When making a patch cable, the wires are placed in the RJ-45 plug in order, and the plug is crimped once they are in place. If a particular wire is named white/orange, that means the bulk of the wire is white in color and it has an orange stripe. If the wire is named orange, it is a solid orange wire.

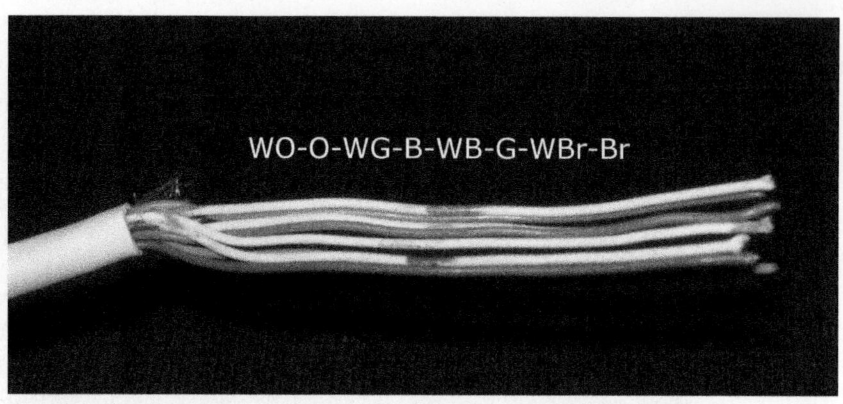

Figure 3-3
Twisted-pair cable with the wires straightened

Table 3-1
568B, 568A, and BOGB Standards

PIN #	568B	568A	BOGB
1	White/Orange	White/Green	White/Blue
2	Orange	Green	Blue
3	White/Green	White/Orange	White/Orange
4	Blue	Blue	Orange
5	White/Blue	White/Blue	White/Green
6	Green	Orange	Green
7	White/Brown	White/Brown	White/Brown
8	Brown	Brown	Brown

There are two types of networking patch cables that you might work with. The first is a ***straight-through cable***. This is the most common type of patch cable, and is the type that you would use to connect a computer to a central connecting device like a switch. It's called straight-through because the wires on each end of the cable are oriented in the same way. Generally, this is 568B on each end. However, there is another type of patch cable—the ***crossover cable***. This is used to connect like devices to each other; for example, a computer to another computer, or a switch to another switch. In this case, the patch cable is wired with the 568B standard on one end and the 568A standard on the other. To make a patch cable, you would use a cutting tool, wire stripper, RJ-45 crimper, RJ-45 plugs, and a patch tester. These tools are illustrated in Figure 3-4.

Generally, Ethernet transmits data signals on the orange and green wires. This means pins one, two, three, and six. Other technologies use different pairs or possibly all four pairs of wires. Usually, twisted-pair networks are wired to the 568B standard. This means that all wiring equipment must comply with 568B, including patch panels, RJ-45 jacks, patch cables, and the actual termination of wiring to each of these devices. To be more specific, the orange pair has a + and – wire, also known as tip and ring (old telco terminology). The green pair is similar. The orange pair transmits data, and the green pair receives. If the connection is half-duplex, only one of these pairs works at any given time. But if the connection is full-duplex, both pairs work simultaneously.

Figure 3-4

Patch cable tools

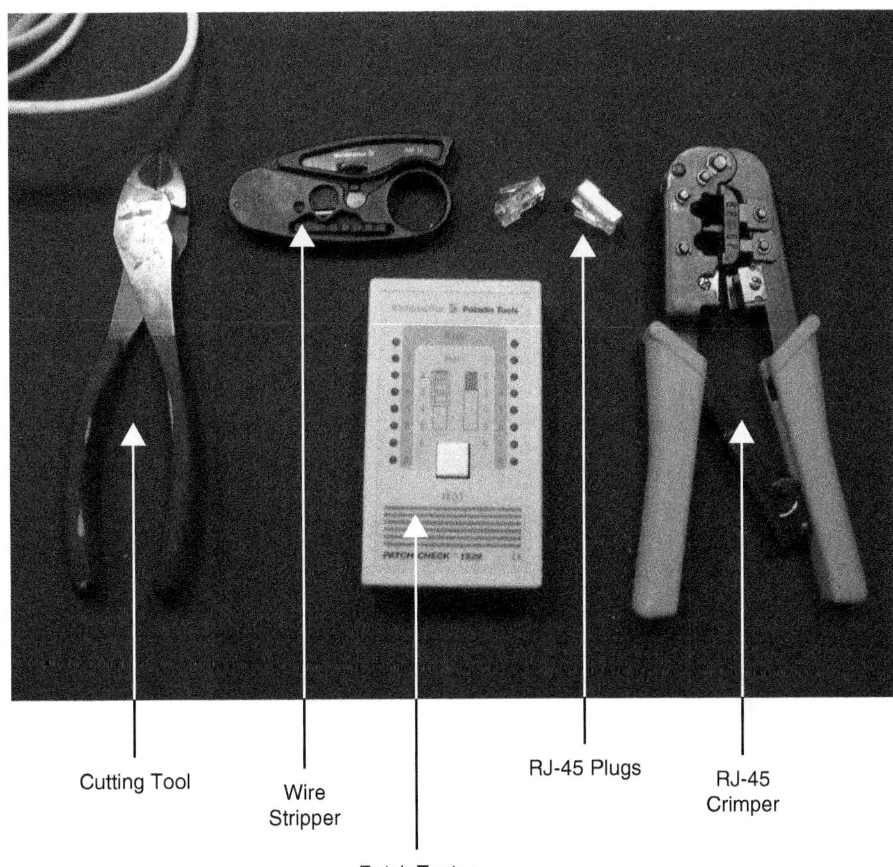

Network adapters normally have a ***MDI*** port; this stands for medium dependent interface. However, in order for computers to communicate with other devices, there has to be a cross in the wires somewhere. In any crossed connection, pin one crosses to pin three, and pin two crosses to pin six. But instead of using crossover cables to connect computers to central connecting devices such as switches, these central connecting devices are equipped with ***MDI-X*** ports (medium dependent interface crossover), which take care of the cross. This way, straight-through cables can be used to connect computers to the central connecting device, which is much easier, plus these cables are cheaper to manufacture. This is why a crossover cable is needed if you want to connect one computer to another computer directly or a switch to another switch directly. However, some switches have a special auto MDI/MDI-X port—sometimes referred to as an auto-sensing port—that will sense whether you're trying to connect a switch to another switch with a straight-through cable or a crossover cable. In other cases, the special port has a button that allows you to select whether it acts as an MDI-X or an MDI port.

Patch cables are a temporary solution. They are meant to be unplugged and plugged in as necessary. But most companies also have permanent cabling solutions, for example, a connection between a patch panel in the server room and an RJ-45 jack at a computer workstation. Figure 3-5 shows examples of both of these pieces of equipment. The cable that connects these two pieces of equipment has the individual wires permanently punched down so that they are immovable. The front of a patch panel simply has a lot of RJ-45 ports. The patch panel works great if a computer is moved to a different area of an office; the patch cable can simply be moved to the correct port on the patch panel.

Figure 3-5

A patch panel and an RJ-45 jack

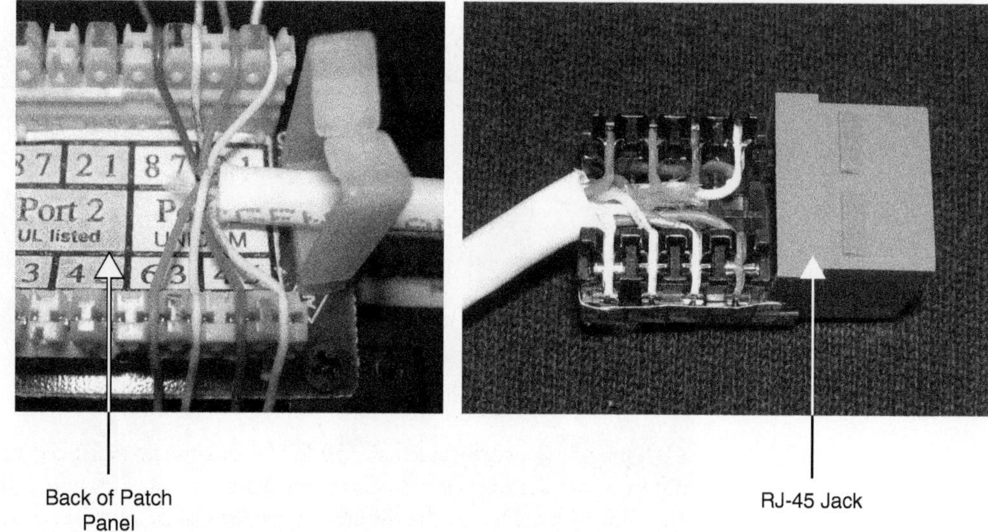

The tools necessary to make the connections between patch panels and RJ-45 jacks include a cutting tool, a wire stripper, a ***punch down tool***, and a testing device known as a ***continuity tester***, which tests all of the pins of a connection one by one. If any of the pins is miswired, the tester will let you know. It does this by testing the entire cable from end to end. The testing device is connected to one end of the run, and a terminating device connects to the other end; signals are bounced back and forth on every wire or pin. These last two tools are illustrated in Figure 3-6. Generally, twisted-pair cables can be run 100 meters before the signal degrades to such a point where it cannot be interpreted by the destination host. This is known as ***attenuation***. If a cable needs to be run farther, a signal repeater, a hub, or a switch can be used. Otherwise, fiber-optic cable will be the solution because it can be run much farther than twisted pair.

Figure 3-6

Punch down tool and continuity tester

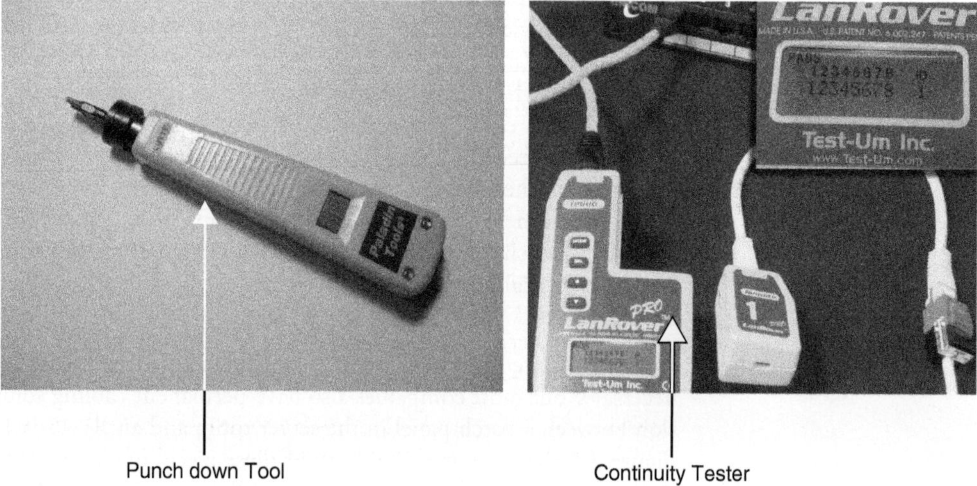

Twisted-pair cables are categorized according to the number of twists per foot, the maximum data rate, and the frequency of the transmit signal that the cable reliably supports. Table 3-2 describes the different categories of twisted-pair cable and the types of network speed they can accommodate.

Table 3-2

Categories of twisted-pair cable

Cable Type	Speed
Category 3	10 Mbps
Category 5	100 Mbps
Category 5e	100 Mbps and Gigabit networks
Category 6	Gigabit networks
Category 7A	10 Gigabit networks

Category 5e is usually rated at 350 MHz, but the actual speed varies depending on several different networking factors. ***Category 6*** already has different versions that run at 250 MHz and 500 MHz. Due to the different types of Cat 5e and Cat 6, it is better to simply say that those are rated for 100-Mbps networks and gigabit networks. Take a look at one of your network cables now. Often, the category type is printed directly on the plastic jacket of the cable. For today's networks, Category 5e or higher is necessary for today's high-bandwidth applications.

Interference can be a real problem with twisted-pair networks, or any networks based on copper wiring. ***Interference*** is anything that disrupts or modifies a signal that is traveling along a wire. There are many types of interference, but there are only a few you should know for the exam, including:

- ***Electromagnetic interference (EMI)*:** This is a disturbance that can affect electrical circuits, devices, and cables due to electromagnetic conduction and possibly radiation. Just about any type of electrical device causes EMI: TVs, air conditioning units, motors, unshielded electrical cables (Romex), and so on. Copper-based cables and network devices should be kept away from these electrical devices and cables if at all possible. If this is not possible, shielded cables can be used, for example ***shielded twisted pair (STP)***. STP cables have an aluminum shield inside the plastic jacket, which surrounds the pairs of wires. Or the device that is emanating EMI can be shielded. For example, an air conditioning unit could be boxed in with aluminum shielding in an attempt to keep the EMI generated by the AC unit's motor to a minimum. In addition, electrical cables should be BX (encased in metal), and not Romex (not encased in metal); in fact, most states require this to meet industrial and office space building code.
- ***Radio frequency interference (RFI)*:** This is interference that can come from AM/FM transmissions and cell phone towers. It is often considered to be part of the EMI family, and will sometimes be referred to as EMI. The closer a business is to one of these towers, the greater the chance of interference. The methods mentioned in the preceding EMI bullet can be employed to help defend against RFI. In addition, filters can be installed on the network to eliminate the signal frequency being broadcast by a radio tower, though this usually does not affect standard wired Ethernet networks.

One serious issue with data networks, especially networks with copper-based cabling, is ***data emanation*** (also known as signal emanation), which is the electromagnetic (EM) field that is generated by a network cable or network device that can be manipulated to eavesdrop on conversations, or to steal data. Data emanation is sometimes also referred to as eavesdropping, although this is not accurate. Data emanation is the most commonly seen security risk when using coaxial cable, but can also be a security risk for other copper-based cables such as twisted pair. There are various ways to tap into these (EM) fields in order to get unauthorized access to confidential data. To alleviate the situation, you could use shielded cabling or run the cabling through metal conduits. Second, you could use electromagnetic shielding on devices that might be emanating an electromagnetic field. This could be done on a small scale by shielding the single device, or on a larger scale by shielding an entire room, perhaps a server room; this would be an example of a ***Faraday cage***.

Another common type of interference is crosstalk. ***Crosstalk*** is when the signal that is transmitted on one copper wire or pair of wires creates an undesired effect on another wire or pair of wires. This first occurred when telephone lines were placed in close proximity to each other. Because the phone lines were so close, the signal could jump from one line to the next intermittently. If you have ever heard another conversation while talking on your home phone (not cell phones), you have been the victim of crosstalk. If the signals are digital, for example Ethernet data transfers or voice over IP, you already have an environment that is less susceptible to crosstalk. Data can still bleed over to other wires, but it is less common. The bleeding can be caused by cables that are bundled too tightly, which lead to crimped or damaged cables. If this is the case, a continuity tester will let you know which cable has failed; normally, this would have to be replaced. When it comes to twisted-pair cabling, crosstalk is broken down into two categories: ***near end crosstalk (NEXT)*** and ***far end crosstalk (FEXT)***. NEXT is when there is measured interference between two pairs in a single cable, measured on the cable end nearest the transmitter. FEXT is when there is similar interference, but this is measured at the cable end farthest from the transmitter. If crosstalk is still a problem, even though twisted-pair cable has been employed, and digital data transmissions have been implemented, shielded twisted pair (STP) could be used. Normally, companies opt for regular twisted-pair cabling, which is unshielded twisted pair (also known as UTP), but sometimes, there is too much interference in the environment to send data effectively, and STP must be utilized.

Cables that are installed inside walls or above drop ceilings where sprinkler systems cannot access in the case of a fire should be ***plenum-rated*** or low smoke rated. Plenum-rated cables have a Teflon coating that makes them more impervious to fire. The reason this is used is due to the fact that standard twisted-pair cables have a PVC jacket that can emit deadly gas into the air, which will ultimately be breathed in as hydrochloric acid.

Finally, the physical plant should be grounded. Often, server rooms or wiring closets are the central connecting point for all the cabling. All of the cables are punched down to patch panels, which are screwed into data racks. These racks should be bolted to the ground and connected with 10-gauge or thicker grounding wire (usually with a green jacket) to a proper earth bonding point, such as an I-beam in the ceiling. This protects all of the cabling (and the devices it connects to) from surges, spikes, lightning strikes, and so on.

That was a lot of information about twisted-pair cabling. We could go on and on, but that should suffice for now. Be sure to review all of the key terms listed at the beginning of this lesson for review.

Identifying and Working with Fiber-Optic Cable

Fiber-optic cable is used when longer distance runs are needed, and even higher data transfer rates are necessary. Fiber-optic cables are used as part of the backbone of the fastest networks. However, they are far more difficult to install, maintain, and troubleshoot.

CERTIFICATION READY
What are the characteristics of a fiber-optic cable used in networking?
Objective 2.3

Fiber-optic cable transmits light instead of electricity. The light (photons) is transmitted over glass or plastic. The glass or plastic strands in fiber-optic cabling are extremely small; they are measured in microns.

Because fiber-optic cable is rarer in networks, and because it is expensive, you can find out more about fiber-optic cable by searching the Internet for the various types of cables and connectors, including fiber-optic cabling. If you happen to have fiber-optic cables, connectors, and devices available, attempt to identify those after you have completed the following steps.

EXAMINE FIBER-OPTIC CABLE

GET READY. To examine fiber-optic cable, perform the following steps.

1. Run a Bing search in the Images section for *optical fiber.*
2. Run Bing searches for the following connector images:
   - FC connector
   - LC connector
   - MT-RJ connector
   - SC connector
   - ST connector
   - TOSLINK
3. Run a Bing image search for the following devices:
   - Fiber-optic network adapter
   - Fiber-optic switch
   - Fiber-optic router
4. If you do have any fiber-optic equipment handy, go ahead and identify these now, based on what you have seen on the Internet.

Fiber-optic cable can be either single mode or multi-mode:

- ***Single-mode*** fiber optic (SMF) is a cable with an optical fiber that is meant to carry a single ray of light: one ray of light, one mode. This type of cable is normally used for longer distance runs, generally 10 km, and up to 80 km.
- ***Multi-mode*** fiber optic (MM) is a cable with a larger fiber core, capable of carrying multiple rays of light. This type of cable is used for shorter distance runs, up to 600 meters. Though much shorter than single-mode fiber runs, this is still six times the length of twisted-pair cable runs.

Usually, fiber-optic cable is used for high-speed connections, backbone connections, storage area networks (SANs), and for direct connections between servers. Speeds of 1 Gbps and 10 Gbps are common, although you will still see 100-Mbps connections. Table 3-3 defines some of the 100-Mbps, 1-Gbps, and 10-Gbps versions of fiber optics as well as their medium type and typical maximum distance.

When it comes to interference, the cable can be its own worst enemy. Generally, fiber-optic cables are not affected by EMI because they are inherently light-based, not electricity-based. Although this cable will still produce a type of electromagnetic radiation, the cable is not traditionally affected by EMI the way copper-based cables are. However, if a fiber run is installed improperly, it can give strange results when it comes to the data signal. Exact installation rules must be followed, including proper termination, specific radii for turns, avoiding bunching, and so on. Improper installation will result in the signal becoming "bent," which causes data loss. Chromatic dispersion is a factor as opposed to attenuation on twisted-pair cables. If the light is refracted too often, again, the signal will degrade. Fiber optic in general is the most secure cable, allows for the longest runs, and offers data transfer rates that are equal to, or greater than, twisted-pair cable. But due to the complexity of installation, cost, and so on, it is not usually a first choice for all the individual client computer runs. Instead, it is used for backbone connections, switch connections at the top of hierarchical star topologies, and other high-bandwidth or long-distance applications.

Table 3-3

Types of fiber-optic cable

Cabling Standard	Medium	Maximum Distance
100BASE-FX	Multi-mode fiber Single-mode fiber	Half-duplex: 400 meters, Full-duplex: 2 km Full-duplex: 10 km
100BASE-SX	Multi-mode fiber	550 meters
100BASE-BX	Single-mode fiber	40 km
100BASE-LX10	Single-mode fiber	10 km
1000BASE-SX	Multi-mode fiber	550 meters
1000BASE-LX	Multi-mode fiber	550 meters
1000BASE-LX	Single-mode fiber	5 km
1000BASE-LX10	Single-mode fiber	10 km
1000BASE-ZX	Single-mode fiber	Up to 70 km
1000BASE-BX10	Single-mode fiber	10 km
10GBASE-SR	Multi-mode fiber	26–82 meters
10GBASE-LR	Single-mode fiber	10–25 km
10GBASE-LRM	Multi-mode	220 meters
10GBASE-ER	Single-mode	40 km

■ Understanding Wireless Networks

Wireless networks are everywhere. There are wireless networks for computers, handheld devices, wide area connections, and more. Chances are you have used a wireless network in the past. To install and troubleshoot wireless networks, you must understand the basics of wireless communications and have knowledge of the devices, standards, frequencies, and security methods.

CERTIFICATION READY
What are the characteristics of a wireless LAN?
Objective 1.2

Identifying Wireless Devices

Wireless devices might allow for central connectivity of client computers and handheld devices. Or, they might offer an extension of connectivity to a preexisting wireless network, and could be used to connect entire local area networks to the Internet. In addition, some wireless devices can be connected directly to each other in a point-to-point fashion.

CERTIFICATION READY
Today, what common wireless standard provides the best performance?
Objective 1.4

By far, the most well-known wireless device is the wireless access point (WAP). This device often also acts as a router, firewall, and IP proxy. It allows for the connectivity of various wireless devices, such as laptops, PDAs, handheld computers, and so on. It does so by making connections via radio waves on specific frequencies. Client computers and handheld devices must use the same frequency in order to connect to the WAP. In the following exercise, you will identify wireless access points, wireless network adapters, and wireless bridges and repeaters.

EXAMINE WIRELESS DEVICES

GET READY. To examine wireless devices, perform the following steps.

1. Execute a Bing search in the images section for the term *wireless access point*. Take a look at some of the various types of WAPs and their connections.
2. Examine Figure 3-7. This displays the front LED panel of a common wireless access point. Notice there is a green LED for the WLAN connection. WLAN is short for wireless local area network; the LED tells us that wireless is enabled on this device. This particular device also acts as a four-port switch; these ports are labeled as "Ethernet," and two of them have green lit LEDs, which means that computers are physically connected to those ports and are active. Finally, the "Internet" LED is lit, which is the physical connection from the WAP to the Internet. Although a WAP by itself is just a wireless transmitter, usually with a single port to connect to the LAN, multifunction network devices like these are very common in small networks and home offices.

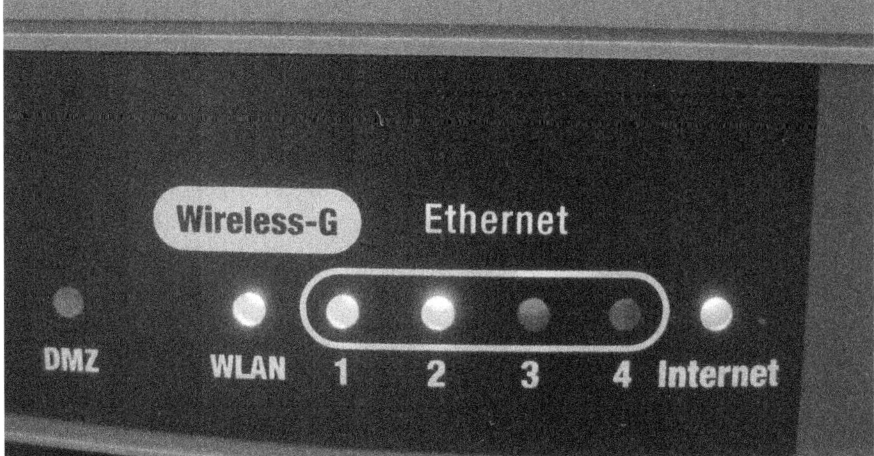

Figure 3-7

A common wireless access point

3. Execute a Bing search in the images section for the term *wireless network adapter*. Examine the results. ***Wireless network adapters*** allow for connectivity between a desktop computer or laptop and the wireless access point. They come in many shapes and sizes, including USB, PC Card, ExpressCard, and of course as an internal PCI or PCI Express adapter card for a personal computer. Most laptops today have built-in wireless network adapters, which are basically a chip on a circuit board with an antenna attached.
4. Access the Internet and execute searches on various wireless manufacturers' websites to find out the latest wireless access points and network adapters they offer. Write down your results for each of the manufacturers' fastest access points and network adapters.
   - www.d-link.com
   - http://www.netgear.com/
   - http://www.belkin.com/
5. Execute a Bing search in the images section for the term *wireless repeater*. Examine the results. A ***wireless repeater*** is used to extend the coverage of a wireless network. Due to the fact that most WLANs only have a range of about 100 feet or so (depending on the standard), wireless repeaters are often needed to extend that signal farther. They can be wired to the access point, but often, they are placed on the perimeter of the existing wireless network area.

6. Execute a Bing search in the images section for the term *wireless bridge*. Examine the results. A ***wireless bridge*** is similar to a wireless repeater, but the bridge can connect different 802.11 standards together; this is known as ***bridge mode***.
7. Access a wireless access point simulator. We will use the D-link DIR-655 emulator later in this lesson. Take a look at the following link now, and log on to the DIR-655 Device UI emulator to become acquainted with its interface. There is no password.
   - http://support.dlink.com/emulators/dir655/

Identifying Wireless Networking Standards

To set up a functional wireless LAN, a network administrator has to know several wireless standards as well as ways to secure the wireless network transmissions.

CERTIFICATION READY
Which encryption algorithm is used to secure wireless communications?
Objective 1.4

A wireless LAN (WLAN) is a network composed of at least one WAP, and at least one computer or handheld device that can connect to the WAP. Usually, these networks are Ethernet-based, but could be based on other networking architectures. To ensure compatibility, the WAP and other wireless devices must all use the same ***IEEE 802.11*** WLAN standard. These standards are collectively referred to as 802.11*x* (not to be confused with 802.1X), and are defined by the Data Link layer of the OSI model. The term WLAN is often used interchangeably with Wi-Fi. However, ***Wi-Fi*** refers to a trademark created by the Wi-Fi Alliance. The Wi-Fi products and technologies are based on the WLAN standards. These WLAN standards dictate the frequency (or frequencies) used, speed, and so on. Table 3-4 shows the most common standards and their maximum data transfer rate and frequency.

Table 3-4
IEEE 802.11 WLAN Standards

IEEE 802.11 Standard	Data Transfer Rate (Max.)	Frequency
802.11a	54 Mbps	5 GHz
802.11b	11 Mbps	2.4 GHz
802.11g	54 Mbps	2.4 GHz
802.11n	600 Mbps (300 Mbps typical)	5 GHz and/or 2.4 GHz

In the United States, 802.11b and g have 11 usable channels starting with channel 1 centered at 2.412 GHz and ending with channel 11 centered at 2.462 GHz. This is a smaller range than other countries may use.

Many of the channels in a WLAN overlap. To avoid this, organizations will often put, for example, three separate WAPs on channels 1, 6, and 11, respectively. This keeps them from overlapping and interfering with each other. If two WAPs on channels 4 and 5 are in close proximity to each other, there will be a decent amount of interference. It's wise to keep WLAN WAPs away from Bluetooth devices and Bluetooth access points because Bluetooth also uses the 2.4-GHz frequency range.

Compatibility is key. However, many WAPs are backward compatible. For example, an 802.11g WAP (such as the Linksys WRT54G) might also allow 802.11b connections. In addition, some specialized equipment may provide wireless bridging by also allowing 802.11a connections. But, generally, companies are looking for the fastest compatible speed possible from all their wireless networking equipment, and today, that means 802.11n. 802.11n is superior to older WLAN standards in the following ways:

- ***Multiple-Input Multiple-Output (MIMO)*:** This means that wireless devices can have more antennas, up to four maximum.
- ***Frame aggregation*:** This is the sending of two or more frames of data in a single transmission. By aggregating frames, the amount of data transferred on the Data Link layer can be doubled in the 802.11n standard.
- ***Channel bonding*:** Two channels that do not overlap are used together, to double the physical data rate (PHY). Channel bandwidth becomes 40 MHz instead of the previously used 20 MHz.

TAKE NOTE*

Today, while the wireless access points may support 802.11b, the 802.11b adapters are rarely used. In addition, 802.11a technology is even rarer.

Of course, all this great technology can be easily manipulated if it is not protected. To mitigate risk, encryption should be used. There are several types of encryption available for wireless networks, but the most secure is WPA2 when used with AES, as shown in Table 3-5. Without the proper encryption turned on at the client, and without knowledge of the correct key or passphrase, a client computer will not be able to connect to the WAP.

WEP also has 128-bit and 256-bit versions, but these versions are not commonly found in wireless network hardware. WEP in general is a deprecated protocol, and it is not recommended. However, if there are no other options available to you, WEP is far superior to *no* encryption!

Table 3-5

Wireless Encryption Options

Wireless Encryption Protocol	Description	Encryption Level (Key Size)
WEP	Wired Equivalent Privacy	64-bit
WPA2	Wi-Fi Protected Access	256-bit
TKIP	Temporal Key Integrity Protocol	128-bit
AES	Advanced Encryption Standard	128-, 192-, and 256-bit

Another way to secure the wireless connection is to use 802.1X. ***IEEE 802.1X*** is ***Port-based Network Access Control (PNAC)***. This provides strong authentication to devices that want to connect to the WLAN; it can also be used for regular wired LANs. There are three components to an 802.1X setup. The first is the supplicant or the computer that is attempting to connect to the WLAN. The second is the authenticator, or the wireless access point. The third is the authentication server; often, this is a RADIUS server, which enables advanced authentication techniques. Windows Server 2008, Windows Server 2008 R2, Windows Server 2012, Windows Server 2012 R2, and Windows Server 2016 include RADIUS within the Network Policy Server (NPS).

There are a couple of different ways to connect to a wireless network—primarily ***infrastructure mode*** and ***ad hoc mode***:

- Infrastructure is more common. It is when wireless clients connect to and are authenticated by a wireless access point. This can be expanded by creating a wireless distribution system, a group of WAPs interconnected wirelessly. When utilizing infrastructure mode, the base unit (normally a WAP) is configured with a ***service set identifier (SSID)***. This then becomes the name of the wireless network, and is broadcast out over the airwaves. When a client wants to connect to the WAP, he can identify it by the SSID.

- Ad hoc is less common, and used more in a handheld computer environment. Ad hoc (also referred to as peer-to-peer or P2P) networks are when all the clients communicate directly with each other. There is no "base" so to speak, meaning a wireless access point. Generally, this is configured so that two individual wireless devices can connect to each other and communicate, perhaps privately.

EXAMINE WIRELESS NETWORKING SETTINGS

GET READY. To access the D-Link DIR-655 emulator and view some standard wireless configurations, perform the following steps.

1. Log on to the DIR-655 emulator and view basic settings:
   a. Connect to the router. The user name cannot be changed, and the password is blank, meaning no password. This displays the main Device Information page. Examine this page. Note the LAN IP address of the device. It should be 192.168.0.1, the default for D-Link WAPs. If a client wants to connect to this device, it has to be configured via DHCP or statically, but must be on the 192.168.0 network.
   b. Scroll down and examine the wireless settings. Wireless should be enabled by default. Note the mode, channel width, channel used, and so on.
2. Modify the SSID:
   a. Click the **Setup** link on the top banner.
   b. Click the **Wireless Settings** link on the left side.
   c. Click the **Manual Wireless Network Setup** button. This should display the Wireless page.
   d. Look for the Wireless Network Name. This is the SSID. The default for D-Link devices is none other than **dlink**. It is highly recommended that you modify the default SSID on any WAP. Change it now to something a bit more complex.
3. Modify the wireless configuration:
   a. Examine the **802.11 Mode** drop-down menu. Note the variety of settings. Modify this so that it says **802.11n only**.
   b. Deselect the **Enable Auto Channel Scan** check box. This should enable the Wireless Channel drop-down menu. Select **channel 11**, which is centered at 2.462 GHz. Subsequent WAPs should be set to channel 6 and channel 1 in order to avoid channel overlapping.
   c. Modify the Channel Width setting to **40 MHz.** This incorporates channel bonding.
4. Enable encryption:
   a. At the Security Mode drop-down menu, select **WPA-Personal.** This should display additional WPA information. You would only select WPA-Enterprise if you have an available RADIUS server.
   b. Scroll down and in the WPA Mode drop-down menu, select **WPA2 Only.**
   c. In the Cipher Type drop-down menu, select **AES.**
   d. Finally, type in a complex pre-shared key. This is the passphrase that clients will need to enter in order to connect to the WLAN.

      This is the highest level of security this device offers (aside from WPA-Enterprise). Your configuration should look similar to Figure 3-8.

Figure 3-8

D-Link DIR-655 wireless configuration

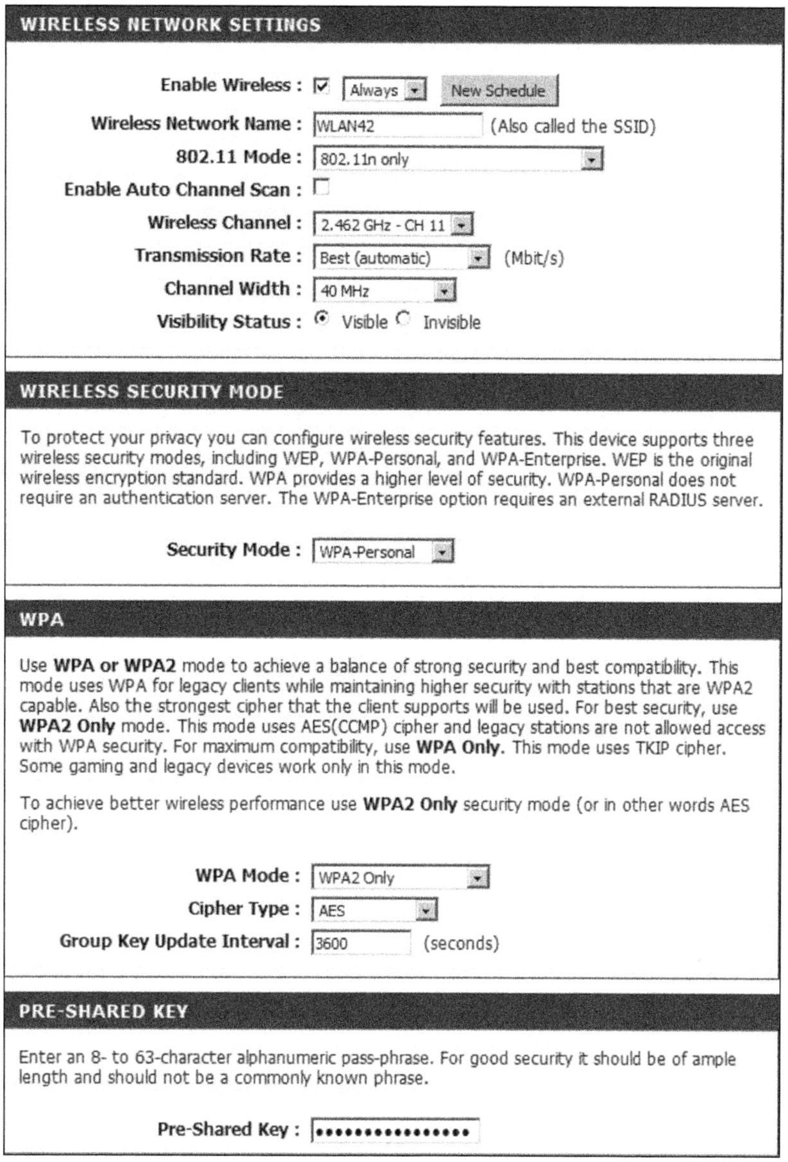

WIRELESS NETWORK SETTINGS

Enable Wireless : ☑ Always New Schedule
Wireless Network Name : WLAN42 (Also called the SSID)
802.11 Mode : 802.11n only
Enable Auto Channel Scan : ☐
Wireless Channel : 2.462 GHz - CH 11
Transmission Rate : Best (automatic) (Mbit/s)
Channel Width : 40 MHz
Visibility Status : ◉ Visible ○ Invisible

WIRELESS SECURITY MODE

To protect your privacy you can configure wireless security features. This device supports three wireless security modes, including WEP, WPA-Personal, and WPA-Enterprise. WEP is the original wireless encryption standard. WPA provides a higher level of security. WPA-Personal does not require an authentication server. The WPA-Enterprise option requires an external RADIUS server.

Security Mode : WPA-Personal

WPA

Use **WPA or WPA2** mode to achieve a balance of strong security and best compatibility. This mode uses WPA for legacy clients while maintaining higher security with stations that are WPA2 capable. Also the strongest cipher that the client supports will be used. For best security, use **WPA2 Only** mode. This mode uses AES(CCMP) cipher and legacy stations are not allowed access with WPA security. For maximum compatibility, use **WPA Only**. This mode uses TKIP cipher. Some gaming and legacy devices work only in this mode.

To achieve better wireless performance use **WPA2 Only** security mode (or in other words AES cipher).

WPA Mode : WPA2 Only
Cipher Type : AES
Group Key Update Interval : 3600 (seconds)

PRE-SHARED KEY

Enter an 8- to 63-character alphanumeric pass-phrase. For good security it should be of ample length and should not be a commonly known phrase.

Pre-Shared Key : ••••••••••••••••

5. Disable the SSID:
    a. When all clients are connected to the WAP, the SSID should be disabled. This does not allow new connections to the WAP unless the person knows the SSID name, but computers that have already connected may continue to do so.
    b. To do so, in the Visibility Status field, click the **Invisible** radio button.
6. Save the settings:
    a. At this point, you would save the settings. The emulator doesn't allow anything to be saved. It reverts back to defaults when you log off or disconnect from the website, so clicking **Save Settings** doesn't do anything. But on an actual DIR-655, the settings would save, and a reboot would be necessary.
    b. It's also important to back up the configuration. This can be done by clicking **Tools** on the top banner, then **System** on the left side, and then **Save Configuration**—a real time-saver, in the case that you have to reset the unit. It is also wise to update the device to the latest firmware. Save your settings before doing so because they will be lost when the upgrade is complete; then, they can be loaded back in.

SKILL SUMMARY

IN THIS LESSON, YOU LEARNED:

- Twisted-pair cable is the most common cable used in local area networks. It's relatively easy to work with, flexible, efficient, and fast. Twisted-pair cables are the most common of all copper-based cables. A single twisted-pair cable has eight wires; they are insulation-covered copper conductors that transmit electric signals.
- Twisted-pair cables are categorized according to the number of twists per foot, the maximum data rate, and the frequency of the transmit signal that the cable reliably supports.
- Fiber-optic cable is used when longer distance runs are needed and even higher data transfer rates are necessary. Fiber-optic cables are used as part of the backbone of the fastest networks. However, they are far more difficult to install, maintain, and troubleshoot.
- Wireless devices might allow for central connectivity of client computers and handheld devices. Or, they might offer an extension of connectivity to a preexisting wireless network, and could be used to connect entire local area networks to the Internet. In addition, some wireless devices can be connected directly to each other in a point-to-point fashion.
- There are a couple of different ways to connect to a wireless network—primarily infrastructure mode and ad hoc mode.

■ Knowledge Assessment

Multiple Choice

Select the correct answer for each of the following questions.

1. When installing 200 twisted-pair cable drops, which wiring standard should be used?
   a. 568A
   b. BOGB
   c. 568B
   d. 586B
2. To connect two laptops directly to each other by way of their network adapters, which kind of cable should be used?
   a. Rolled cable
   b. Crossover cable
   c. Straight-through cable
   d. Patch cable
3. When making a specialized wired connection for a server that will operate on an Ethernet network, which two wiring colors should be used?
   a. Orange and green
   b. Orange and blue
   c. Orange and brown
   d. White and blue

4. One of the network connections to a programmer's computer has failed. She suspects it is the twisted-pair cable. Which tool should be used to test for any problems in the cable?
   a. Patch tester
   b. Wireshark
   c. Continuity tester
   d. Fox and hound
5. You need to connect three new supercomputers to the backbone of the network that runs at 1 Gbps. Which type of cable will be sufficient for this task?
   a. Category 3
   b. Category 5
   c. Category 5e
   d. Category 10a
6. A network contains many fiber-optic connections. Which of the following does *not* belong in the fiber network?
   a. FC connector
   b. ST connector
   c. TOSLINK
   d. 8P8C
7. When connecting 802.11a, 802.11b, and 802.11n wireless networks together, which wireless device will guarantee connectivity between these networks?
   a. Wireless network adapter
   b. Wireless hub
   c. Wireless router
   d. Wireless bridge
8. You need to connect three new laptops to the wireless network "WLAN42." It runs at a speed of 54 Mbps only and a frequency of 2.4 GHz only. Which IEEE 802.11 standard should be implemented when connecting the laptops to the WAP?
   a. 802.11a
   b. 802.11b
   c. 802.11g
   d. 802.11n
9. A desktop computer needs to be connected to a WLAN using the strongest encryption type possible. Which of the following is the strongest?
   a. WEP
   b. RADIUS
   c. WPA2
   d. WPA
10. Thirteen PCs and laptops have been connected to a wireless network. To make the WLAN more secure, which of the following tasks disallows additional client access to the WAP?
    a. Enabling channel bonding
    b. Enabling frame aggregation
    c. Disabling SSID broadcasting
    d. Disabling WPA2

Fill in the Blank

Fill in the correct answer in the blank space provided.

1. To connect a computer to an RJ-45 jack a _____ cable should be used.
2. A twisted-pair cable was run 140 meters without any repeaters. The signal cannot be picked up by the destination host. This cable is the victim of _____.
3. A network uses Category 3 cabling. It needs to be upgraded so that it can support faster 100-Mbps applications. _____ is the minimum cable needed to accomplish this.
4. The type of cable known as _____ cable protects the copper wires inside the cable from EMI.
5. A manager complains about hearing a second conversation when he is talking on the phone. This is an example of _____.
6. The LANs in two separate buildings in a campus area network need to be connected. They are several kilometers apart. _____ fiber-optic cable is needed to accomplish this.
7. A manager doesn't know exactly how to do it, but he knows that he wants port-based authentication for his network. He is searching for an _____ implementation.
8. To connect to WLANs that are faster than 54 Gbps, the IEEE _____ standard should be utilized.
9. The _____ wireless encryption mode can be as strong as 256-bit.
10. A(n) _____ is when two or more wireless clients communicate directly with each other, without the need for a WAP.

■ Business Case Scenarios

Scenario 3-1: Selecting Channels for a WLAN

Proseware, Inc., requires you to implement an infrastructure mode WLAN that will have three WAPs. How should these WAPs be configured so that there is no overlap of signal between the three?

Scenario 3-2: Running Cable Drops Properly

The ABC Company requires you to run several cabling drops between patch panels and RJ-45 jacks. Which tools are necessary for this task?

Scenario 3-3: Selecting Network Adapters for Your WLAN Computers

A company you are consulting for needs five new computers installed with wireless connections. The wireless network adapter in each computer should be able to communicate at 300 Mbps. Which wireless Ethernet standard should be selected and which layer of the OSI model does this deal with?

Scenario 3-4: Securing a WLAN

Proseware, Inc., needs you to secure its wireless LAN. Describe three tasks you can perform to make the wireless LAN more secure.

Workplace Ready

The 802.11n Explosion

The IEEE 802.11n standard took several years to be finalized, and has been causing quite a stir since the standard was first ratified as a draft version. Aside from enabling speeds that approach gigabit wired connections, which are 6 to 12 times the speed of earlier wireless standards, it is more secure and more efficient. Lots of companies have jumped on the 802.11n bandwagon.

Access the Internet and look up the following wireless devices:

- **Cisco Aironet:** https://www.cisco.com/en/US/products/ps8382/index.html
- **HP ProCurve:** http://www.procurve.com/products/wireless/420_series/overview.htm
- **Bluesocket:** http://www.bluesocket.com/products
- **D-Link:** http://www.dlink.com/products/?pid=396

Compare the products and define which would be the best for a network with 275 wireless users who need speed and a high level of security.

In your analysis, consider the total amount of wireless connections allowed, IEEE 802.11 standards, encryption types, and ease of administration.

Understanding Internet Protocol

OBJECTIVE DOMAIN MATRIX

Skills/Concepts	Objective Domain Description	Objective Domain Number
Working with IPv4	Understand IPv4	3.2
	Understand local area networks (LANs)	1.2
Working with IPv6	Understand IPv6	3.3

KEY TERMS

anycast address
APIPA
broadcast address
classful network architecture
classless interdomain routing (CIDR)
default gateway
DNS server address
dual IP stack
dynamic IP address
global routing prefix
interface ID
IP conflict
IPv4
IPv4-mapped addresses
IPv6
IPv6 subnet
IPv6 tunneling
logical IP address
loopback IP addresses
masked
multicast address
multicasting
Network Address Translation (NAT)
node
private IP addresses
public IP addresses
static IP address
subnetting
Transmission Control Protocol/Internet Protocol (TCP/IP)
truncated
unicast address
unmasked
variable-length subnet masking (VLSM)

As a network administrator, you will use the ***Transmission Control Protocol/Internet Protocol (TCP/IP)*** communications protocol suite most often. Most technicians refer to this simply as Internet Protocol or IP. Although the newer IPv6 has many advances over its predecessor, IPv4 is still used in the majority of local area networks. However, this lesson covers both. To truly be a master of IP networks, a network administrator must know how the different versions of IP work, and how to configure, analyze, and test them in the GUI and in the command line. By utilizing knowledge about IP classes and reserved ranges, a well-planned network can be implemented. Further, by taking advantage of technologies like Network Address Translation and subnetting, a more efficient and secure network can be developed. Finally, by incorporating IPv6 whenever possible, you open the door to the future of data communications and enable easier administration, bigger and more powerful data transmissions, and a more secure IP network. Proseware, Inc., expects its network administrators to be able to set up a fully functional IPv4/IPv6 network. This lesson discusses how to enable computers on the LAN or the Internet to communicate through Layer 3 IP addressing. By the end of this lesson, you will be able to configure advanced IP network connections on the LAN, WAN, and Internet.

Working With IPv4

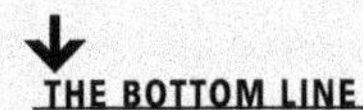

Internet Protocol version 4 or ***IPv4*** is the most frequently used communications protocol. IP resides on the Network layer of the OSI model, and IP addresses consist of four numbers, each between 0 and 255. The protocol suite is built into most operating systems and is used by most Internet connections in the United States and many other countries. As mentioned in Lesson 1, it is composed of a network portion and a host portion, which are defined by the subnet mask. For an IP address to function, there must be a properly configured IP address and compatible subnet mask. To connect to the Internet, you also need a gateway address and DNS server address. Advanced examples of IP configurations include subnetting, NAT, and CIDR.

Categorizing IPv4 Addresses

CERTIFICATION READY
Which default subnet mask is used by the Class C network and how many hosts can you put on the Class C network?
Objective 3.2

CERTIFICATION READY
Which address is assigned to the loopback IPv4 address?
Objective 1.2

To better understand IPv4 addresses, they have been categorized as five IP classes. Some have been reserved for private use, whereas the rest are utilized by public connections. This classification system helps to define what networks can be used on the LAN and what IP addresses can be used on the Internet.

The IPv4 classification system is known as the ***classful network architecture*** and is broken down into five sections, three of which are commonly used by hosts on networks; these are Classes A, B, and C. All five sections are displayed in Table 4-1. The first octet of the IP address defines the network class.

Table 4-1

IPv4 Classful Network Architecture

CLASS	IP RANGE (1ST OCTET)	DEFAULT SUBNET MASK	NETWORK/NODE PORTIONS	TOTAL NUMBER OF NETWORKS	TOTAL NUMBER OF USABLE ADDRESSES
A	0–127	255.0.0.0	Net.Node.Node.Node	2^7 or 128	$2^{24} - 2$ or 16,777,214
B	128–191	255.255.0.0	Net.Net.Node.Node	2^{14} or 16,384	$2^{16} - 2$ or 65,534
C	192–223	255.255.255.0	Net.Net.Net.Node	2^{21} or 2,097,151	$2^8 - 2$ or 254
D	224–239	N/A	N/A	N/A	N/A
E	240–255	N/A	N/A	N/A	N/A

Class A network addresses are used by government, ISPs, big corporations, and large universities. Class B network addresses are used by midsized companies and smaller ISPs. Class C network addresses are used by small offices and home offices.

The term ***node*** in the table is synonymous with "host." If an IP address is Class A, then the first octet is the "network" portion. The other three octets are the node or host portion of the address. So, a computer might be on the 11 network, and have an individual host ID of 38.250.1, making the entire IP address: 11.38.250.1. Observe the pattern. Class B addresses use two octets as the network portion (for example, 128.1). The other two octets are the host portion. Class C addresses use the first three octets as the network portion (for example, 192.168.1). The last octet is the host portion.

There are several other notations we need to make to this table.

First, the range for Class A is 0-127. Although this is true mathematically, the 127 network number isn't used by hosts as a ***logical IP address***. Instead, this network is used for ***loopback IP addresses***, which allow for testing. For example, every computer that runs IPv4 is assigned a logical IP address such as 192.168. In fact, any address on the 127 network (for example, 127.200.16.1) redirects to the local loopback. It is used for testing, as discussed in Lesson 1. So, this network number cannot be used when designing your logical IP network—rather it can be used to aid in testing.

Second, note the default subnet masks for each class. Notice how they ascend in a corresponding fashion to the network/node portions. Memorize the default subnet masks for Classes A, B, and C.

Third, the total number of usable addresses is always going to be two less than the mathematical number. For example, in a Class C network such as 192.168.50.0, there are 256 mathematical values, the numbers including and between 0 and 255. However, the first and last addresses, 0 and 255, cannot be used. The number 0 and the number 255 cannot be used as logical IP addresses for hosts. This is because they are already committed for a different use. The 0 in the last octet of 192.168.50.0 defines a network number, not a single IP address; it is the entire network. And 192.168.50.255 is known as the ***broadcast address***. The broadcast address is used to communicate with all hosts on the network. So, because you can never use the first and last addresses, you are left with two less addresses—in this case, 254 usable IP addresses. This applies to bigger networks as well. A Class A network can use 16,777,214 addresses instead of 16,777,216. If you examine this more carefully, you will see that the number 0 in binary equals 00000000 and the number 255 in binary is 11111111. So, you can't use the "all 0s" octet and the "all 1s" octet. This rule applies to total hosts, but not to total networks within a particular class. This concept will be built upon in the "Subnetting" section later in this lesson. One other related notion is the network 0. This generally isn't used, but is listed in the table because it is technically considered to be part of Class A.

Next, Class D and Class E are not used by regular hosts. Therefore, they are not given a network/node classification, and as a result of that, they are not given a specific number of networks or total hosts they can utilize. Instead, Class D is used for what is known as ***multicasting***, which is the transmitting of data to multiple computers (or routers). Class E was reserved for future use, but this has given way to IPv6 instead.

Finally, try to get into the habit of converting IP octets into their binary form. For example, the binary range of the first octet in Class A (0–127) is 00000000–01111111. For Class B, it is 10000000–10111111, and for Class C, it is 11000000–11011111. To practice this, you can use one of many decimal-to-binary conversion methods (such as the one shown in Table 4-2), or you can use the scientific calculator in Windows by navigating to the Run prompt and typing calc.exe. Then, click View on the calculator's menu bar and select Scientific. This will help you when it comes to more complex IP networks and when you attempt to create subnetworks. Keep in mind that computer certification exams might not allow the use of a calculator.

Table 4-2

Decimal-to-Binary Conversion Table

Conversion Area								Decimal Equivalent
128	64	32	16	8	4	2	1	
1	1	1	0	0	0	0	0	224
1	0	1	0	1	0	1	0	170
0	1	0	1	0	1	0	1	85

Table 4-2 shows a very simple method of converting from decimal to binary, or vice versa with three examples. Try this on paper as well. Simply make a table that begins with a 1 in the upper-right corner. Then, double the 1, moving to the left each time as you do so, until you have eight placeholders that will act as column headers. They should be 1, 2, 4, 8, 16, 32, 64, and 128.

To convert a decimal number to binary, place the decimal number to the right or left of the table. If the number is 224, for example, see if the placeholders can fit inside that number starting with the placeholder on the left. Because 128 fits into 224, place a binary 1 under the 128 column. Then, move to the right one step at a time. If you add 128 to 64, this equals 192, which also fits inside 224, so place a binary 1 in that column as well. Next, add 192 + 64 +32, which equals 224. This fits (exactly) with the number you are trying to convert, so place a binary 1 in the 32 column and leave the rest of the columns as 0s. As a second example, consider the number 170; 128 fits inside of it, so place a 1 in the first column. However, because 128 + 64 = 192, which is larger than 170, place a 0 in the second column. But you carry the 128 over, so next is 128 + 32, which equals 160. This does fit inside 170, so you place a 1 in the third column, and so on. Keep going through the octet until the binary number is equal to the decimal number.

To convert a binary number to decimal, just place the binary octet from left to right under the placeholders. In the third example, you placed 01010101 underneath the placeholders. To convert, just multiply down and add across. Or, you could think of it as just adding all the placeholders that have 1s in the column together to get the final result. In the third example, the 1s inhabit the 64, 16, 4, and 1 columns, so 64 + 16 + 4 + 1 = 85.

Again, this is an important skill for network administrators, and is especially vital for networking certification exams. Try a few more of these conversions, in both directions. Then, use the scientific calculator to check your work. By default, the calculator works in decimal, but you can simply type a number such as 5, and click the Bin radio button to make the conversion. The F8 key also activates this button. Notice that leading 0s (any on the left side) are omitted from the final results. By the way, the F6 key activates the Dec radio button.

In the following exercise, you will configure two computers with Class A IP addresses, and verify the configuration through the use of `ipconfig` and `ping`. Pay very close attention to the exact IP addresses that you type and their corresponding subnet masks.

CONFIGURE CLASS A ADDRESSES

GET READY. To configure two computers with Class A IP addresses and verify the configuration through the use of `ipconfig` and `ping`, perform the following steps.

1. Access the Local Area Connection Properties dialog box.
2. Click **Internet Protocol Version 4** and then click the **Properties** button. The Internet Protocol Version 4 Properties dialog box opens. Write down the current settings so that you can return the computer to these settings at the end of the exercise.
3. Click the **Use the following IP address** radio button. This enables the other fields so you can enter the IP information. Type the following:
   - For the IP address of the first computer, type **10.0.0.1**.
   - For the IP address of the second computer, type **10.0.0.2**.
   - If necessary, configure the router to act as a host on this network as well (for example, using 10.0.0.3). Do this for subsequent exercises also, but only if the router gets in the way of the computers pinging each other.
   - For the Subnet mask of both computers, type **255.0.0.0**.
   - Leave the Default gateway and the Preferred DNS server fields blank.
   - When you are finished, the first computer's configuration should look like Figure 4-1.
   - If you have other computers, try configuring their IP addresses as well; the host portion of the IP address should ascend once for each computer: .3, .4, .5, and so forth.

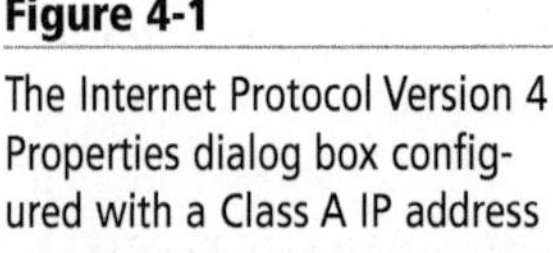

Figure 4-1

The Internet Protocol Version 4 Properties dialog box configured with a Class A IP address

4. Click **OK.** Then, in the Local Area Connection Properties dialog box, click **OK.** This completes and binds the configuration to the network adapter.
5. Now, it's time to test your configuration. You will do this in two ways: first with the `ipconfig` command and second with the `ping` command in the Command Prompt window:
    a. Type the **`ipconfig`** command and press **Enter**. Verify that the IP configuration is accurate and corresponds to what you typed in the Internet Protocol Version 4 (TCP/IPv4) Properties window. If not, check your Internet Protocol Version 4 (TCP/IPv4) Properties dialog box.
    b. Ping the other computer. Also, try to ping any other computers that were configured as part of this Class A network (for example, `ping 10.0.0.2`). Make sure you get replies. If you do not, check the IP configurations of both computers. Also, make sure they are physically connected to the same network. In addition, as mentioned in previous exercises, verify that firewalls are disabled, if necessary. It is very important to avoid an ***IP conflict***. IP conflicts occur when two computers are configured with the same IP address. If this happens, a small pop-up alert appears at the lower right of your screen, as shown in Figure 4-2. When configuring computers statically as you are in this exercise, it is all too easy to become confused as to which computers are which. Consider labeling every computer you work on with a different number: Computer1, Computer2, and so on. Use that number as the last octet of the computer's IP address in each exercise. This helps to reduce the chances of an IP conflict.

Figure 4-2

IP conflict pop-up

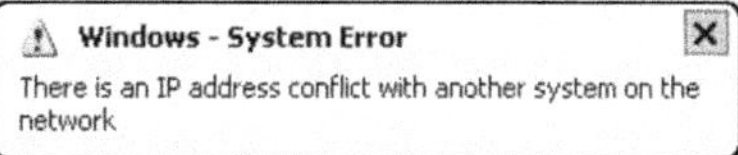

In the following exercise, you will configure two computers with Class B IP addresses and verify the configuration through the use of `ipconfig` and `ping`.

CONFIGURE CLASS B ADDRESSES

GET READY. To configure two computers with Class B IP addresses and verify the configuration through the use of `ipconfig` and `ping`, perform the following steps.

1. Access the Local Area Connection Properties dialog box.
2. Click **Internet Protocol Version 4** and then click the **Properties** button. The Internet Protocol Version 4 Properties dialog box opens. Write down the current settings so that you can return the computer to these settings at the end of the exercise.
3. Click the **Use the following IP address** radio button. This enables the other fields so you can enter the IP information. Type the following:
    - For the IP address of the first computer, type **172.16.0.1**.
    - For the IP address of the second computer, type **172.16.0.2**.
    - For the Subnet mask of both computers, type **255.255.0.0**.
    - Leave the Default gateway and the Preferred DNS server fields blank.
    - When you are finished, the first computer's configuration should look like Figure 4-3.
    - If you have other computers, try configuring their IP addresses as well; the host portion of the IP address should ascend once for each computer: .3, .4, .5, and so forth.
4. Click **OK**. Then, in the Local Area Connection Properties dialog box, click **OK**. This completes and binds the configuration to the network adapter.

Figure 4-3

The Internet Protocol Version 4 Properties dialog box configured with a Class B IP address

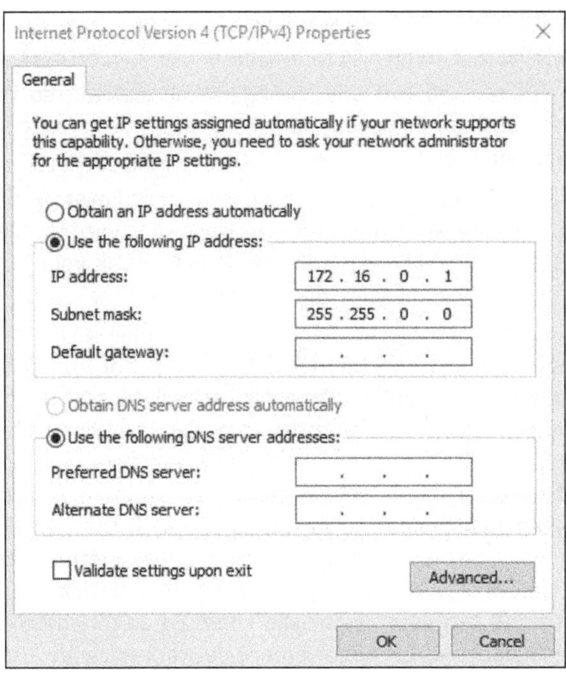

5. Now, it's time to test your configuration. You will do this in two ways: first with the `ipconfig` command and second with the `ping` command:
   a. Execute the **`ipconfig`** command. Verify that the IP configuration is accurate and corresponds to what you typed in the Internet Protocol Version 4 (TCP/IPv4) Properties window. If not, go back and check your Internet Protocol Version 4 (TCP/IPv4) Properties dialog box.
   b. Ping the other computer. Also, try to ping any other computers that were configured as part of this Class B network (for example, **`ping 172.16.0.2`**). Make sure you get replies. If you do not, check the IP configurations of both computers. Also, make sure they are physically connected to the same network.

IPv4 addresses are further classified as either public or private. ***Public IP addresses*** are ones that are exposed to the Internet; any other computers on the Internet can potentially communicate with them. ***Private IP addresses*** are hidden from the Internet and any other networks. They are usually behind an IP proxy or firewall device. There are several ranges of private IP addresses that have been reserved by the IANA, as shown in Table 4-3. Most of the other IPv4 addresses are considered to be public.

Table 4-3

Private IPv4 Addresses as Assigned by the IANA

Class	Start of Range	End of Range
A	10.0.0.0	10.255.255.255
B	172.16.0.0	172.31.255.255
C	192.168.0.0	192.168.255.255

The only private Class A network is 10. However, there are multiple Class B and Class C private networks. For example, 172.16, 172.17, and so on through 172.31 are all valid private Class B networks. And 192.168.0, 192.168.1, 192.168.2, and so on all the way through 192.168.255 are all valid private Class C networks. Remember, that for an address to be Class C, the first three octets must be part of the network portion. For Class B, the first and second octets must be part of the network portion, and for Class A, only the first octet must be part of the network portion.

Another type of private range was developed by Microsoft for use on small peer-to-peer Windows networks. It is called ***APIPA***, which is an acronym for Automatic Private IP Addressing. It uses a single Class B network number: 169.254.0.0. If a Windows client cannot get an IP address from a DHCP server, and has not been configured statically, it will auto-assign a number on this network. If for some reason APIPA assigns addresses even though a DHCP server exists, APIPA can be disabled in the registry. See the Microsoft Support site for details.

Although most people understand the difference, it would be wise to revisit the topic of static versus dynamic IP addresses. All of the exercises we have done in this lesson have been examples of setting up a ***static IP address***. But most commonly, computers are set up to obtain an IP address (and other IP information) automatically. In this example of a ***dynamic IP address***, it means that the computer broadcasts out to the network in an attempt to find a DHCP server, be it a four-port SOHO router, DHCP server, or other appliance. The server then replies with the required information. This is accomplished through a four-step process known as DORA that is covered in more depth in Lesson 6.

In the following exercise, you will configure two computers with Class C private IP addresses and verify the configuration through the use of `ipconfig` and `ping`.

CONFIGURE CLASS C PRIVATE ADDRESSES

GET READY. To configure two computers with Class C private IP addresses and verify the configuration through the use of `ipconfig` and `ping`, perform the following steps.

1. Access the Local Area Connection Properties dialog box.
2. Click **Internet Protocol Version 4** and then click the **Properties** button. The Internet Protocol Version 4 Properties dialog box opens. Write down the current settings so that you can return the computer to these settings at the end of the exercise.
3. Click the **Use the following IP address** radio button. This enables the other fields so you can enter the IP information. Type the following:
   - For the IP address of the first computer, type **192.168.50.1**.
   - For the IP address of the second computer, type **192.168.50.2**.
   - For the Subnet mask of both computers, type **255.255.255.0**.
   - Leave the Default gateway and the Preferred DNS server fields blank.
   - When you are finished, the first computer's configuration should look like Figure 4-4.

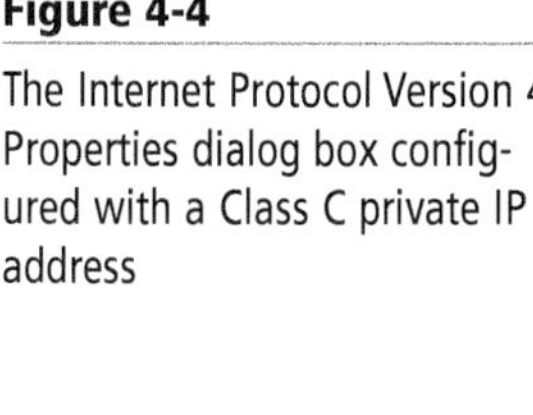

Figure 4-4

The Internet Protocol Version 4 Properties dialog box configured with a Class C private IP address

- If you have other computers, try configuring their IP addresses as well; the host portion of the IP address should ascend once for each computer: .3, .4, .5, and so forth.

4. Click **OK**. Then, in the Local Area Connection Properties dialog box, click **OK**. This completes and binds the configuration to the network adapter.
5. Test your configuration. You will do this in two ways: first with the `ipconfig` command and second with the `ping` command:
   a. Open the Command Prompt window. Execute **`ipconfig`**. Verify that the IP configuration is accurate and corresponds to what you typed in the Internet Protocol 4 (TCP/IPv4) Properties window. If not, go back and check your Internet Protocol 4 (TCP/IPv4) Properties dialog box.
   b. Ping the other computer. Also, try to ping any other computers that were configured as part of this Class C network (for example, **`ping 192.168.50.2`**). Make sure you get replies. If you do not, check the IP configurations of both computers. Also, make sure they are physically connected to the same network.

Default Gateways and DNS Servers

To complete the IP configuration, you need a default gateway address and a DNS server address. This will help your client computers access the Internet.

CERTIFICATION READY
Why does a client need access to a gateway?
Objective 3.2

Up until now, you have only configured the IP address and Subnet mask fields of the IP Properties dialog box. To have a fully functional computer, you need to configure two more fields.

The first is the Default gateway field. The ***default gateway*** is the first IP address of the device that a client computer will look for when attempting to gain access outside of the local network. This device could be a router, server, or other similar device; it is the device that grants access to the Internet or other networks. This device's address will be on the same network number as the client. So, for example, if the client is 192.168.50.1, the gateway might be 192.168.50.100. Many gateway devices come preconfigured with their own LAN IP, but this is almost always configurable. For example, the D-Link DIR-655 you accessed in the previous lesson was configured as 192.168.0.1, but you could change that if you desire. Without a default gateway address configured within the local computer's Internet Protocol 4 (TCP/IPv4) Properties dialog box, it will not be able to gain access to any other networks. It is possible to have more than one gateway address, in the case that the default gateway device fails. This can be done in Windows 10 by navigating to the Network Connections window, right-clicking the network adapter in question (for example, Local Area Connection) and choosing **Properties**. Then, select **Internet Protocol Version 4 (TCP/IPv4)** and click the **Properties** button. In the Internet Protocol Version 4 Properties dialog box, click the **Advanced** button. Additional gateway addresses can be added to the Default gateway field.

The second field you need to configure is the DNS server address field. The ***DNS server address*** is the IP address of the device or server that resolves DNS addresses to IP addresses. This could be a Windows server or an all-in-one multifunction network device. It depends on the network environment. Also, it could be on the LAN (common in big networks) or located on the Internet (common in smaller networks). An example of a name resolution would be the domain name microsoft.com, which currently resolves to the IP address 104.40.211.35. To demonstrate this, try this command in the Command Prompt window: `ping www.microsoft.com`. You should get results similar to "Reply from 104.40.211.35. . .". Microsoft can change its IP address at any time, but the results should be similar. By the way, this is an example of a public IP address. The whole concept here is that computers ultimately communicate by IP address. But it is easier for a person to remember www.microsoft.com than an IP address. The DNS server will resolve domain names like www.proseware.com, host names like server1.proseware.com, and so on. Without this DNS server address, a client computer will not be able to connect by name to any resources on the Internet. DNS servers are also necessary in Microsoft domain environments. If your computer is a member of one, and the DNS server address is not configured properly, domain resources will most likely be inaccessible.

In the following exercise, you will configure two computers with Class C private IP addresses, subnet masks, default gateways, and DNS server addresses. Then, you will verify the configuration through the use of `ipconfig` and `ping`. Additional documentation is required for Steps 7–9.

CONFIGURE CLASS C ADDRESSES, SUBNET MASKS, GATEWAY ADDRESSES, AND DNS SERVER ADDRESSES

GET READY. To configure two computers with Class C private IP addresses, subnet masks, default gateways, and DNS server addresses—and then verify the configuration through the use of `ipconfig` and `ping`—perform the following steps. Additional documentation is required for Steps 7–9.

1. Access the Local Area Connection Properties dialog box.
2. Click **Internet Protocol Version 4** and then click the **Properties** button. The Internet Protocol Version 4 Properties dialog box opens. Write down the current settings so that you can return the computer to these settings at the end of the exercise.
3. Click the **Use the following IP address** radio button. This enables the other fields so you can enter the IP information. Type the following:
   - For the IP address of the first computer, type **192.168.50.1**.
   - For the IP address of the second computer, type **192.168.50.2**.
   - For the Subnet mask of both computers, type **255.255.255.0**.
   - For the Gateway address of both computers, type **192.168.50.100**.
   - Then, in the next field, type a Preferred DNS server address of **192.168.50.201**. Do this for both computers.
   - When you are finished, the first computer's configuration should look like Figure 4-5.

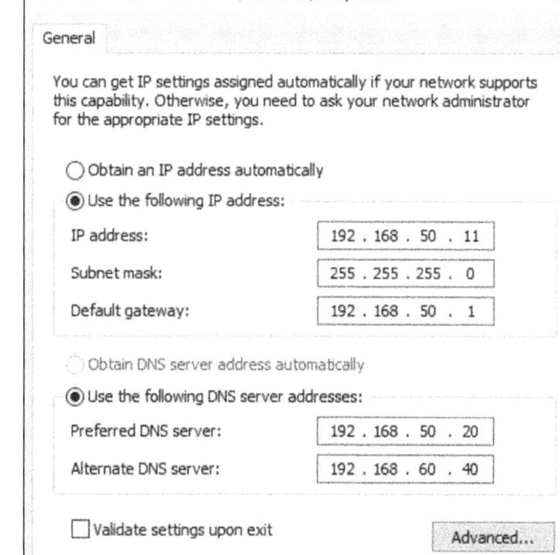

Figure 4-5

The Internet Protocol Version 4 Properties dialog box configured with a Class C private IP address, subnet mask, default gateway, and DNS server address

- If you have other computers, try configuring their IP addresses as well; the host portion of the IP address should ascend once for each computer: .3, .4, .5, and so forth.

4. Click **OK**. Then, in the Local Area Connection Properties dialog box, click **OK**. This completes and binds the configuration to the network adapter.
5. Now test your configuration. You will do this in two ways: first with the `ipconfig` command and second with the `ping` command:
   a. Execute **`ipconfig`**. Verify that the IP configuration is accurate and corresponds to what you typed in the IP Properties window. If not, go back and check your Internet Protocol Properties dialog box.
   b. Ping the other computer. Also, try to ping any other computers that were configured as part of this Class C network (for example, **`ping 192.168.50.2`**). Make sure you get replies. If you do not, check the IP configurations of both computers. Also, make sure they are physically connected to the same network.
6. Now, attempt to connect to the Internet. You should not be able to! That is because we used fictitious gateway and DNS server addresses.
7. Find out the following from your instructor, or from documentation elsewhere:
   - At least two static IP addresses that you can use for your client computers that will be allowed access to the gateway
   - The proper subnet mask, default gateway, and DNS server address that corresponds with the static IPs
8. Configure the computers with the new information and save the configuration.
9. Test the LAN connection with **`ping`** and then test the Internet connections by using a web browser to connect to a website. If either fails, check each address individually for any typos, IP conflicts, or other configuration mistakes.

Defining Advanced IPv4 Concepts

Methods such as Network Address Translation, subnetting, and classless interdomain routing (CIDR) can make networks more efficient, faster, and more secure. These advanced IP configurations can be found in most networks today. To be a proficient network engineer, you must master these concepts.

UNDERSTANDING NETWORK ADDRESS TRANSLATION

CERTIFICATION READY
How can you share multiple internal addresses with a single public address?
Objective 3.2

Network Address Translation (NAT) is the process of modifying an IP address while it is in transit across a router, computer, or similar device. This is usually so one larger address space (private) can be remapped to another address space, or even to a single public IP address. It is also known as IP masquerading, and was originally implemented due to the problem of IPv4 address exhaustion. Today, NAT also hides a person's private internal IP address, making it more secure. Some routers only allow for basic NAT, which carries out IP address translation only. But more advanced routers allow for *Port Address Translation (PAT)*, a subset of NAT, which translates both IP addresses and port numbers. A NAT implementation on a firewall hides an entire private network of IP addresses (for example, the 192.168.50.0 network) behind a single, publicly displayed IP address. Many SOHO routers, servers, and similar devices offer this technology to protect a company's computers on the LAN from outside intrusion.

Figure 4-6 illustrates how NAT might be implemented with some fictitious IP addresses. The router has two network connections. One goes to the LAN—it is 192.168.50.254. This is a private IP address. This is also known as an Ethernet address and is sometimes referred to as E^0, Ethernet 0, or the first Ethernet address. The other connection goes to the Internet or WAN. This is 64.51.216.27 and is a public IP address. Sometimes, this is referred to as S^0,

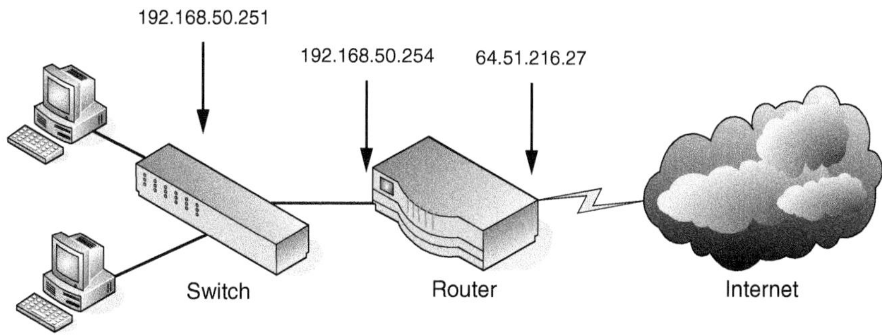

Figure 4-6

An example of NAT

which denotes a serial address (common to vendors such as Cisco). So, the router is employing NAT to protect all of the organization's computers (and switch) on the LAN from possible attacks that could be initiated by mischievous persons on the Internet or other location outside of the LAN.

An example of a D-Link DIR-655 multifunction network device that implements NAT is shown in Figure 4-7. This screen capture is displaying the main Device Information page. Notice in the WAN section that there is a public IP address of 216.164.145.27. This is

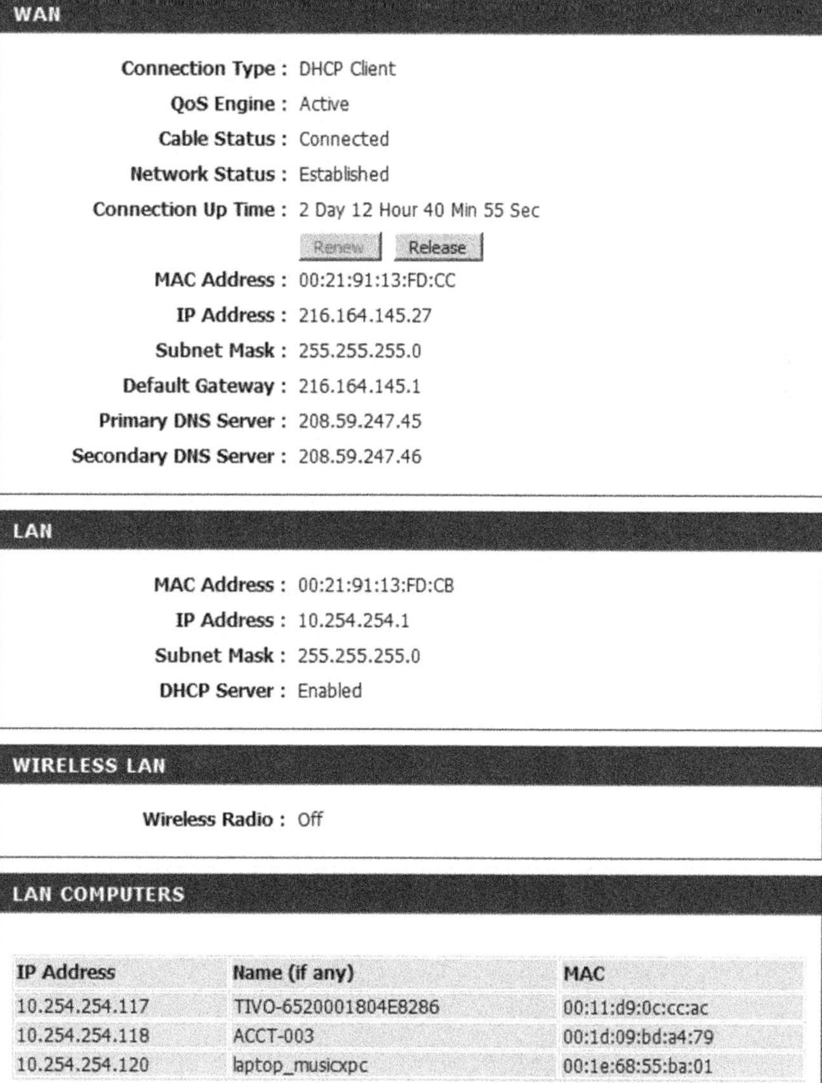

IP Address	Name (if any)	MAC
10.254.254.117	TIVO-6520001804E8286	00:11:d9:0c:cc:ac
10.254.254.118	ACCT-003	00:1d:09:bd:a4:79
10.254.254.120	laptop_musicxpc	00:1e:68:55:ba:01

Figure 4-7

NAT on a DIR-655 router

the WAN address, and on this particular testing device, it obtains that address (and the subsequent WAN information) from an ISP's DHCP server. Notice also the LAN IP address of 10.254.254.1. That is the private IP address on the local side of the router. So, this device is translating for all computers on the 10.254.254.0 network and allowing them to communicate with the Internet, but is only displaying one IP address to the Internet: 216.164.145.27.

UNDERSTANDING SUBNETTING

CERTIFICATION READY
How can you divide a class network into multiple smaller networks?
Objective 3.2

Subnetting could be considered one of the most difficult concepts in networking. However, it can be simplified with some easy equations and a well-planned implementation process. Until now, you have used default subnet masks. However, one of the reasons for having a subnet mask is to have the ability to create subnetworks logically by IP addresses. So, what is a subnet? It is a subdivision of your logical IP network; by default, all computers are on a single subnet or network with no divisions involved. And. . . what is a mask? It is any binary number that is a 1. If a binary digit is a 1, it is ***masked***, meaning the corresponding IP address bit is part of the network ID. If the binary digit is a 0, it is ***unmasked***, meaning the corresponding IP address bit is part of the host ID. Let's review the standard default subnet masks, as shown in Table 4-4.

Table 4-4
Standard Subnet Mask Review

TYPE	DECIMAL	BINARY
Class A	255.0.0.0	11111111.00000000.00000000.00000000
Class B	255.255.0.0	11111111.11111111.00000000.00000000
Class C	255.255.255.0	11111111.11111111.11111111.00000000

Note the binary numbers that are 1s and the binary numbers that are 0s in the table. ***Subnetting*** is the act of dividing a network into smaller logical subnetworks. It is done by transforming the default subnet mask into something else, by borrowing bits. One or more of the 0s in the subnet masks in Table 4-4 will become masking 1 bits, thus changing the amount of subnets and hosts per subnet. In other words, some of the host bits are converted to network bits, which are then used to define subnets (smaller networks located within the bigger network).

Subnetting is implemented by network administrators to organize and compartmentalize networks, reduce broadcast traffic, and increase network security. By default, computers in one subnet cannot communicate with computers on another subnet, even if they are part of the same total IP network.

For the upcoming exercise, you will use a Class C network to show how you can subdivide it into smaller subnetworks. You will use the network number 192.168.50.0. By default, the subnet mask would be 255.255.255.0. But what if you wanted to divide the network into four distinct IP subnetworks?

There are a lot of different subnetting options, but one example could be this:

255.255.255.*240*

The corresponding CIDR notation (to be discussed further, shortly) is 192.168.1.0 /28. That is because the binary equivalent of the subnet mask has 28 masked bits and 4 unmasked bits.

The first three 255s are the same and you can pretty much ignore them, but the fourth octet (240) tells how many subnetworks (subnet IDs) and how many hosts you can have per subnetwork. All you need is the ability to convert to binary and the usage of two equations:

- Equation #1: $2^n = x$
- Equation #2: $2^n - 2 = x$

Here's how you do it:

1. Convert 240 to binary. It equals 11110000.
2. Break the octet up like this: 1111 and 0000. Use the parts that are 1s for the subnet IDs and the parts that are 0s for the host IDs.
3. To find out the total number of subdivisions (or subnet IDs) you can have in your network, input the number of 1s into equation #1. So, there are four 1s in 11110000. That number 4 replaces ", so the equation then becomes $2^4 = x$. Because $2^4 = 16$, the maximum number of subnets is 16. However, the first and last numbered subnets cannot be used as subnets. That leaves you with 14 usable subnets.
4. You can never use the first and the last IP address for a host ID. "All ones" and "all zeros" cannot be used as they are for identifying the subnetwork and for doing broadcasting. To find out the total number of hosts *per subnet* you can use in your network, this time input the number of 0s into equation #2. There are four 0s in 11110000. That number 4 replaces ", so the equation becomes $2^4 - 2 = x$. Because $2^4 - 2 = 14$, the maximum number of hosts per subnet is 14.

So now you have 14 possible subnets and 14 possible hosts per subnet. That gives you a total of 196 usable hosts on your whole network. Although you lose out on total hosts when you subnet, it should work fine for the original plan of having four subnetworks. Table 4-5 shows all the subnets and hosts that are possible for this particular scenario.

Table 4-5

Possible Subnets and Hosts in the 192.168.50.0/28 Subnetworking Scenario

Subnet ID#	Subnet ID Binary Equivalent	Host IP Range in Binary	Host IP in Decimal
0	0000	0000–1111	0–15 (not recommended)
1	0001	0000–1111	16–31
2	0010	0000–1111	32–47
3	0011	0000–1111	48–63
4	0100	0000–1111	64–79
5	0101	0000–1111	80–95
6	0110	0000–1111	96–111
7	0111	0000–1111	112–127
8	1000	0000–1111	128–143
9	1001	0000–1111	144–159
10	1010	0000–1111	160–175
11	1011	0000–1111	176–191
12	1100	0000–1111	192–207
13	1101	0000–1111	208–223
14	1110	0000–1111	224–239
15	1111	0000–1111	240–255 (not recommended)

As you can see, there are 16 values in each subnet host range, but you can't use the first and last because they are all 0s and all 1s respectively. So, for example, in subnet ID #1, the 16 and the 31 are unavailable. The actual subnet ID is 16, and the broadcast address is 31 for that subnet. The usable IP addresses in that subnet are 17–30. In subnet ID #2, 32 and 47 are unavailable. The usable range is 33–46. Keep in mind that computers in different subnets cannot communicate with each other by default. So, the IP address 192.168.50.17 cannot communicate with 192.168.50.33 and vice versa. Another item to note is that most operating systems (including Windows) either discourage or flat out do not allow usage of the first and last subnet IDs. This is to avoid confusion with the main network number (prior to subnetting) and the broadcasting segment. That was a lot of information. So, the best way to really explain this is to do it.

SUBNET A NETWORK

GET READY. To create a working subnet, use the following information to create your working subnetwork and then perform the following steps.

- **Network:** 192.168.50.0
- **Subnet mask:** 255.255.255.240
- **Subnet ID to be used:** ID 7

Be sure to write this on paper as you perform the exercise.

1. Go to the first computer (we will call this Computer1).
2. Disable any secondary network adapters. Make sure only one adapter is enabled; this is the one you will use for the exercise.
3. Access the Internet Protocol Version 4 (TCP/IPv4) Properties window of Computer1 and change the IP settings to reflect the above subnet information. If you look back at Table 4-5, you will notice that subnet ID 7 dictates that you can use IP addresses between 192.168.50.112 and 192.168.50.127. However, remember that golden rule! You cannot use the first and last addresses. That will leave you with 113–126. You can use any of those IP addresses that you want; just make sure that no two computers get the *same* IP address. For the purposes of simplicity, we chose the first valid IP for Computer1, as shown in Figure 4-8. No gateway address or subnet mask is necessary.

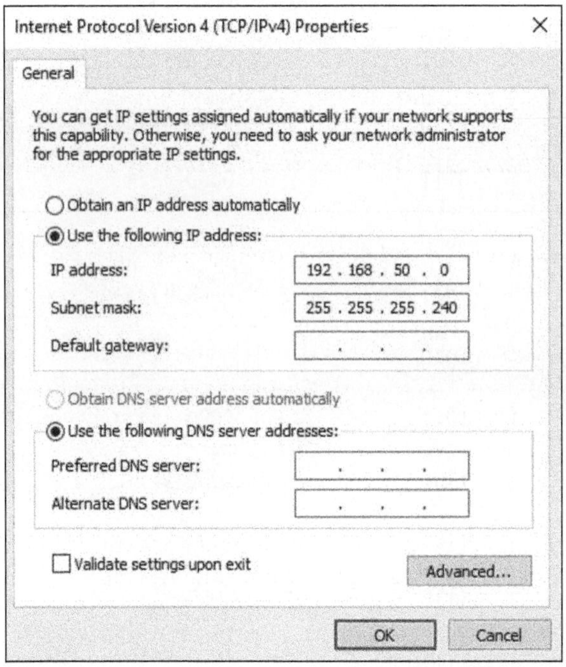

Figure 4-8

IP Properties of Computer1

4. Click **OK** for both dialog boxes
5. Go to a second computer (we will call this Computer2).
6. Disable any secondary network adapters. Make sure only one adapter is enabled; this is the one you will use for the exercise.
7. Access the Internet Protocol Version 4(TCP/IPv4) Properties window of Computer2 and change the IP settings to reflect the above subnet information. This time, select 192.168.50.114. Again, no gateway address or subnet mask is necessary.
8. Click **OK** for both dialog boxes.
9. Return to Computer1 and open the Command Prompt window.
10. Execute `ipconfig/all` and verify that your settings are as they should be.
11. Now execute `ping 192.168.50.114`. You should get replies. If not, double-check your configuration on both computers.
12. Now try pinging a host that is not within your network (for example, 192.168.1.1). Execute **`ping 192.168.1.1`**. It should not reply and you should get either a transmit failed error or a message similar to: Destination Host unreachable, depending on the OS used. Either way, the connection will fail because it is on a different network number. Even if a device does exist on that network number, it will not reply to you.
13. Now try pinging a host that is not within your network (for example, 192.168.50.17). Execute **`ping 192.168.50.17`**. It should not reply and you should get a similar error message to the one shown in Step 12. This is shown in Figure 4-9. This is because it is on a different *subnet* and by default cannot communicate with computers on your subnet.

Figure 4-9

Failed ping from a computer on a subnet

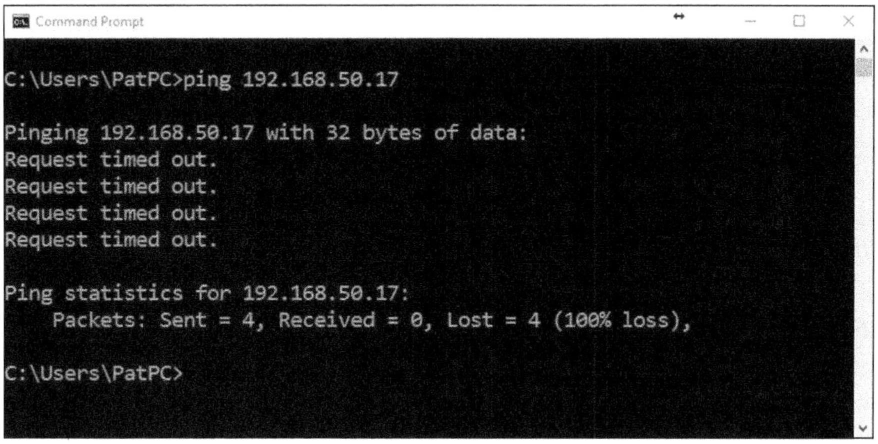

```
Command Prompt

C:\Users\PatPC>ping 192.168.50.17

Pinging 192.168.50.17 with 32 bytes of data:
Request timed out.
Request timed out.
Request timed out.
Request timed out.

Ping statistics for 192.168.50.17:
    Packets: Sent = 4, Received = 0, Lost = 4 (100% loss),

C:\Users\PatPC>
```

You now have a working subnet that compartmentalizes the two computers from the other subnets on the network. Network engineers create subnets to compartmentalize the network. This could be to decrease broadcasts, increase data throughput, add security, limit access, and use the IP addresses more wisely. There are many other examples of subnetting. There are other kinds of subnet masks that you can use than just the subnet mask 255.255.255.240. For example, 255.255.255.224 gives you the ability to have eight subnets (recommended six usable) and 30 usable IP addresses per subnet. You can also create subnets within Class A networks and Class B networks as well. Tables 4-6 through 4-8 show all the possibilities when it comes to subnetting within any of the three IP classes. These tables take into account the fact that most OS and IOS (internetwork operating system) manufacturers recommend not using the first or last subnet for any given subnetting scheme.

Table 4-6

Class A Subnetting Matrix

Net ID	Subnet ID	Host ID	Mask		# of Usable Subnets	# of Hosts per Subnet
8	0	24	255.0.0.0	/8	N/A	16,777,14
8	1	23	255.128.0.0	/9	N/A	N/A
8	2	22	255.192.0.0	/10	2	4,194,302
8	3	21	255.224.0.0	/11	6	2,097,150
8	4	20	255.240.0.0	/12	14	1,048,574
8	5	19	255.248.0.0	/13	30	524,286
8	6	18	255.252.0.0	/14	62	262,142
8	7	17	255.254.0.0	/15	126	131,070
8	8	16	255.255.0.0	/16	254	65,534
8	9	15	255.255.128.0	/17	510	32,766
8	10	14	255.255.192.0	/18	1,022	16,382
8	11	13	255.255.224.0	/19	2,046	8,190
8	12	12	255.255.240.0	/20	4,094	4,094
8	13	11	255.255.248.0	/21	8,190	2,046
8	14	10	255.255.252.0	/22	16,382	1,022
8	15	9	255.255.254.0	/23	32,766	510
8	16	8	255.255.255.0	/24	65,534	254
8	17	7	255.255.255.128	/25	131,070	126
8	18	6	255.255.255.192	/26	262,142	62
8	19	5	255.255.255.224	/27	524,286	30
8	20	4	255.255.255.240	/28	1,048,574	14
8	21	3	255.255.255.248	/29	2,097,150	6
8	22	2	255.255.255.252	/30	4,194,302	2
8	23	1	255.255.255.254	/31	N/A	N/A
8	24	0	255.255.255.255	/32	N/A	N/A

Table 4-7

Class B Subnetting Matrix

NetID	SubnetID	HostID	Mask		# of Usable Subnets	# of Hosts per
16	0	16	255.255.0.0	/16	N/A	65,534
16	1	15	255.255.128.0	/17	N/A	N/A
16	2	14	255.255.192.0	/18	2	16,382
16	3	13	255.255.224.0	/19	6	8,190
16	4	12	255.255.240.0	/20	14	4,094
16	5	11	255.255.248.0	/21	30	2,046
16	6	10	255.255.252.0	/22	62	1,022
16	7	9	255.255.254.0	/23	126	510
16	8	8	255.255.255.0	/24	254	254
16	9	7	255.255.255.128	/25	510	126
16	10	6	255.255.255.192	/26	1,022	62
16	11	5	255.255.255.224	/27	2,046	30
16	12	4	255.255.255.240	/28	4,094	14
16	13	3	255.255.255.248	/29	8,190	6
16	14	2	255.255.255.252	/30	16,382	2
16	15	1	255.255.255.254	/31	N/A	N/A
16	16	0	255.255.255.255	/32	N/A	N/A

Table 4-8

Class C Subnetting Matrix

NetID	SubnetID	HostID	Mask		# of Usable Subnets	# of Hosts per
24	0	8	255.255.255.0	/24	N/A	254
24	1	7	255.255.255.128	/25	N/A	N/A
24	2	6	255.255.255.192	/26	2	62
24	3	5	255.255.255.224	/27	6	30
24	4	4	255.255.255.240	/28	14	14
24	5	3	255.255.255.248	/29	30	6
24	6	2	255.255.255.252	/30	62	2
24	7	1	255.255.255.254	/31	N/A	N/A
24	8	0	255.255.255.255	/32	N/A	N/A

DEFINING CLASSLESS INTERDOMAIN ROUTING (CIDR)

Classless interdomain routing (CIDR) is a way of allocating IP addresses and routing Internet Protocol packets. You have already seen CIDR notation in the previous section. It was intended to replace the prior classful IP addressing architecture in an attempt to slow the exhaustion of IPv4 addresses. Classless interdomain routing is based on ***variable-length subnet masking (VLSM)***, which allows a network to be divided into different-sized subnets and make an IP network that would have previously been considered a class (such as Class A) appear to look like Class B or Class C. This can help network administrators efficiently use subnets without wasting IP addresses.

One example of CIDR is the IP network number 192.168.0.0/16. The /16 means that the subnet mask has 16 masked bits (or 1s), making the subnet mask 255.255.0.0. Usually, that would be a default Class B subnet mask, but because we are using it in conjunction with what used to be a Class C network number, the whole kit and caboodle becomes classless.

In the following exercise, you will configure two computers with classless private IP addresses and verify the configuration through the use of `ipconfig` and `ping`. In this particular exercise, the IP network (10.254.254.0), which would have previously appeared to be a Class A network, will use a Class C subnet mask. This effectively makes it classless.

CONFIGURE A CIDR-BASED IP NETWORK

GET READY. To configure two computers with classless private IP addresses and verify the configuration through the use of `ipconfig` and `ping`, perform the following steps.

> **TAKE NOTE***
> In this particular exercise, the IP network (10.254.254.0), which would have previously appeared to be a Class A network, will use a Class C subnet mask. This effectively makes it classless.

1. Access the Local Area Connection Properties dialog box.
2. Click **Internet Protocol Version 4** and then click the **Properties** button. The Internet Protocol Version 4 Properties dialog box opens. Write down the current settings so that you can return the computer to these settings at the end of the exercise.
3. Click the **Use the following IP address** radio button. This enables the other fields so you can type the IP information. Type the following:
   - For the IP address of the first computer, type **10.254.254.115.**
   - For the IP address of the second computer, type **10.254.254.116.**
   - For the Subnet mask of both computers, type **255.255.255.0.** This would be written out as 10.254.254.0/24 signifying that you are creating a classless 10.254.254.0 network with a subnet mask that has 24 masked bits.
   - Leave the Default gateway and the Preferred DNS server fields blank.
   - When you are finished, the first computer's configuration should look like Figure 4-10.

Figure 4-10

The Internet Protocol Version 4 Properties dialog box configured with a classless IP address

Internet Protocol Version 4 (TCP/IPv4) Properties

General

You can get IP settings assigned automatically if your network supports this capability. Otherwise, you need to ask your network administrator for the appropriate IP settings.

Obtain an IP address automatically

Use the following IP address:

IP address: 10 . 254 . 254 . 115

Subnet mask: 255 . 255 . 255 . 0

Default gateway:

Obtain DNS server address automatically

Use the following DNS server addresses:

Preferred DNS server:

Alternate DNS server:

Validate settings upon exit

Advanced...

OK Cancel

4. Click **OK**. Then, in the Local Area Connection Properties dialog box, click **OK**. This completes and binds the configuration to the network adapter.
5. Now test your configuration. You will do this in two ways: first with the `ipconfig` command and second with the `ping` command:
   a. Execute **`ipconfig`**. Verify that the IP configuration is accurate and corresponds to what you typed in the IP Properties window. If not, go back and check your Internet Protocol Properties dialog box.
   b. Ping the other computer. Also try to ping any other computers that were configured as part of this classless network (for example, **`ping 10.254.254.116`**). Make sure you get replies. If you do not, check the IP configurations of both computers, watch for IP conflicts, and make sure they are physically connected to the same network.

Working With IPv6

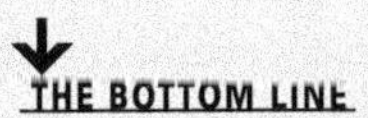

IPv6 is the new generation of IP addressing for the Internet, but it can also be used in small office networks and home networks. It was designed to meet the limitations of IPv4's address space and security.

CERTIFICATION READY
Can you define IPv6?
Objective 3.3

Understanding IPv6

Before you can configure IPv6, you first need to understand a few concepts, some of which are similar to IPv4, others of which are quite different. This section categorizes the types of IPv6 addresses and explains specifically why it is to be the successor to IPv4, even though IPv4 is still the dominant IP protocol.

IPv6 has been defined for over a decade and has slowly been gaining acceptance in the networking world, though it is still considered to be in its infancy. The number one captivating reason to use IPv6 is its large address space. IPv6 is a 128-bit system compared with its still dominating predecessor IPv4, which is only a 32-bit system. What does this mean? Well, whereas IPv4 can have approximately 4 billion IP addresses in the whole system, IPv6 can have 340 undecillion addresses. That's 340 with 36 zeros after it! Of course, various limitations in the system will reduce that number, but the final result is still far greater than the IPv4 system. However, another reason to use IPv6 is advanced integrated security; for example, IPsec is a fundamental component of IPv6 (IPsec is discussed in more depth in Lesson 6). IPv6 also has many advancements and simplifications when it comes to address assignment, which is covered in more detail later in this section. Table 4-9 summarizes some of the differences between IPv4 and IPv6.

Table 4-9
Summary of IPv4 Versus IPv6

IPv4		IPv6	
32-bit	4 billion addresses	128-bit	340 undecillion addresses
Less security in general		More security, IPsec is mandatory	
N/A		Simplification of address assignment	

IPv6 also has support for jumbograms. These are much larger packets than IPv4 can handle. IPv4 packets are normally around 1,500 bytes in size, but can go as large as 65,535 bytes. IPv6 packets can optionally be as big as approximately 4 billion bytes.

As mentioned previously, IPv6 addresses are 128-bit numbers. They are also hexadecimal in format, they are divided into eight groups of four numbers each, and each group is separated by a colon. These colon separators contrast IPv4's dot-decimal notation. In Windows, IPv6 addresses are automatically assigned, autoconfigured, and are known as link-local addresses. There are three main types of IPv6 addresses:

- ***Unicast address:*** These addresses define a single address on a single interface. There are two types of unicast addresses. The first, global unicast addresses, are routable and are displayed directly to the Internet. These addresses start at the 2000 range. The other is the aforementioned link-local address. These are further broken down into two types, the Windows autoconfigured address, which starts at either FE80, FE90, FEA0, or FEB0, and the loopback address, which is known as ::1. ::1 and is the equivalent of IPv4's 127.0.0.1.
- ***Anycast address:*** These are addresses assigned to a group of interfaces, most likely on separate hosts. Packets that are sent to these addresses are delivered to only one of the interfaces, generally, the first or closest available. These are used in failover systems.
- ***Multicast address:*** These are also assigned to a group of interfaces, and are also most likely on separate hosts, but packets sent to the address are delivered to all the interfaces in the group. This is similar to IPv4 broadcast addresses (such as 192.168.1.255). Multicast addresses do not suffer from broadcast storms the way their IPv4 counterparts do.

Table 4-10 summarizes these three types of addresses.

Table 4-10

Summary of IPv6 Address Types

IPv6 Type	Address Range	Purpose
Unicast	Global unicast starts at 2000 Link-local ::1 and FE80::/10	Address assigned to one interface of one host. ::/10 means that addresses starting with FE80, FE90, FEA0, and FEB0 are part of the range. These are assigned by the IANA and this range has many more addresses than the entire IPv4 system.
Anycast	Structured like unicast addresses	Address assigned to a group of interfaces on multiple nodes. Packets are delivered to the first or closest interface only.
Multicast	FF00::/8	Address assigned to a group of interfaces on multiple nodes. Packets are delivered to all interfaces.

Here is an example of a global unicast address. It used to be one of Google's public IPv6 addresses: 2001:4860:0000:2001:0000:0000:0000:0068. It used to correspond to their website: ipv6.google.com. However, as of this writing, they are using a new address (that we will ping later), and the address could easily change again in the future.

IPv6 addresses are broken down into three parts:

- ***Global routing prefix:*** This is the first three groups of numbers and defines the "network" of the address.

- ***IPv6 subnet*:** This defines the individual subnet of the network that the address is located on.
- ***Interface ID*:** This is the individual host IP portion. It can be assigned to one interface or more than one interface depending on the type of IPv6 address.

Table 4-11 breaks down an example of an IPv6 address.

Table 4-11

Global Unicast Address Breakdown

Global Routing Prefix	Subnet	Interface ID
2001:4860:0000	2001	0000:0000:0000:0068

This address can be abbreviated or ***truncated*** by removing unnecessary and/or leading 0s. For example, the address in Table 4-11 can be truncated in the following manner:

- **Original IP:** 2001:4860:0000:2001:0000:0000:0000:0068
- **Truncated IP:** 2001:4860:0:2001::68

Notice that the first group of 0s has been changed from **0000** to just **0**. Well, in hexadecimal (just like in any other numbering system), 0 is 0. So, the leading 0s can be removed, and this can be done within an individual group of four 0s as many times as necessary in one IPv6 address. Also, multiple groups of consecutive 0s can be abbreviated to a double colon. So, 0000:0000:0000:0068 is abbreviated to ::68. However, this can only be done once in an IPv6 address.

Here is an example of an abbreviated link-local unicast address that was auto-assigned by Windows: fe80::260:8ff:fec0:98d%4. Notice that it starts with FE80, defining it as a link-local address. The % sign specifies the interface index of the interface where traffic is sent from. Sometimes, this is a tunneling interface that corresponds to an IPv4 address.

Packet structure works pretty much the same way in IPv6 as it does in IPv4. An IPv6 packet is broken down into three parts:

- **Header:** This is also known as a fixed header. This is 40 bytes and contains the source and destination addresses plus other forwarding information. Because IPv6 addresses have more characters (and are therefore bigger) than IPv4 addresses, a larger fixed header is necessary. However, due to the maximum size available for an IPv6 packet (jumbograms), the percentage of total overhead can actually be less in an IPv6 packet. Even without jumbograms, the increase in header size is negligible.
- **Optional extension header:** This incorporates options for special treatment of the packet, such as routing and security.
- **Payload:** By default, this is 64-KB maximum just like IPv4 packets. But again, this can be increased much further if jumbograms are used.

Let's go ahead now and run through some IPv6 exercises.

Configuring IPv6

Configuring IPv6 is in some ways easier than IPv4 and in other ways more difficult. For example, the installation of the IPv6 protocol is quite painless, but the configuration of a static IPv6 address can be a bit trickier given the length and complexity of an IPv6 address. In general, though, IPv6 is designed to be easier to work with once you learn the basics.

In the following exercises, you will install IPv6, work with autoconfigured addresses, add static addresses, and test connections. This exercise will function better if Windows 10 client computers are used. Different Windows operating systems may require slightly different navigation to the various dialog boxes.

INSTALL, CONFIGURE, AND TEST IPv6

GET READY. To install, configure, and test IPv6, perform the following steps.

1. Right-click the network icon on the taskbar and choose **Open Network and Sharing Center.**
2. In the Network and Sharing Center, click your network connection.
3. In the status dialog box, click the **Details** button.
4. In the Network Connection Details dialog box, notice the IPv6, which is a link-local IPv6 address that is automatically configured on any interface using the link-local prefix FE80, similar to how APIPA works. Click **Close** to close the Network Connection Details dialog box.
5. Look at the new address by opening the Command Prompt window and executing **`ipconfig/all`**. The results should be similar to the link-local IPv6 address entry shown in Figure 4-11. Be sure to locate your primary network adapter.

Figure 4-11

TCP/IPv6 address as shown with `ipconfig/all`

```
Administrator: Command Prompt
C:\WINDOWS\system32>ipconfig /all

Windows IP Configuration

   Host Name . . . . . . . . . . . . : win2016Svr
   Primary Dns Suffix  . . . . . . . :
   Node Type . . . . . . . . . . . . : Hybrid
   IP Routing Enabled. . . . . . . . : No
   WINS Proxy Enabled. . . . . . . . : No

Ethernet adapter External:

   Connection-specific DNS Suffix  . :
   Description . . . . . . . . . . . : Broadcom NetXtreme Gigabit Ethernet #2
   Physical Address. . . . . . . . . : 20-47-47-88-94-C0
   DHCP Enabled. . . . . . . . . . . : No
   Autoconfiguration Enabled . . . . : Yes
   IPv6 Address. . . . . . . . . . . : 2001:db8:1::1002(Preferred)
   Lease Obtained. . . . . . . . . . : Sunday, May 21, 2017 5:44:09 PM
   Lease Expires . . . . . . . . . . : Saturday, June 3, 2017 5:27:26 AM
   Link-local IPv6 Address . . . . . : fe80::c980:9c92:dcb9:1bf1%8(Preferred)
   IPv4 Address. . . . . . . . . . . : 192.168.3.200(Preferred)
   Subnet Mask . . . . . . . . . . . : 255.255.255.0
   Default Gateway . . . . . . . . . : 192.168.3.1
   DHCPv6 IAID . . . . . . . . . . . : 69224263
   DHCPv6 Client DUID. . . . . . . . : 00-01-00-01-1F-7F-7C-72-20-47-47-88-94-8E
   DNS Servers . . . . . . . . . . . : 192.168.3.1
   NetBIOS over Tcpip. . . . . . . . : Enabled
```

6. Ping the local loopback address. This can be done by executing **`ping ::1`**. The results should look similar to Figure 4-12. If you do not get replies, verify that IPv6 is installed. You can also execute **`ping -6 ::1`** if it appears that IPv4 results are getting in the way.

```
Command Prompt
C:\Users\PatPC>ping ::1

Pinging ::1 with 32 bytes of data:
Reply from ::1: time<1ms
Reply from ::1: time<1ms
Reply from ::1: time<1ms
Reply from ::1: time<1ms

Ping statistics for ::1:
    Packets: Sent = 4, Received = 4, Lost = 0 (0% loss),
Approximate round trip times in milli-seconds:
    Minimum = 0ms, Maximum = 0ms, Average = 0ms

C:\Users\PatPC>_
```

Figure 4-12

Testing the IPv6 loopback address with `ping`

7. Ping another computer on the network that is also running IPv6. Do so by pinging its IPv6 link-local address. For example:
   a. Ping by IPv6 address. For example:

      ping fe80::5549:3176:540a:3e09%10

      The exact IP address will be different depending on what computer you ping. Results should look similar to Figure 4-13.
   b. Ping by host name. For example:

      ping computer1

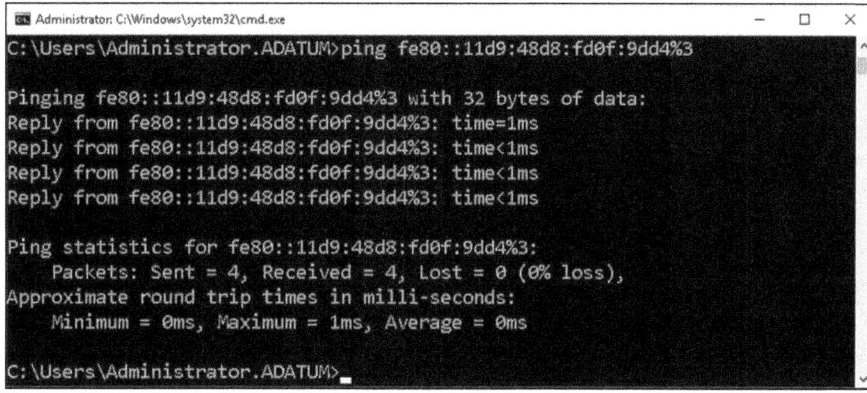
Administrator: C:\Windows\system32\cmd.exe
C:\Users\Administrator.ADATUM>ping fe80::11d9:48d8:fd0f:9dd4%3
Pinging fe80::11d9:48d8:fd0f:9dd4%3 with 32 bytes of data:
Reply from fe80::11d9:48d8:fd0f:9dd4%3: time=1ms
Reply from fe80::11d9:48d8:fd0f:9dd4%3: time<1ms
Reply from fe80::11d9:48d8:fd0f:9dd4%3: time<1ms
Reply from fe80::11d9:48d8:fd0f:9dd4%3: time<1ms
Ping statistics for fe80::11d9:48d8:fd0f:9dd4%3:
Packets: Sent = 4, Received = 4, Lost = 0 (0% loss),
Approximate round trip times in milli-seconds:
Minimum = 0ms, Maximum = 1ms, Average = 0ms
C:\Users\Administrator.ADATUM>_

Figure 4-13

Testing another computer's IPv6 link-local address with `ping`

8. Configure a global unicast address in the GUI:
   a. This can be done in the Internet Protocol Version 6 Properties dialog box. Just click **Internet Protocol Version 6** and click **Properties** in the Local Area Connection Properties dialog box (which should now be the Ethernet Properties dialog box).
   b. Click the **Use the following IPv6 address** radio button. This enables the IPv6 configuration fields.
   c. Type an address and press **Enter**. For example:

      2001:ab1:442e:1323::1

      The address can be on any network of your choosing. If the number is not valid, Windows will inform you when you attempt to go to the next field.

d. Type an address that is one higher for the second computer. For example:

   2001:ab1:442e:1323::2

e. Ascend from there for each additional computer.

f. For the Subnet prefix length, either tab through or type **64**. That is the default length; if you tab through, it will be entered automatically.

g. For the Default gateway on all computers, type:

   2001:ab1:442e:1323::9

   This is just an example. If you are using a different network, just make sure your gateway address is on the same network but uses a different host number (in this case, the last octet). If you have specific network documentation with a real IPv6 gateway address, utilize it!

h. For the Preferred DNS server on all computers, type:

   2001:ab1:442e:1323::8

   This is just an example. If you have specific network documentation with an IPv6 gateway address, utilize it. The DNS server could even be on a different network; it all depends on the network configuration. Your configuration should look similar to Figure 4-14.

Figure 4-14

IPv6 GUI configuration

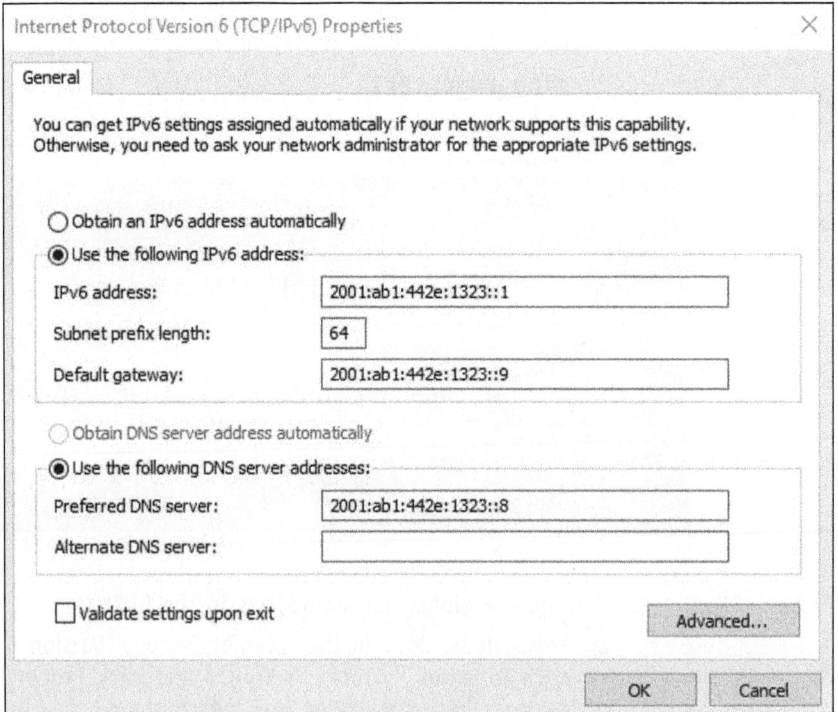

9. In the IPv6 Properties dialog box, click **OK**.
10. In the Ethernet Properties dialog box, click **Close**. That should bind the information to the network adapter.
11. Verify the configuration in the Command Prompt window by executing **`ipconfig/all`**. Your results should be similar to Figure 4-15. The address you just added should show up in the IPv6 Address field. This is usually just above the Link-local IPv6 Address field. Also, check for the IPv6 gateway and DNS server addresses.

Figure 4-15

`Ipconfig/all` results of added IPv6 address

```
Administrator: C:\Windows\system32\cmd.exe
   Connection-specific DNS Suffix  . :
   Description . . . . . . . . . . . : Microsoft Hyper-V Network Adapter
   Physical Address. . . . . . . . . : 00-15-5D-03-C8-2D
   DHCP Enabled. . . . . . . . . . . : No
   Autoconfiguration Enabled . . . . : Yes
   IPv6 Address. . . . . . . . . . . : 2001:ab1:442e:1323::1(Preferred)
   Link-local IPv6 Address . . . . . : fe80::7170:259f:9e38:6b8%3(Preferred)

   IPv4 Address. . . . . . . . . . . : 172.16.0.40(Preferred)
   Subnet Mask . . . . . . . . . . . : 255.255.255.0
   Default Gateway . . . . . . . . . : 172.16.0.1
   DHCPv6 IAID . . . . . . . . . . . : 33559901
   DHCPv6 Client DUID. . . . . . . . : 00-01-00-01-20-3E-BF-27-00-15-5D-03-C
8-2D
```

12. Verify connectivity to another IPv6 host. For example, this can be done by executing the following command in the Command Prompt window:

    ping -6 2001:abl:442e:1323::2

    You should get replies. If not, check the configuration of both computers.
13. Configure a global unicast address in the Command Prompt window. For this, use the Net Shell command, which is **netsh**. Netsh is a tool that administrators can use to configure and monitor Windows computers from the Command Prompt window. This is a complex command with lots of variables. It is commonly used to configure TCP/IP and other networking functions. Add the following example:

    netsh interface ipv6 add address interface=ethernet address=2001:abl:442e:1323::7

    You should get a simple OK as a result. If there are other computers you want to configure with the netsh command, make sure they all get separate host IDs.
14. Check that the new address has been added by executing **ipconfig/all**.
15. Verify connectivity to other computers by using **ping**.
16. Delete the address you just added by using the netsh command. Use the following syntax:

    netsh interface ipv6 delete address interface=ethernet address=2001:abl:442e:1323::7

    If you have any issues deleting it, try using a nontruncated number. The equivalent for this address would be:

    2001:0abl:442e:1323:0000:0000:0000:0007
17. Reset the GUI IPv6 Properties dialog box by clicking the **Obtain an IPv6 address automatically** radio button. If you want, execute **ipconfig** to find out your auto-assigned address and another computer's address. Try pinging those addresses as well.

To learn more information about configuring IPv6, visit the Microsoft TechNet site.

DEFINING THE DUAL IP STACK

A ***dual IP stack*** is when there is the presence of two Internet Protocol software implementations in an operating system, one for IPv4 and another for IPv6. Dual-stack IP hosts can run IPv4 and IPv6 independently, or can use a hybrid implementation, which is the most commonly used method for modern operating systems.

Dual stack TCP/IP implementations enable programmers to write networking code that works transparently on IPv4 or IPv6. The software can use hybrid sockets designed to accept both IPv4 and IPv6 packets. When used in IPv4 communications, hybrid stacks use IPv6 methodologies but represent IPv4 addresses in a special IPv6 address format known as the IPv4-mapped address.

IPv4-mapped addresses have the first 80 bits set to 0s (note the double colon below) and the next 16 bits set to 1s (shown as ffff), while its last 32 bits are populated by the IPv4 address. These addresses look like IPv6 addresses, other than the last 32 bits, which are written in the customary dot decimal notation. Here is an example:

::ffff:10.254.254.1

This is an IPv4-mapped IPv6 address for the IPv4 address 10.254.254.1.

DEFINING IPv4 TO IPv6 TUNNELING

The transition from IPv4 to IPv6 is expected to take several more years. In the meantime, expect to see a mix of IPv4, IPv4/IPv6 (dual stack), and IPv6-only networks. To help with the transition from IPv4 to IPv6, several methods were developed, including Teredo and Intra-Site Automatic Tunnel Addressing Protocol (ISATAP).

IPv6 packets can be encapsulated inside IPv4 datagrams. This is known as ***IPv6 tunneling*** or IP 6 to 4. In Microsoft operating systems, this is generally done with the Teredo adapter. It is a virtual adapter or "pseudo-interface," not a physical network adapter. This allows connectivity for IPv6 hosts that are behind an IPv4 device or IPv6 unaware device. It ensures backward compatibility. An example of one of these addresses is:

Fe80::5efe:10.0.0.2%2

Notice it is a link-local address and that the IPv4 address (10.0.0.2) is actually part of the whole IPv6 address. IPv6 tunneling requires little router configuration and no client computer configuration whatsoever, so it is fairly easy to implement, enabling IPv6 clients to interact with IPv6 servers on the Internet, even though their router is not IPv6 aware.

SKILL SUMMARY

IN THIS LESSON, YOU LEARNED:

- Internet Protocol version 4, or IPv4, is the most frequently used communications protocol. IP resides on the Network layer of the OSI model, and IP addresses consist of four numbers, each between 0 and 255. The protocol suite is built into most operating systems and is used by most Internet connections in the United States and many other countries.
- The IPv4 classification system is known as the classful network architecture and is broken down into five sections, three of which are commonly used by hosts on networks; these are Classes A, B, and C.
- To complete an IP configuration, you need a default gateway address and a DNS server address. This helps the client computers access the Internet.
- Network Address Translation (NAT) is the process of modifying an IP address while it is in transit across a router, computer, or similar device. This is usually so one larger address space (private) can be remapped to another address space, or remapped to a single, public IP address.
- One of the reasons for having a subnet mask is to have the ability to create subnetworks logically by IP address. It is a subdivision of your logical IP network and host IDs. Subnetting is the act of dividing a network into smaller, logical subnetworks.

- Classless interdomain routing (CIDR) is a way of allocating IP addresses and routing Internet Protocol packets. It was intended to replace the prior classful IP addressing architecture in an attempt to slow the exhaustion of IPv4 addresses.
- Classless interdomain routing is based on *variable-length subnet masking* (VLSM), which allows a network to be divided into different-sized subnets and make an IP network that would have previously been considered a class (such as Class A) appear to look like Class B or Class C.
- IPv6 is the new generation of IP addressing for the Internet, but it can also be used in small office networks and home networks. It was designed to meet the limitations of IPv4 address space and security.
- The transition from IPv4 to IPv6 is expected to take several more years. In the meantime, expect to see a mix of IPv4, IPv4/IPv6 (dual stack), and IPv6-only networks. To help with the transition from IPv4 to IPv6, several methods were developed, including Teredo and Intra-Site Automatic Tunnel Addressing Protocol (ISATAP).

Knowledge Assessment

Multiple Choice

Select the correct answer for each of the following questions.

1. If a customer requires the installation of 284 computers on a single IP network, which IP class is the best option?
   a. Class A
   b. Class B
   c. Class C
   d. Class D
2. To set up three computers on a classful network with a default subnet mask of 255.0.0.0, which class should be used?
   a. Class A
   b. Class B
   c. Class C
   d. Class D
3. Proseware, Inc., needs to set up 100 computers on a private Class A network. Which of the following IP network numbers meets all the criteria for a private Class A network?
   a. 100.10.1.0
   b. 192.168.1.0
   c. 172.16.0.0
   d. 10.0.0.0
4. A 192.168.1.0 network needs to be subnetted using the 255.255.255.240 subnet mask. Which of the following is equal to 240 in binary?
   a. 11100000
   b. 11000000
   c. 11110000
   d. 10000000

5. You need to set up 14 separate IP networks that can each have up to 400 computers. Which IANA private IP range should be used?
   a. 10.0.0.0–10.255.255.255
   b. 172.16.0.0–172.31.255.255
   c. 192.168.0.0–192.168.255.255
   d. 169.254.0.0–169.254.255.255
6. A computer cannot obtain the proper IP address from a DHCP server. The `ipconfig/all` command shows that it has automatically obtained the address 169.254.67.110. Which of the following has occurred?
   a. The DHCP server has auto-assigned an IP address to the computer.
   b. APIPA has auto-assigned an IP address to the computer.
   c. A SOHO router has auto-assigned an IP address to the computer.
   d. The ISP has auto-assigned an IP address to the computer.
7. Which of the following represents the beginning of an IPv6 link-state address?
   a. 127
   b. 172
   c. 2001
   d. FE80
8. A manager's computer cannot connect to the Internet. Examine the following `ipconfig` results and select the best answer as to why this has occurred.

```
IPv4 Address.............................: 10.254.254.1
Subnet Mask..............................: 255.255.255.0
Default Gateway..........................: 10.254.254.255
```

   a. The subnet mask is incorrect.
   b. The IP address is incorrect.
   c. The default gateway is incorrect.
   d. The subnet mask and the IP address are incorrect.
9. A user cannot connect to any websites. Examine the following `ipconfig` results and select the best answer as to why this has occurred.

```
Windows IP Configuration
   Host Name............................: Computer1
   Primary Dns Suffix...................:
   Node Type............................: Hybrid
   IP Routing Enabled...................: No
   WINS Proxy Enabled...................: No
  Ethernet adapter lan:
   Connection-specific DNS Suffix.........:
   Description..........................: Intel(R)
     82566DC-2 Gigabit Network Connection
   Physical Address.....................: 00-1C-C0-A1-55-16
   DHCP Enabled.........................: No
   Autoconfiguration Enabled............: Yes
   IPv4 Address.........................:
  10.254.254.105(Preferred)
   Subnet Mask..........................: 255.255.255.0
   Default Gateway......................: 10.254.254.1
   DNS Servers..........................: 10.255.254.1
```

a. The MAC address is incorrect.
b. The DNS server address is incorrect.
c. The default gateway address is incorrect.
d. The computer has no IP address.

10. A device has been installed that has two IP addresses. One, 64.51.216.27, is displayed to the Internet. The other, 192.168.50.254, communicates with the LAN. Which type of technology has been implemented?
    a. Subnetting
    b. IPv6
    c. Network Address Translation
    d. Class A public IP address

Fill in the Blank

Fill in the correct answer in the blank space provided.

1. You want to subnet a group of computers on the 192.168.50.0/28 network. This will provide _____ subnets.
2. You configure an IP network 192.168.1.0 with the subnet mask 255.255.255.240. Two computers have the IP addresses 192.168.1.113 and 192.168.1.114. Another computer cannot communicate with them. It is using the IP address 192.168.1.145. The third computer cannot communicate with the first two computers because the third computer is on subnet ID _____.
3. A network uses the subnetted IP network: 192.168.100.0/26. Its subnet mask is _____.
4. You are troubleshooting an IP network with the following number: 10.254.254.0/24. This type of IP network number is known as _____.
5. A manager is concerned about how many IPv4 addresses remain and inquires about installing IPv6. Whereas IPv4 is a 32-bit system, IPv6 is a _____ system.
6. You need to set up a group of IPv6 network interfaces in such a way that each will have all packets delivered to them. You should implement a _____ address.
7. A server needs to connect directly to the Internet. The `ipconfig/all` command shows that the server has been auto-assigned the IPv6 address fe80::260:8ff:fec0:98d%4. It won't connect to the Internet because it is a _____ address, which does not have Internet access.
8. To save time when working with IPv6 addresses in the command line, they can be truncated. The truncated version of:
   2001:4860:0000:2001:0000:0000:0000:0068 is _____.
9. An IPv6 address is displayed as fe80::5efe:10.0.0.2%2. This is an example of _____.
10. A client's network is using the following IP network scheme:

    IP network: 192.168.50.0

    Subnet mask: 255.255.255.240

    They have 196 computers that are functioning properly. However, another 30 computers will not connect to the network. This is because _____.

Business Case Scenarios

Scenario 4-1: Defining a Private Class C IP Network

Proseware, Inc., requires that you implement a private Class C network for its 200 computers. What is the range of IP networks that you can select from?

Scenario 4-2: Specifying the Correct Device

Proseware, Inc., wants to protect its LAN computers. The company would like a device that displays one public IP address to the Internet, yet allows all the local clients with private IPs on the LAN to communicate out to the Internet. Which kind of device is required and which network technology should be implemented on that device?

Scenario 4-3: Implementing the Correct Class Network

A client wants you to design a single IP network that can support 84,576 computers. Complete Table 4-12, listing the correct IP class to use.

Table 4-12

IPv4 Class Analysis

Class	IP Range (1st Octet)	Default Subnet Mask	Network/Node Portions	Total Number of Networks	Total Number of Usable Addresses
A					
B					
C					
D	224–239	N/A	N/A	N/A	N/A
E	240–255	N/A	N/A	N/A	N/A

Scenario 4-4: Implementing the Correct Subnet Mask

Proseware, Inc., wants you to set up a Class C subnetting scheme that will allow for six subnets and 30 hosts per subnet. Complete Table 4-13, listing the correct subnet mask. Explain why your selected subnet mask is the correct answer.

Table 4-13

Class C Subnetting Analysis

Subnet Mask	Subnets (Recommended Usable)	Hosts per Subnet	Total Hosts
255.255.255.192			
255.255.255.224			
255.255.255.240			
255.255.255.248			

Workplace Ready

IPv6—Here, Yet Still in Waiting

IPv6 has been defined since 1998, but it has yet to become the powerhouse that analysts expect is bound to happen. Even though IPv6 has advancements in packet structure, packet size, security, and, of course, the amount of addresses it can support, it is still in its infancy.

Search the Internet and make a list of organizations, companies, and governmental bodies that already use IPv6. Also, describe how they use it. Is it internal only? Do they have servers that support IPv6 directly to the Internet? Or does an organization or other body have a sort of hybrid IPv4/IPv6 network?

Next, search the Internet (and in your local library if you have the time) for articles about IPv6. See what the analysts have to say about it. Pool your knowledge together, analyze it, and imagine a time frame for when IPv6 will become the dominant IP technology in use. Pick an approximate year when you think this will become a reality, and state your case to support your theory.

Implementing TCP/IP in the Command Line

OBJECTIVE DOMAIN MATRIX

Skills/Concepts	Objective Domain Description	Objective Domain Number
Using Basic TCP/IP Commands	Understand TCP/IP	3.6
Working with Advanced TCP/IP Commands	Understand TCP/IP	3.6
	Understand routers	2.2

KEY TERMS

Border Gateway Protocol (BGP)
cmdlets
Command Prompt window
elevated mode
FTP
`ipconfig`
`nbtstat`
`net`
`netsh`
`netstat`
`nslookup`
Open Shortest Path First (OSPF)
`pathping`
`ping`
`route`
Routing Information Protocol (RIP)
Telnet
`tracert`
Universal Naming Convention (UNC)
Windows PowerShell

Proseware, Inc., doesn't tolerate delays. If there is an issue on the network, the network administrator needs to straighten it out ASAP. One way to work quickly and efficiently is to use the command-line interface (CLI). It might seem counterintuitive, but typing commands to run network tests can be quicker than using the GUI. TCP/IP commands, in particular, if used properly, can increase your speed and accuracy when analyzing network issues and when troubleshooting. This lesson defines what you need to know in order to use basic and advanced TCP/IP commands in the Command Prompt window. This will develop important skills you will need as a network administrator.

Using Basic TCP/IP Commands

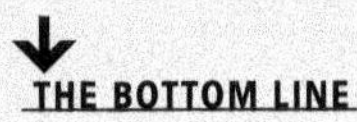

`Ipconfig` and `ping` are some of the best friends to a network administrator. These basic TCP/IP commands can help to analyze and troubleshoot networking issues that might occur. They also offer a certain amount of configurative ability, as well as the ability to create performance baselines. They are accessed through the Command Prompt window, a tool that every network administrator should have confidence in using.

Working with the Command Prompt Window

To better understand how to work with TCP/IP in the command line, it is necessary to discuss how to access the Command Prompt window as an administrator. It is also important to show some of the ways to make the Command Prompt window work for you and show how to view help files.

CERTIFICATION READY
Which tool can be used to view IP configuration and which tool can be used to verify connectivity to a server?
Objective 3.6

The ***Command Prompt window*** is the Microsoft version of a command-line interface (CLI). Just about anything you can accomplish in the GUI can also be done in the Command Prompt window, and when it comes to TCP/IP commands, the Command Prompt window can be even more effective. Today's Command Prompt window is the executable file cmd.exe. This is located in C:\Windows\system32. The older command.com is not recommended when working with TCP/IP commands.

Some of the commands you will be using in this lesson require administrative privileges. Some operating systems use User Account Control (UAC) to check if you are an administrator. Be sure to log on as an administrator of the computer in question before going through the exercises. If you are using a system with UAC enabled, open the Command Prompt window as an administrator in one of the following ways:

- Click Start > All Programs > Accessories; then, right-click Command Prompt and choose Run as Administrator.
- Click Start and type cmd in the search field. Instead of pressing Enter, press Ctrl+Shift+Enter.

Running the Command Prompt window as an Administrator is also known as running it in ***elevated mode***. Of course, you could turn off UAC, but that is not recommended.

Once opened, the Command Prompt window should look similar to Figure 5-1. Notice in the title bar that the directory path is preceded by the word *Administrator*. This is how you know that the Command Prompt window has been opened in elevated mode.

Figure 5-1

The Command Prompt window

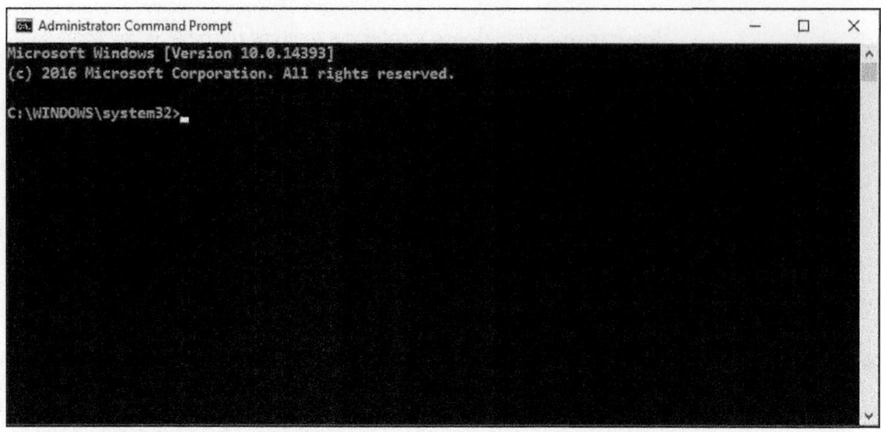

Open the Command Prompt window now, and configure it as you desire, including size, colors, and so on.

You might be familiar with the Command Prompt window. If you aren't, the command line in general can be daunting. But we will cover some tips and tricks to make the transition to the command line a bit easier. In the following exercise, you will learn some quick pointers as to how to work with the Command Prompt window quickly.

USE THE COMMAND PROMPT

GET READY. To use the Command Prompt window, perform the following steps.

1. Log on to a server running Windows Server 2016 as **adatum\administrator** with the password of **Pa$$w0rd**.
2. Click **Start**. Type cmd and press **Enter**. The Administrator: Command Prompt window opens.
3. To execute a command, type the command and press **Enter**. For example, type the command **cd** and then press **Enter**.

   This should change the prompt to C:\>, without any additional folders. This can help when you are dealing with long lines of code because the prompt takes up less space.
4. Execute the **cls** command.

   This clears the Command Prompt screen and any history buffer. However, you can still bring up older commands that you previously typed. This can be done by pressing the up (and down) arrow keys or by using F3, F5, or F7. The arrow keys can cycle back and forth though the history of commands. F3 only goes back one command and F7 allows you to see a table of previously typed commands that you can select from.
5. Try using the arrow keys and function keys to bring up previous commands.
6. Execute the **cls /?** command.

   This displays the help file for the cls command telling you that cls clears the screen. This is a basic help file, but more complex commands have more in-depth help files.
7. Execute the **dir /?** command.

   This shows the help file for the directory command, as shown in Figure 5-2, which has much more content than the previous help file we displayed.

Figure 5-2

The `dir` command help file

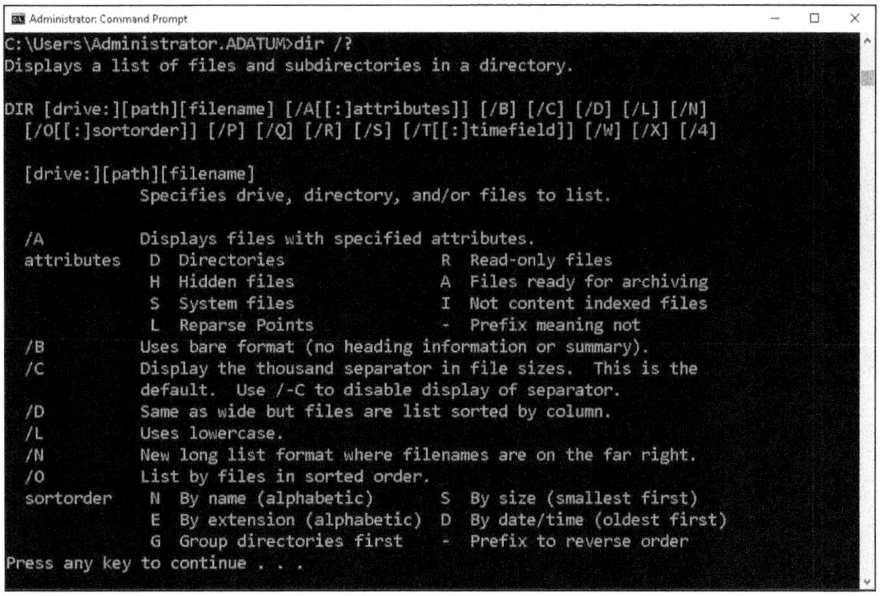

```
C:\Users\Administrator.ADATUM>dir /?
Displays a list of files and subdirectories in a directory.

DIR [drive:][path][filename] [/A[[:]attributes]] [/B] [/C] [/D] [/L] [/N]
  [/O[[:]sortorder]] [/P] [/Q] [/R] [/S] [/T[[:]timefield]] [/W] [/X] [/4]

  [drive:][path][filename]
              Specifies drive, directory, and/or files to list.

  /A          Displays files with specified attributes.
  attributes   D  Directories                R  Read-only files
               H  Hidden files               A  Files ready for archiving
               S  System files               I  Not content indexed files
               L  Reparse Points             -  Prefix meaning not
  /B          Uses bare format (no heading information or summary).
  /C          Display the thousand separator in file sizes.  This is the
              default.  Use /-C to disable display of separator.
  /D          Same as wide but files are list sorted by column.
  /L          Uses lowercase.
  /N          New long list format where filenames are on the far right.
  /O          List by files in sorted order.
  sortorder    N  By name (alphabetic)       S  By size (smallest first)
               E  By extension (alphabetic)  D  By date/time (oldest first)
               G  Group directories first    -  Prefix to reverse order
Press any key to continue . . .
```

Use the /? option when you need to find out more information about a TCP/IP command. In some cases, you will have to type the command followed by -? instead.

Sometimes, a help file, or the results of a command, will be too large to fit in one screen. In some cases, you might be able to press a key to see more. In other cases, you will need to add the `| more` option to the end of your syntax (spoken as "pipe more"). The | or pipe sign shares the backslash key. Use this when faced with extremely long results! For example, go to the root of C by typing `cd\`. Then, change to the System 32 directory by typing `cd\windows\system32`. This should bring you directly to the System32 directory. Now, type `dir`. This flashes hundreds of line items across the screen. But to see this one page at a time, type `dir | more`. You will see that it displays the information one page at a time showing "more" at the bottom of each screen full of information. Press the spacebar to show the next screen of information. Or, to show one line at a time, press Enter.

Using ipconfig and ping

`Ipconfig` and `ping` can be used to analyze, test, troubleshoot, and configure IPv4 and IPv6 connections. Before moving on to advanced TCP/IP commands, it is important to master these by learning what each of the commands and their options do, as well as why you would use those options in a real-world scenario.

TAKE NOTE*

Microsoft has a command-line reference from A to Z on its website with in-depth explanations of most commands. The `Help` command also gives a list of shell commands, but does not include TCP/IP commands.

The ***ipconfig*** command displays information pertaining to your network adapter, namely TCP/IP configurations. The ***ping*** command is used to test connectivity to other hosts; it tells you by way of command-line results whether a remote host is "alive" on the network.

The `ipconfig` and `ping` commands are probably the two most commonly used commands when analyzing and troubleshooting networking issues. Although `ipconfig` displays information, it can also be used to make basic configuration changes and resets of certain facets of DHCP and DNS.

ANALYZE AND CONFIGURE IP CONNECTIONS USING IPCONFIG AND PING

TAKE NOTE*

Disable any firewalls (hardware or software) that might interfere with the following exercises and tests.

GET READY. To analyze and configure IP connections using `ipconfig` and `ping`, perform the following steps.

1. Execute **ipconfig**

   This should display results similar to Figure 5-3.

   Your IP address and other actual configurations are probably different. Regardless, this is where you can find out the IP address, subnet mask, and default gateway

Figure 5-3

The `ipconfig` command

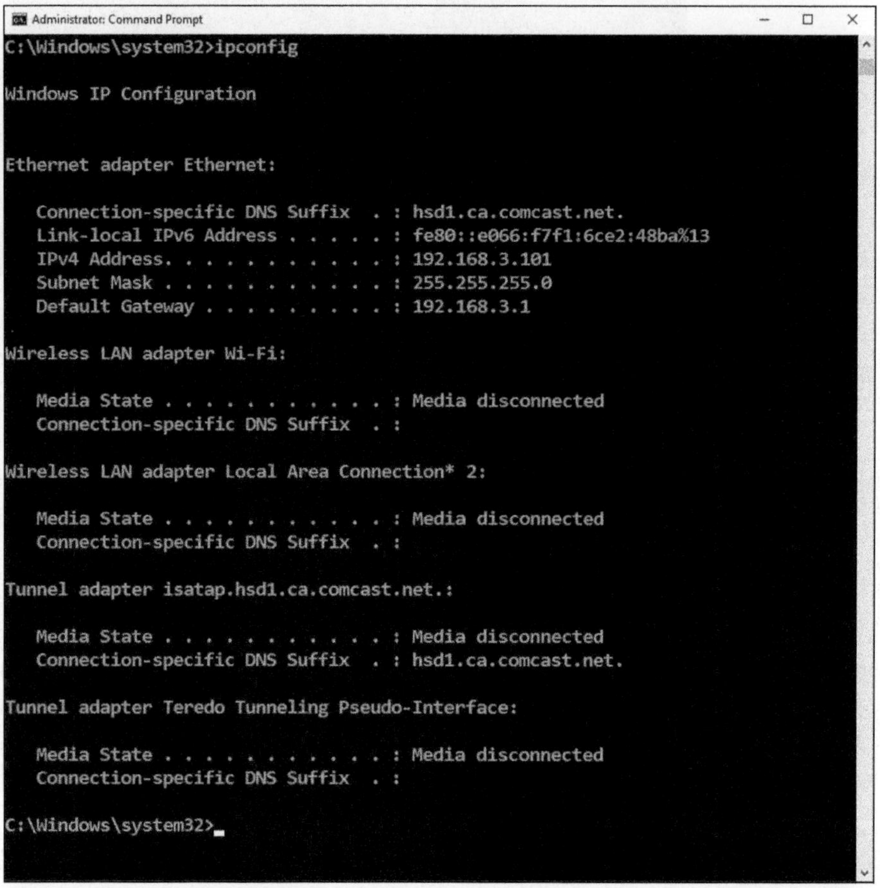

```
Administrator: Command Prompt
C:\Windows\system32>ipconfig

Windows IP Configuration


Ethernet adapter Ethernet:

   Connection-specific DNS Suffix  . : hsd1.ca.comcast.net.
   Link-local IPv6 Address . . . . . : fe80::e066:f7f1:6ce2:48ba%13
   IPv4 Address. . . . . . . . . . . : 192.168.3.101
   Subnet Mask . . . . . . . . . . . : 255.255.255.0
   Default Gateway . . . . . . . . . : 192.168.3.1

Wireless LAN adapter Wi-Fi:

   Media State . . . . . . . . . . . : Media disconnected
   Connection-specific DNS Suffix  . :

Wireless LAN adapter Local Area Connection* 2:

   Media State . . . . . . . . . . . : Media disconnected
   Connection-specific DNS Suffix  . :

Tunnel adapter isatap.hsd1.ca.comcast.net.:

   Media State . . . . . . . . . . . : Media disconnected
   Connection-specific DNS Suffix  . : hsd1.ca.comcast.net.

Tunnel adapter Teredo Tunneling Pseudo-Interface:

   Media State . . . . . . . . . . . : Media disconnected
   Connection-specific DNS Suffix  . :

C:\Windows\system32>_
```

   of your network adapter. IPv4 and possibly IPv6 information will be listed, depending on your configuration.

   This is not all the information `ipconfig` can display. For example, if you want to know the MAC address of the network adapter, you would use one of several options of `ipconfig`.

2. Execute **ipconfig /all**

   The results should have much more information, including the MAC address, as shown in Figure 5-4 (the field is named Physical Address). The space after the word `ipconfig` is not necessary in this case; however, some commands will not function properly without it. So it's best to always use the space, unless specifically instructed by the command syntax.

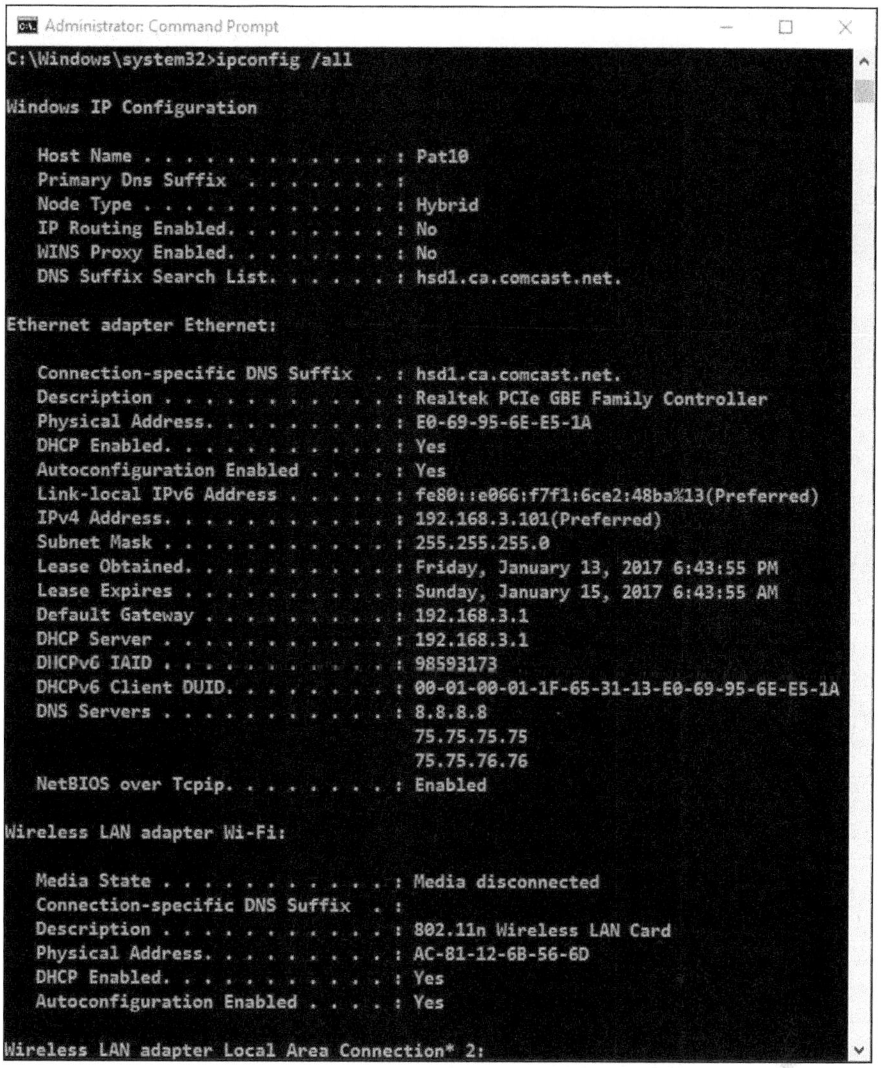

Figure 5-4

Results from the `ipconfig /all` command

```
Administrator: Command Prompt
C:\Windows\system32>ipconfig /all

Windows IP Configuration

   Host Name . . . . . . . . . . . . : Pat10
   Primary Dns Suffix  . . . . . . . :
   Node Type . . . . . . . . . . . . : Hybrid
   IP Routing Enabled. . . . . . . . : No
   WINS Proxy Enabled. . . . . . . . : No
   DNS Suffix Search List. . . . . . : hsd1.ca.comcast.net.

Ethernet adapter Ethernet:

   Connection-specific DNS Suffix  . : hsd1.ca.comcast.net.
   Description . . . . . . . . . . . : Realtek PCIe GBE Family Controller
   Physical Address. . . . . . . . . : E0-69-95-6E-E5-1A
   DHCP Enabled. . . . . . . . . . . : Yes
   Autoconfiguration Enabled . . . . : Yes
   Link-local IPv6 Address . . . . . : fe80::e066:f7f1:6ce2:48ba%13(Preferred)
   IPv4 Address. . . . . . . . . . . : 192.168.3.101(Preferred)
   Subnet Mask . . . . . . . . . . . : 255.255.255.0
   Lease Obtained. . . . . . . . . . : Friday, January 13, 2017 6:43:55 PM
   Lease Expires . . . . . . . . . . : Sunday, January 15, 2017 6:43:55 AM
   Default Gateway . . . . . . . . . : 192.168.3.1
   DHCP Server . . . . . . . . . . . : 192.168.3.1
   DHCPv6 IAID . . . . . . . . . . . : 98593173
   DHCPv6 Client DUID. . . . . . . . : 00-01-00-01-1F-65-31-13-E0-69-95-6E-E5-1A
   DNS Servers . . . . . . . . . . . : 8.8.8.8
                                       75.75.75.75
                                       75.75.76.76
   NetBIOS over Tcpip. . . . . . . . : Enabled

Wireless LAN adapter Wi-Fi:

   Media State . . . . . . . . . . . : Media disconnected
   Connection-specific DNS Suffix  . :
   Description . . . . . . . . . . . : 802.11n Wireless LAN Card
   Physical Address. . . . . . . . . : AC-81-12-6B-56-6D
   DHCP Enabled. . . . . . . . . . . : Yes
   Autoconfiguration Enabled . . . . : Yes

Wireless LAN adapter Local Area Connection* 2:
```

Notice that there is a section at the beginning of the results called Windows IP Configuration. This displays the name of the computer or host name. (You can also find this out by executing **hostname**.) It also shows a DNS suffix field, which is blank in this instance, but if the computer was a member of a domain, it would be populated, as shown in Figure 5-5. In the figure, the DNS suffix is Adatum.com, which is the domain name that this computer belongs to. If the computer does belong to a domain, an additional field called "DNS Suffix Search List" is added.

The `ipconfig/all` command also defines whether IP routing or WINS proxy is enabled. We will cover these services in more depth in Lesson 6.

Until now, this might be review. But there are many options for `ipconfig`. You might hear IT professionals refer to the word *options* as *switches* or *parameters* as well.

3. Execute **ipconfig /?**

   This displays the help file for `ipconfig`, which as can be seen, is rather extensive. It describes what `ipconfig` is, what it does, and shows the various options you can use with the command as well as some examples. Results of this command are shown in Figure 5-6.

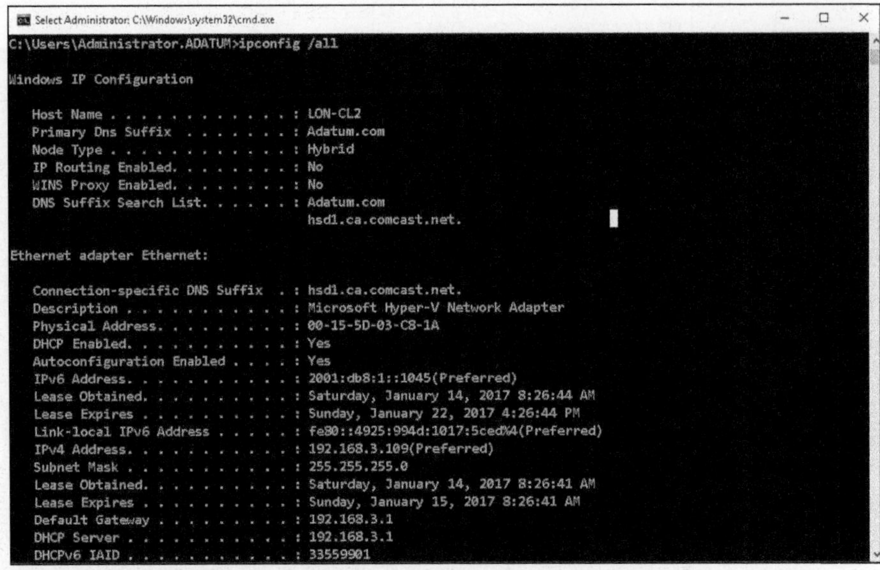

Figure 5-5

Results from the `ipconfig /all` command on a second host

Figure 5-6

Results from the `ipconfig /?` command

```
Administrator: Command Prompt
C:\Users\Administrator.ADATUM>ipconfig /?

USAGE:
    ipconfig [/allcompartments] [/? | /all |
                                 /renew [adapter] | /release [adapter] |
                                 /renew6 [adapter] | /release6 [adapter] |
                                 /flushdns | /displaydns | /registerdns |
                                 /showclassid adapter |
                                 /setclassid adapter [classid] |
                                 /showclassid6 adapter |
                                 /setclassid6 adapter [classid] ]

where
    adapter             Connection name
                       (wildcard characters * and ? allowed, see examples)

    Options:
       /?               Display this help message
       /all             Display full configuration information.
       /release         Release the IPv4 address for the specified adapter.
       /release6        Release the IPv6 address for the specified adapter.
       /renew           Renew the IPv4 address for the specified adapter.
       /renew6          Renew the IPv6 address for the specified adapter.
       /flushdns        Purges the DNS Resolver cache.
       /registerdns     Refreshes all DHCP leases and re-registers DNS names
       /displaydns      Display the contents of the DNS Resolver Cache.
       /showclassid     Displays all the dhcp class IDs allowed for adapter.
       /setclassid      Modifies the dhcp class id.
       /showclassid6    Displays all the IPv6 DHCP class IDs allowed for adapter.
       /setclassid6     Modifies the IPv6 DHCP class id.


The default is to display only the IP address, subnet mask and
default gateway for each adapter bound to TCP/IP.
```

4. Execute **`ipconfig /allcompartments`**

   Network adapters can be compartmentalized so that traffic from one doesn't leak to the other, for example, VPN traffic on one adapter and private LAN traffic on another. This command shows the adapters in their compartmentalized format. You can also use **`ipconfig /allcompartments /all`** to see extended information about each compartment (similar to `ipconfig /all`).

5. Work with the dynamically assigned address:

   a. On a computer that obtains its IP information automatically, execute the **`ipconfig /release`** command.

The `ipconfig /release` command releases any IP configurations it received from a DHCP server. Figure 5-7 shows an example of a released IP address.

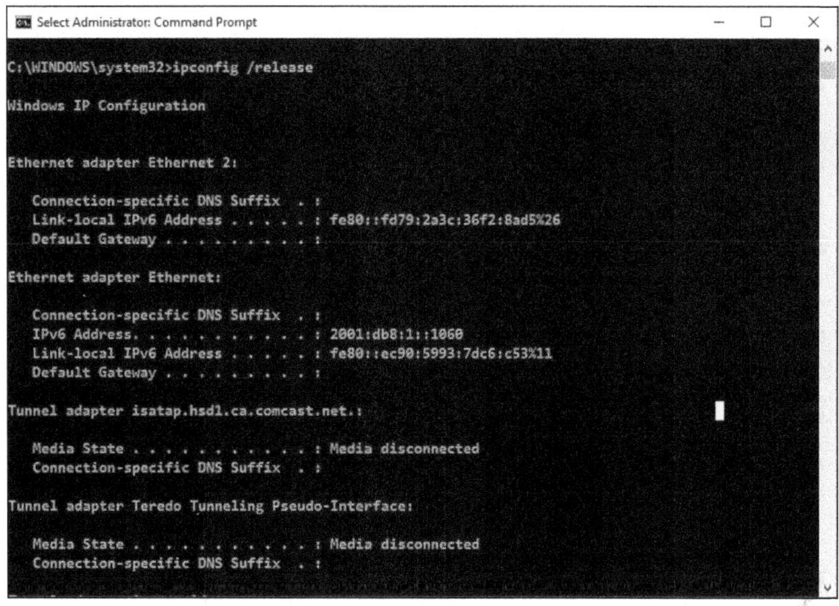

Figure 5-7

A released IP configuration

b. Execute **`ipconfig /renew`** to retrieve an IP address and other IP configurations.

   This should reconfigure the computer with the same IP address it used before. If the IP address has only been released for a short time, the `/renew` option will reconfigure the address based on information stored in the registry. If no information is available, or the address has expired after a certain amount of time, the computer will seek out a DHCP server on the network from which to obtain an IP address. These commands can be useful if a new DHCP server has been placed on the network, or the current DHCP server has been reconfigured. The commands are also helpful if an error has occurred in the network adapter's IP configuration, or if APIPA has gotten in the way, and has self-assigned a 169.254.0.0 address to the client. The commands issued in Steps 5a and 5b pertain to IPv4; however, to release and renew IPv6 addresses, simply add a 6 to the option (for example, **`ipconfig /release6`**). More information about this process and DHCP is covered in Lesson 6.

6. Display, flush, and register DNS information:

   a. Execute **`ipconfig /displaydns`**

      This command displays Domain Name System records for the client computer, including localhost connections.

   b. Execute **`ipconfig /flushdns`**

      This command empties the DNS cache.

   c. Execute **`ipconfig /registerdns`**

      This command registers the computer with the nearest DNS server. The last two commands can be useful if there is an error with the DNS configuration on the client, or if a new DNS server, or newly configured DNS server, becomes live on the network.

      As you can see, the `ipconfig` command has a lot of uses. It can be used to analyze and troubleshoot the basic networking connection, as well as troubleshoot DHCP and DNS issues.

Let's move on to the ping command. As previously noted, ping is used to test the existence of other hosts on the network. However, there are many permutations of ping.

7. Execute **ping /?**

   This command displays the help file for the ping command. Note the various options available to you.

8. Ping the local host computer and other computers on the network:

   a. Execute **ping localhost**

   b. Execute **ping loopback**

   c. Execute **ping 127.0.0.1**

      The first two commands are basically the same. However, when you ping 127.0.0.1, the results do not include any host name resolution information. This is the best way to ping the localhost when testing IPv4. When pinging 127.0.0.1, no traffic is placed on the network segment; all traffic is kept inside the computer or local loopback.

      Now select another computer to ping; it could be a partner's computer, a secondary computer, or a router. Make note of its IP address. For this example, use the address 10.254.254.252.

   d. Execute **ping [IP address]**

      For example, **ping 172.16.0.12**

      This basic ping command tests whether another host on the network is live. You can also ping another computer on the network by host name. To find out the host name of a computer, execute either **hostname** or **ipconfig**. Examples of pinging an IP address and pinging the corresponding host name are shown in Figure 5-8. Notice the IP address in the first ping (172.16.0.12) as well as the host name (LON-SVR2) and resolved IP address (172.16.0.12) in the second ping.

TAKE NOTE*

Disable IPv6 in the Local Area Connection Properties dialog box before continuing this portion. If you get replies that include ::1 in the address, IPv6 is still functioning.

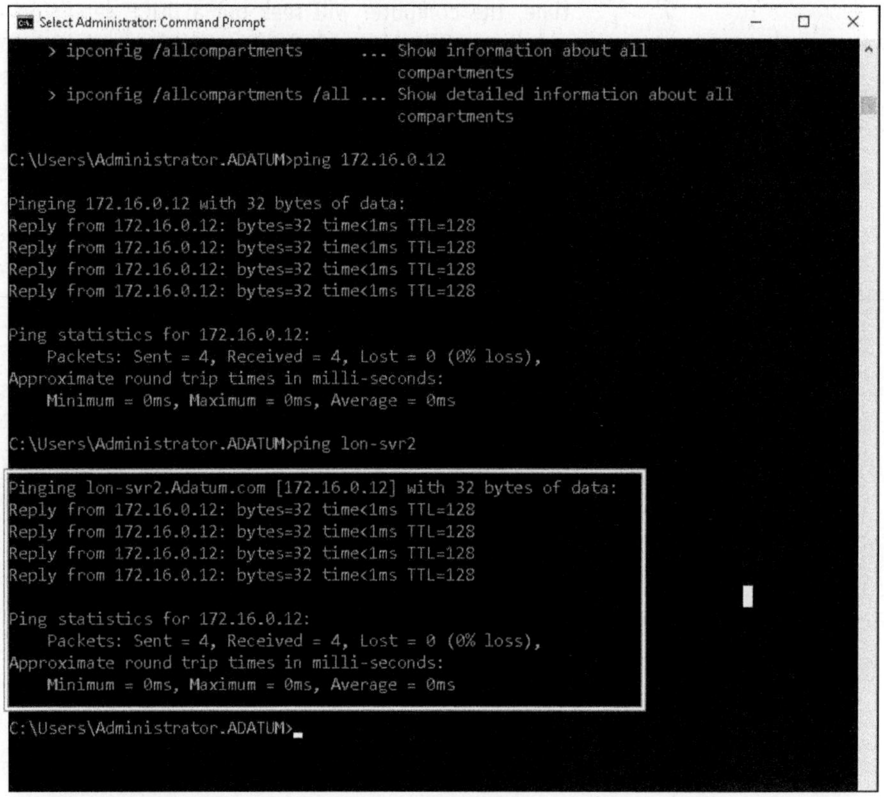

Figure 5-8

Pinging computers by IP address and by host name

```
Select Administrator: Command Prompt
    > ipconfig /allcompartments      ... Show information about all
                                         compartments
    > ipconfig /allcompartments /all ... Show detailed information about all
                                         compartments

C:\Users\Administrator.ADATUM>ping 172.16.0.12

Pinging 172.16.0.12 with 32 bytes of data:
Reply from 172.16.0.12: bytes=32 time<1ms TTL=128
Reply from 172.16.0.12: bytes=32 time<1ms TTL=128
Reply from 172.16.0.12: bytes=32 time<1ms TTL=128
Reply from 172.16.0.12: bytes=32 time<1ms TTL=128

Ping statistics for 172.16.0.12:
    Packets: Sent = 4, Received = 4, Lost = 0 (0% loss),
Approximate round trip times in milli-seconds:
    Minimum = 0ms, Maximum = 0ms, Average = 0ms

C:\Users\Administrator.ADATUM>ping lon-svr2

Pinging lon-svr2.Adatum.com [172.16.0.12] with 32 bytes of data:
Reply from 172.16.0.12: bytes=32 time<1ms TTL=128
Reply from 172.16.0.12: bytes=32 time<1ms TTL=128
Reply from 172.16.0.12: bytes=32 time<1ms TTL=128
Reply from 172.16.0.12: bytes=32 time<1ms TTL=128

Ping statistics for 172.16.0.12:
    Packets: Sent = 4, Received = 4, Lost = 0 (0% loss),
Approximate round trip times in milli-seconds:
    Minimum = 0ms, Maximum = 0ms, Average = 0ms

C:\Users\Administrator.ADATUM>_
```

If the computer pinged is alive, the pinging computer will get replies. However, if a computer is not live, or is not available, you will get one of several error messages, for example, "Request timed out," "Destination host unreachable," or a similar error.

When troubleshooting network connectivity issues, start with the local computer and then branch out. For example, start with a `ping 127.0.0.1`, and then try pinging other hosts on the same network, ultimately ending up with the router. Then, try pinging hosts on other networks.

9. Ping a computer with a larger packet size:
   a. Select another computer to ping; it could be a partner's computer, a secondary computer, or a router. Make note of its IP address. For this example, use the address 172.16.0.12.
   b. Execute **ping -l 1500 [IP address]**

      For example, **ping -l 1500 172.16.0.12**

      The results should be similar to Figure 5-9. Notice that each of the replies equals 1,500 bytes instead of the standard 32 bytes. The `-l` option allows you to modify the packet size of the ICMP echoes that are sent. The most bytes that you can send in this fashion is 65,500; however, this will create fragmented packets. This `ping` option can help to simulate network traffic to a particular host.

Figure 5-9

`Ping` used with the `-l` option

```
Administrator: Command Prompt
Reply from 172.16.0.12: bytes=32 time<1ms TTL=128
Reply from 172.16.0.12: bytes=32 time<1ms TTL=128

Ping statistics for 172.16.0.12:
    Packets: Sent = 4, Received = 4, Lost = 0 (0% loss),
Approximate round trip times in milli-seconds:
    Minimum = 0ms, Maximum = 0ms, Average = 0ms

C:\Users\Administrator.ADATUM>ping lon-svr2

Pinging lon-svr2.Adatum.com [172.16.0.12] with 32 bytes of data:
Reply from 172.16.0.12: bytes=32 time<1ms TTL=128
Reply from 172.16.0.12: bytes=32 time<1ms TTL=128
Reply from 172.16.0.12: bytes=32 time<1ms TTL=128
Reply from 172.16.0.12: bytes=32 time<1ms TTL=128

Ping statistics for 172.16.0.12:
    Packets: Sent = 4, Received = 4, Lost = 0 (0% loss),
Approximate round trip times in milli-seconds:
    Minimum = 0ms, Maximum = 0ms, Average = 0ms

C:\Users\Administrator.ADATUM>ping -l 1500 172.16.0.12

Pinging 172.16.0.12 with 1500 bytes of data:
Reply from 172.16.0.12: bytes=1500 time=1ms TTL=128
Reply from 172.16.0.12: bytes=1500 time<1ms TTL=128
Reply from 172.16.0.12: bytes=1500 time<1ms TTL=128
Reply from 172.16.0.12: bytes=1500 time<1ms TTL=128

Ping statistics for 172.16.0.12:
    Packets: Sent = 4, Received = 4, Lost = 0 (0% loss),
Approximate round trip times in milli-seconds:
    Minimum = 0ms, Maximum = 1ms, Average = 0ms
```

10. Ping a computer *X* amount of times:
    a. Use the same computer you pinged in Step 9.
    b. Execute **ping -n 10 [IP address]**

       For example, **ping -n 10 172.16.0.12**

The results should be similar to Figure 5-10. Notice that there were a total of 10 ICMP echo replies. The -n option allows you to ping with as many ICMP packets as you want. This option works well if you are creating a performance baseline. By executing a command such as **ping -n 1000 172.16.0.12** every day, you could compare the results and see if the destination computer is performing better or worse than usual.

Figure 5-10

`Ping` used with the -n option

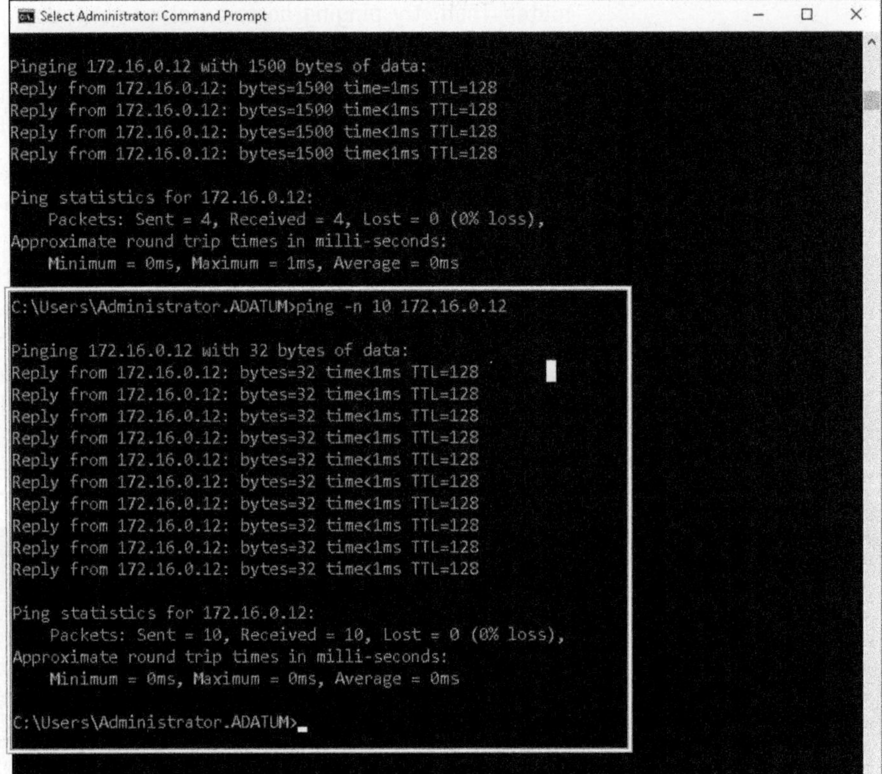

11. Ping a computer continuously:
    a. Use the same computer you pinged in Steps 9 and 10.
    b. Execute **ping -t [IP address]**

       For example, **ping -t 172..16.0.12**

       This command option sends pings endlessly to a destination IP address. This can only be stopped by pressing Ctrl+C on the keyboard or by closing the Command Prompt window altogether. This option works well if you need to test whether a network connection is being made. For example, if you aren't sure which patch cable to use, or which RJ-45 port to connect to, you could run this command, then test one connection at a time, and check the results on the screen each time until you get replies.

By the way, most of the time the option can be typed after the IP address as well. But it is a good habit to place options directly after the command they are modifying.

These are just a few of the `ping` options, but they are some of the more commonly used options. Do your best to memorize the various switches that we employed during this exercise.

Working with Advanced TCP/IP Commands

THE BOTTOM LINE

Advanced TCP/IP commands like `netstat`, `nbtstat`, and `tracert` allow us to analyze more facets of our TCP/IP connection than `ipconfig` and `ping` can. FTP, `Telnet`, `netsh`, and `route` enable us to go much further than just analyze our system—they help to configure the system.

CERTIFICATION READY
How do you configure TCP/IP commands with TCP/IP?
Objective 3.6

In the following exercises, we will be showing results from two computers. One is a server computer; its Command Prompt windows will be displayed with a black background. The other is a client computer; its Command Prompt windows will be displayed with a white background. The results work basically the same way on both types of computers; however, a server computer will often have more results because it will generally have more networking connections.

Using netstat and nbtstat

In the following exercise, you will analyze your system with the ***netstat*** and ***nbtstat*** commands. Both show statistics of the network connection, but `netstat` centers on the local computer, whereas `nbtstat` can also show statistics for remote machines.

ANALYZE A TCP/IP CONFIGURATION WITH NETSTAT AND NBTSTAT

GET READY. To analyze your system with the `netstat` and `nbtstat` commands, perform the following steps.

1. Execute the **`netstat`** command and view the results. They might take up to a minute to show up depending on your network configuration and amount of current network connections. Your results should look similar to Figure 5-11, although you might have fewer line items of information.

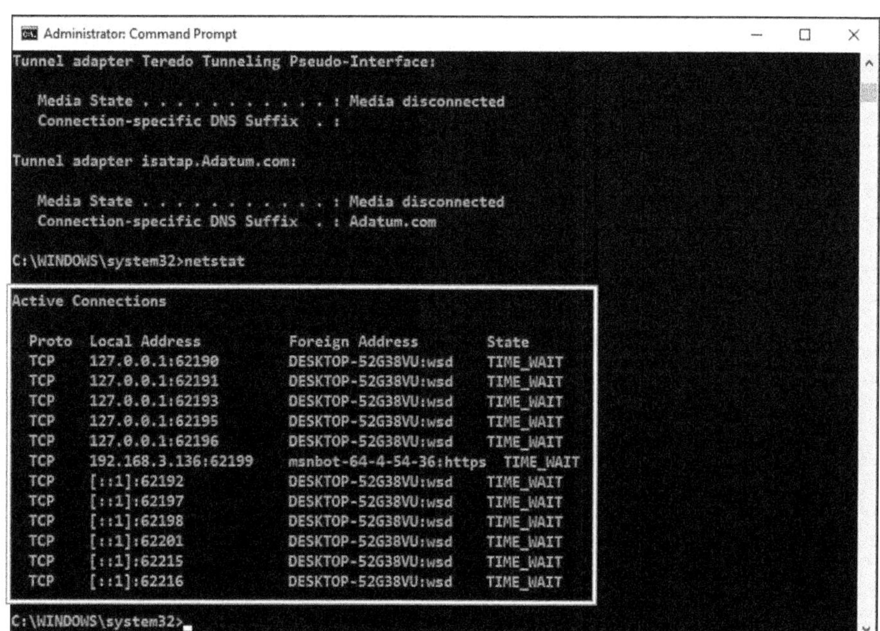

Figure 5-11
`Netstat` results

The `netstat` command is used to display active TCP (or UDP) connections as well as a host of other statistics that we will cover later in the exercise. Note that there are four columns. The Proto column shows the Transport layer protocol being used for the connection. The `netstat` command by itself only shows TCP connections in this column. The Local Address column displays the local computer by name (server2003) followed by the outbound port number. The Foreign Address column shows the remote computer that is being connected to; in some cases, this can be the same computer. The State column shows what the status of the connection is, for example Established, Close_Wait, Closed, Listen, and so on. They are self-explanatory, but let's show another example of an established session.

2. Open Internet Explorer and connect to www.microsoft.com. Move ahead to Step 3 right away.
3. Execute **netstat** again. Now you should see additional entries, as shown in Figure 5-12.

Figure 5-12

`Netstat` results with additional entries

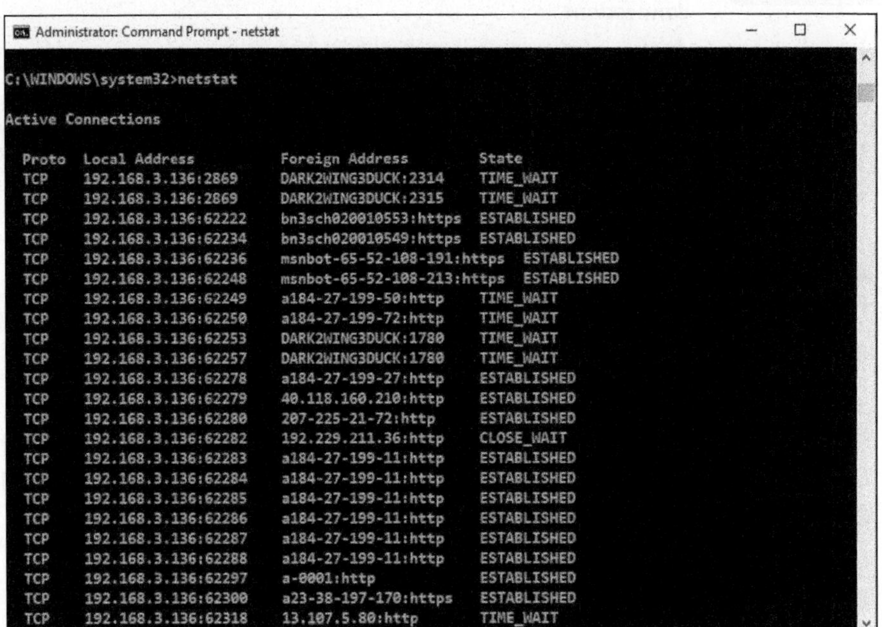

Notice in the figure the two extra entries in the Foreign Address column that start with the letters *lga*. This is part of the domain name called 1e100.net, which is controlled by four name servers at google.com. These two connections were made when the computer browsed to www.microsoft.com; they are established connections. The host names are followed by the inbound port called https, which is the equivalent of port 443. The local computer is making connections to Microsoft (msnbot-65-52-108-191) and msnbot-65-52-208-213) on outbound ports 62222 and 62234. Note that the ports used by your computer will be different because they are dynamically assigned. This command and the following two commands can be very helpful when tracking applications and the network connections they make.

4. Execute **netstat -a**

   This displays TCP and UDP connections.

5. Execute **netstat -an**

   This displays TCP and UDP connections in numeric format. For many administrators, being able to view IP addresses and port numbers is easier than going by name. `Netstat -n` shows numerical results but for TCP connections only.

6. Execute **netstat -e**

   This displays Ethernet statistics such as the number of packets and bytes sent and received, as shown in Figure 5-13.

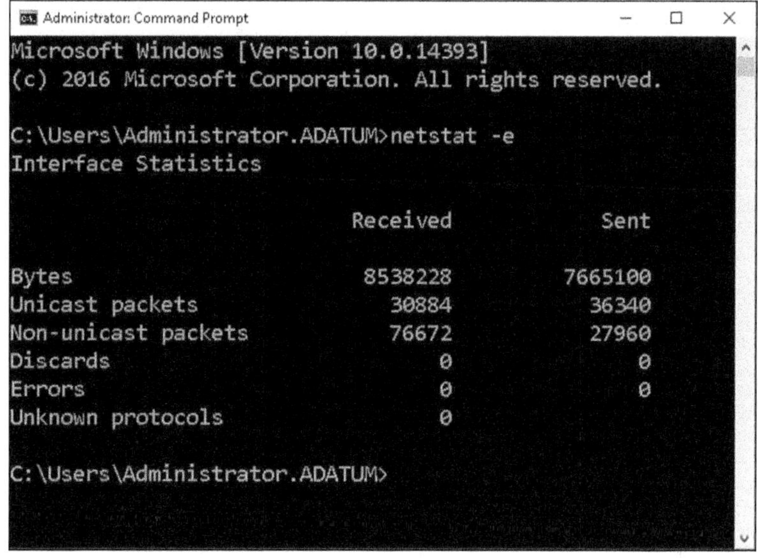

Figure 5-13

`Netstat -e` results

7. Execute **netstat -r**

   This displays the route table and produces the same results as executing **route print**, which is covered in more depth later.

8. Execute **netstat -s**

   This displays statistics per protocol, such as TCP, UDP, ICMP, IP, and so on.

   Check out the rest of the options for `netstat`. Note that you can fine-tune the results of the `netstat` command in several ways.

   Let's move on to `nbtstat`.

9. Execute **nbtstat**

   This displays the help file for the command. `Nbtstat` displays NetBIOS over TCP/IP statistics for local and remote computers. NetBIOS was developed in the 1980s to allow applications to communicate over the network via the Session layer of the OSI model. NetBIOS over TCP/IP sends the NetBIOS protocol within TCP and UDP sessions.

10. Execute **nbtstat -a [local computername]**

    For example, execute **nbtstat -a LON-SVR2** (see Figure 5-14). The same results can also be achieved by executing **nbtstat -n**.

11. Execute **nbtstat -a [remotename]**

    Use the name of a computer on your network that you can connect to with `ping`.

    The results of the `nbtstat` command display the major services that are running on that machine. For example, <00> is the workstation service, used to allow connections to remote computers. <20> is the server service, used to allow other computers to connect to the local computer. If you see <03>, this is the messenger service. Many organizations have policies stating that this should be turned off. This command works very well to discern the services running on a local or remote machine and can help when troubleshooting why the computer cannot make selected network connections. You can also connect by IP address.

Figure 5-14

`Nbtstat -a` results

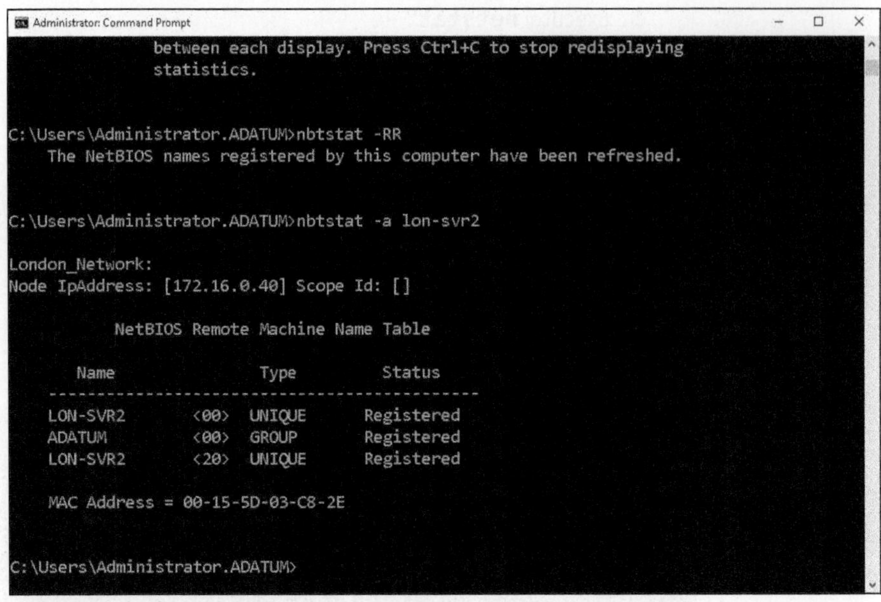

12. Execute **nbtstat** **-A [IPAddress]**

    For example, execute **nbtstat -A 10.254.254.205**, which provides the same information but allows you to connect via IP address. So, the lowercase *a* option is used for names, and the uppercase *A* is used for IP addresses. Let's attempt to stop a service and view the results with `nbtstat`:

    a. Stop the workstation service on a remote computer. This can be done in the Computer Management console or by executing **net stop workstation**.
    b. Next, execute **nbtstat -A** to that remote computer's IP address. You should see that the <00> service is no longer listed.
    c. Restart the service on the remote computer within Computer Management.
    d. Execute **nbtstat -A** again to verify that it is listed. A restart of the remote computer might be necessary.

13. Execute **nbtstat -r** to display NetBIOS name resolution statistics.
14. Execute **nbtstat -R** to purge the contents of the NetBIOS name cache table.
15. Execute **nbtstat -RR** to release and refresh NetBIOS names.

    The previous two commands are used in conjunction with Lmhosts and WINS respectively, and are not commonly used in today's networks.

16. Execute **nbtstat -s** to display NetBIOS sessions and convert the remote IP addresses to a name. You might have to make a network connection or two before this command displays any results.
17. Execute **nbtstat -S** to display the same sessions as with the `-s` parameter. The only difference is that remote computers will be listed by IP address.

    Generally, it is wise to use uppercase options, such as -A and -S. These provide results by IP address, which is usually what a network administrator prefers.

Using tracert and pathping

Next, you will learn how to analyze network paths with `tracert` and `pathping`. Both show paths to remote destinations, extending beyond one or more routers, but their syntax, and results, will differ. Plus, ***pathping*** analyzes the trace after it makes it, further differentiating it from `tracert`. An Internet connection is required.

ANALYZE NETWORK PATHS WITH TRACERT AND PATHPING

GET READY. To analyze network paths with `tracert` and `pathping`, perform the following steps. Remember, an Internet connection is required.

1. Execute **`tracert`** and view the results. This command or **`tracert /?`** displays the help file for the command. Review the details in the help file. The `tracert` command shows paths to a destination on another network. It does this by pinging each step along the way three times. The Time to Live (TTL) for the pings increases with each "hop" to another network.
2. Trace to www.microsoft.com by executing the **`tracert www.microsoft.com`** command. The results should be similar to Figure 5-15.

Figure 5-15

`Tracert` results

```
Administrator: Command Prompt
  TCP    192.168.3.136:62402    a184-27-109-102:https  ESTABLISHED
  TCP    192.168.3.136:62403    a184-27-109-102:https  ESTABLISHED
  TCP    192.168.3.136:62404    a184-27-109-102:https  ESTABLISHED
  TCP    192.168.3.136:62405    a184-27-111-10:https   ESTABLISHED
  TCP    192.168.3.136:62406    a184-27-111-10:https   ESTABLISHED
  TCP    192.168.3.136:62407    40.112.223.14:https    ESTABLISHED

C:\WINDOWS\system32>tracert www.microsoft.com

Tracing route to e1863.dspb.akamaiedge.net [23.200.140.34]
over a maximum of 30 hops:

  1     1 ms    <1 ms    <1 ms  DARK2WING3DUCK [192.168.3.1]
  2     1 ms     1 ms     1 ms  10.0.0.1
  3    12 ms    11 ms    14 ms  96.120.14.61
  4    12 ms    11 ms    11 ms  ae214-rur01.sacramento.ca.ccal.comcast.net [68.87.212.193]
  5    10 ms    19 ms    13 ms  ae-2-ar01.sacramento.ca.ccal.comcast.net [162.151.18.133]
  6    18 ms    19 ms    17 ms  be-33667-cr01.9greatoaks.ca.ibone.comcast.net [68.86.93.25]
  7    19 ms    13 ms    14 ms  hu-0-13-0-1-pe03.11greatoaks.ca.ibone.comcast.net [68.86.83.138]
  8    23 ms    33 ms    23 ms  ae-13.r02.snjsca04.us.bb.gin.ntt.net [129.250.66.33]
  9    19 ms    13 ms    14 ms  ae-11.r23.snjsca04.us.bb.gin.ntt.net [129.250.6.118]
 10    37 ms    33 ms    43 ms  ae-3.r21.sttlwa01.us.bb.gin.ntt.net [129.250.3.125]
 11    40 ms    33 ms    33 ms  ae-29.r05.sttlwa01.us.bb.gin.ntt.net [129.250.2.89]
 12    35 ms    38 ms    33 ms  a23-200-140-34.deploy.static.akamaitechnologies.com [23.200.140.34
]

Trace complete.

C:\WINDOWS\system32>
```

Each step along the way to microsoft.com is referred to as a hop. Each line in the results is a new network that has been hopped to. Notice the name of each router and its corresponding IP address. Usually, you can track geographically where the ICMP packets are going step-by-step, just by looking at the router name.

3. Execute **`tracert -d www.microsoft.com`** to run the same trace numerically (as shown in Figure 5-16). This is a real time-saver. Notice how much faster the results are shown without any name resolution to get in the way.

   The idea behind this `tracert` command is that it allows you to find out if a router has malfunctioned. By comparing the `tracert` results with your network documentation, you should be able to alert the correct network person to the problem, or perhaps fix the problem yourself. Often, a router simply needs to be rebooted or turned back on.

4. Execute the **`pathping www.microsoft.com`** command. `Pathping` is similar to `tracert`, but will also compute the degree of packet loss, as shown in Figure 5-17. If there was packet loss, it would show up under the Lost/Sent column and would display a percentage as well.
5. Execute **`pathping -n www.microsoft.com`** to prevent name resolution in the way that `tracert -d` does. This can display the results faster than the standard `pathping` command.

TAKE NOTE*

If `tracert` doesn't work on your computer or is not allowed on your network, you can use web-based reverse tracing tools, such as the tools offered on speedguide.net's website.

Figure 5-16

`Tracert -d` results

```
Administrator: Command Prompt
   -h maximum_hops    Maximum number of hops to search for target.
   -j host-list       Loose source route along host-list (IPv4-only).
   -w timeout         Wait timeout milliseconds for each reply.
   -R                 Trace round-trip path (IPv6-only).
   -S srcaddr         Source address to use (IPv6-only).
   -4                 Force using IPv4.
   -6                 Force using IPv6.

C:\WINDOWS\system32>tracert -d www.microsoft.com

Tracing route to e1863.dspb.akamaiedge.net [23.200.140.34]
over a maximum of 30 hops:

  1    <1 ms    <1 ms    <1 ms  192.168.3.1
  2     1 ms     1 ms     1 ms  10.0.0.1
  3    10 ms    19 ms    11 ms  96.120.14.61
  4    12 ms    13 ms    29 ms  68.87.212.193
  5    11 ms    13 ms    11 ms  162.151.18.133
  6    15 ms    13 ms    19 ms  68.86.93.25
  7    15 ms    13 ms    16 ms  68.86.83.138
  8    19 ms    18 ms    18 ms  129.250.66.33
  9    21 ms    28 ms    28 ms  129.250.6.118
 10    33 ms    36 ms    48 ms  129.250.3.125
 11    32 ms    33 ms    34 ms  129.250.2.89
 12    33 ms    35 ms    33 ms  23.200.140.34

Trace complete.

C:\WINDOWS\system32>
```

Figure 5-17

`Pathping` results

```
Administrator: Command Prompt
C:\WINDOWS\system32>pathping www.microsoft.com

Tracing route to e1863.dspb.akamaiedge.net [23.200.140.34]
over a maximum of 30 hops:
  0  DESKTOP-52G38VU.hsd1.ca.comcast.net. [192.168.3.136]
  1  DARK2WING3DUCK [192.168.3.1]
  2  10.0.0.1
  3  96.120.14.61
  4  ae214-rur01.sacramento.ca.ccal.comcast.net [68.87.212.193]
  5  ae-2-ar01.sacramento.ca.ccal.comcast.net [162.151.18.133]
  6  be-33667-cr01.9greatoaks.ca.ibone.comcast.net [68.86.93.25]
  7  hu-0-13-0-1-pe03.11greatoaks.ca.ibone.comcast.net [68.86.83.138]
  8  ae-13.r02.snjsca04.us.bb.gin.ntt.net [129.250.66.33]
  9  ae-11.r23.snjsca04.us.bb.gin.ntt.net [129.250.6.118]
 10  ae-3.r21.sttlwa01.us.bb.gin.ntt.net [129.250.3.125]
 11  ae-29.r05.sttlwa01.us.bb.gin.ntt.net [129.250.2.89]
 12  a23-200-140-34.deploy.static.akamaitechnologies.com [23.200.140.34]

Computing statistics for 300 seconds...
            Source to Here   This Node/Link
Hop  RTT    Lost/Sent = Pct  Lost/Sent = Pct  Address
  0                                           DESKTOP-52G38VU.hsd1.ca.comcast.net. [192.168.3.136]

                                0/ 100 =  0%   |
  1    0ms     0/ 100 =  0%     0/ 100 =  0%  DARK2WING3DUCK [192.168.3.1]
                                0/ 100 =  0%   |
  2    1ms     0/ 100 =  0%     0/ 100 =  0%  10.0.0.1
                                0/ 100 =  0%   |
  3   12ms     0/ 100 =  0%     0/ 100 =  0%  96.120.14.61
                                0/ 100 =  0%   |
  4   14ms     0/ 100 =  0%     0/ 100 =  0%  ae214-rur01.sacramento.ca.ccal.comcast.net [68.87.21
2.193]
                                0/ 100 =  0%   |
  5   13ms     0/ 100 =  0%     0/ 100 =  0%  ae-2-ar01.sacramento.ca.ccal.comcast.net [162.151.18
.133]
                                0/ 100 =  0%   |
  6   17ms     0/ 100 =  0%     0/ 100 =  0%  be-33667-cr01.9greatoaks.ca.ibone.comcast.net [68.86
```

Using nslookup

In the following exercise, you will analyze DNS information with the `nslookup` command. ***Nslookup*** displays information about DNS names and their corresponding IP addresses, and can be used to diagnose DNS servers. An Internet connection is required.

ANALYZE DOMAIN NAMES WITH NSLOOKUP

GET READY. To analyze DNS information with the `nslookup` command, perform the following steps. Remember, an Internet connection is required.

1. Execute **nslookup www.microsoft.com** and view the results. You should see google.com's corresponding IP address. Try the command with a few other well-known website domain names.
2. Execute **nslookup** to bring you to the `nslookup` shell, where you can enact more commands.
3. Press **?** and then press **Enter**. This displays the various commands you can use in the `nslookup` shell.
4. Execute **exit** to get out of the `nslookup` shell. We'll work with this command in more depth during Lesson 6.

Using ftp and telnet

In the following exercise, you will make network connections using FTP and Telnet. ***FTP*** is the File Transfer Protocol. It is an Application layer protocol as well as an application. The FTP command is used in the Command Prompt window to connect to FTP servers.

Whereas FTP is used to transfer files, ***Telnet*** is used to take control of a remote computer. Basically, a network administrator would connect to a remote computer, server, router, or switch by typing `telnet [IPAddress]`. This would either display a C:\ prompt of the remote system if connecting to a Windows computer, or a menu-based system if connecting to a router or switch. Telnet is an older deprecated protocol, and as such should be replaced with a more secure program such as SSH. Newer operating systems don't have the Telnet service installed by default, and do not allow the use of the command in the Command Prompt window.

MAKE NETWORK CONNECTIONS WITH FTP

GET READY. To make connections to remote systems with `ftp`, perform the following steps. An Internet connection is required.

1. Execute **ftp /?** and view the results.
2. Connect to an FTP server:
   a. Execute **ftp ftp.ipswitch.com** to make a connection to the IPswitch FTP server.
   b. When the FTP server prompts for a user (user name), type **anonymous** and press **Enter**.
   c. When prompted for a password, press **Enter**, as no password is necessary. Once logged in, this should look like Figure 5-18.

Figure 5-18

An FTP connection

```
Administrator: Command Prompt
C:\Windows\system32>ftp ftp.ipswitch.com
Connected to ftp.ipswitch.com.
220 ftp7.ipswitch.com X2 WS_FTP Server 7.5.1(15912000)
503 Command OPTS UTF8 ON not accepted during Connected
User (ftp.ipswitch.com:(none)): anonymous
331 Enter password
Password:
230 User logged in
ftp> ls
200 Command PORT succeed
```

d. Press the **?** key to display a list of commands you can use in the FTP shell.

3. Execute **dir** to show a list of folders and files within your current directory like how DOS would display them.
4. Execute **cd ipswitch** to change to the ipswitch directory.
5. Execute **dir** again. Examine the folders inside.
6. Execute **cd manuals** to change to the manuals directory. (Of course, longer path names can be used to save time if you know where you are going.)
7. Executing **get wsftp80.pdf** to download one of the manuals.

   The get command downloads the file and stores it in the working directory in Windows 10. Other versions of Windows store the file in the root of C: by default. This can be changed with the lcd command. View the manual in the root of C:. It should be a manual for WS_FTP Pro version 8 written in English.

   Execute **mget** to grab multiple files at once.

   Execute **put** or **mput** to upload a file. These commands can do this one at a time or more than one at a time, respectively.

   Although the ftp command is a small program, it is not your only option. If you can use a third-party GUI-based program, such as Filezilla, you will be able to work much faster.
8. When finished, execute **quit** to end the FTP session and return to the C:\ prompt.

Using Windows PowerShell

Windows PowerShell is a command-line interface used mainly by IT professionals to run cmdlets (pronounced command-lets), complete background jobs (processes or programs that run in the background without a user interface), and run scripts to perform administrative tasks. ***Cmdlets*** (pronounced *command-let*) are native commands available in Windows PowerShell.

Cmdlets follow a verb-noun naming pattern, such as get-process, get-service, get-help, set-date, or stop-process. Common verbs include:

- **Add:** Add a resource to a container, or attach an item to another item.
- **Get:** Retrieve data from a resource.
- **New:** Create a new resource.
- **Remove:** Delete a resource from a container.
- **Set:** Modify a resource, such as data or system parameters.
- **Start:** Begin an operation, such as a process or program.

Knowing the legal verbs and remembering the singular noun rule really helps guessing cmdlet names.

In the next exercise, you will work with Windows PowerShell, using the netsh command and the route command. ***Netsh*** is a built-in command-line scripting utility that enables you to display and modify network configurations of the local computer. ***Route*** enables you to display and modify network configurations of the local computer.

CONFIGURE IPv4 WITH WINDOWS POWERSHELL

GET READY. To configure IPv4 with the Windows PowerShell cmdlet, perform the following steps.

1. Click **Start**, type **PowerShell**, and then press **Enter**. The Windows PowerShell window opens, as shown in Figure 5-19.

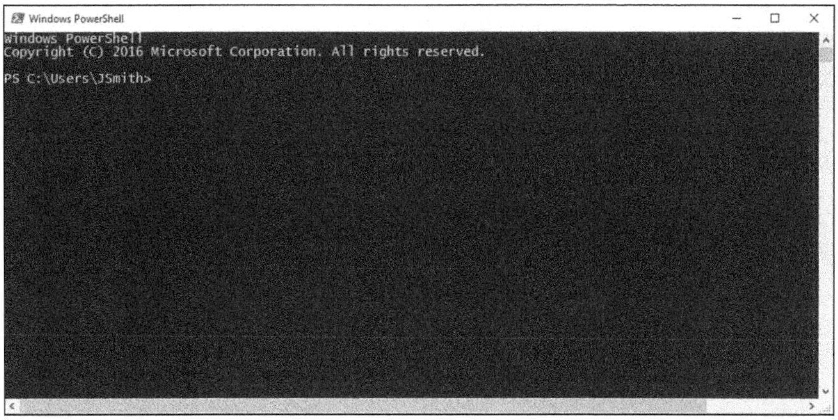

Figure 5-19

Opening a Windows PowerShell window

2. In the Windows PowerShell window, execute the following command, as shown in Figure 5-20:

```
New-NetIPAddress -InterfaceAlias "Local Area Network"
-IPv4Address 192.168.1.101 -PrefixLength "24" -DefaultGateway
192.168.1.1
```

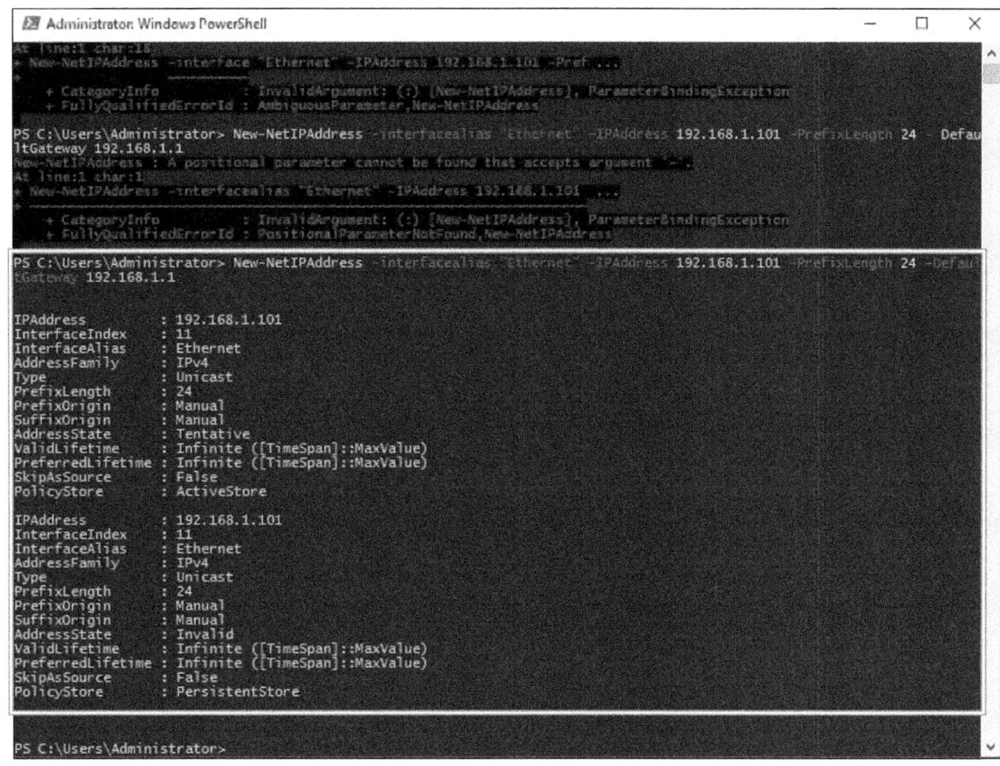

Figure 5-20

Configuring the IP address using the New-`NetIPAddress` cmdlet

3. To specify a DNS server, execute the following command:

```
Set-DnsClientServerAddress -InterfaceAlias "Ethernet"
-ServerAddresses "10.10.20.1","10.10.20.2"
```

4. Execute **ipconfig** to see the new address and DNS servers.
5. To change the adapter to DHCP-enabled, execute the following Windows PowerShell command:

```
Set-NetIPInterface -interfacealias "Ethernet" -Dhcp enabled
```

6. Execute **ipconfig** to verify that the address was removed.

CERTIFICATION READY
Which command is used to view static routes on a computer running Windows Server 2016?
Objective 2.2

The `route` command enables you to display and make changes to the local IP routing table of the computer. The local IP routing table displays IP connections to other networks as well as testing networks. Generally, a client computer will not have routes to other actual networks, mainly because a client computer is not normally intended for that role. Also, most client computers have only one network adapter. To create routes to other networks, a second network adapter is required. When a computer has two network adapters, it is known as a multihomed machine. If it has two and only two network adapters, it is specifically known as a dual-homed machine.

CONFIGURE ROUTING WITH THE ROUTE COMMAND

GET READY. To analyze and configure your system with the `route` command, perform the following steps.

1. Click **Start**, type **cmd**, and then press **Enter**.
2. In a Command Prompt window, execute **`route print`**. This should display results similar to Figure 5-21. This command gives the same result as `netstat -r`, but is more commonly used.

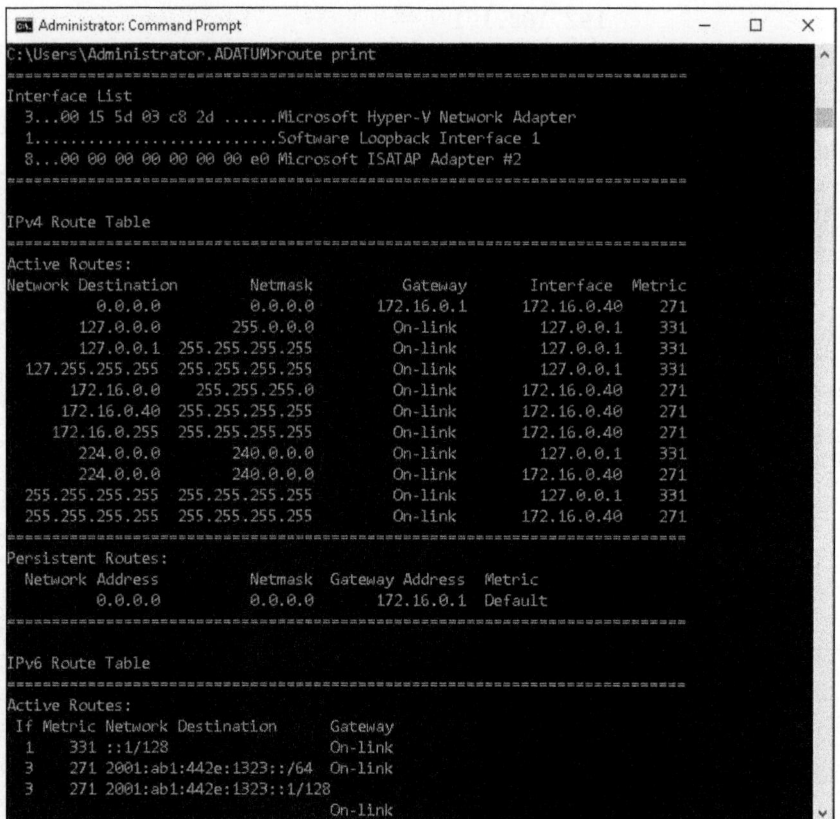

```
Administrator: Command Prompt
C:\Users\Administrator.ADATUM>route print
===========================================================================
Interface List
  3...00 15 5d 03 c8 2d ......Microsoft Hyper-V Network Adapter
  1...........................Software Loopback Interface 1
  8...00 00 00 00 00 00 00 e0 Microsoft ISATAP Adapter #2
===========================================================================

IPv4 Route Table
===========================================================================
Active Routes:
Network Destination        Netmask          Gateway       Interface  Metric
          0.0.0.0          0.0.0.0       172.16.0.1     172.16.0.40    271
        127.0.0.0        255.0.0.0         On-link        127.0.0.1    331
        127.0.0.1  255.255.255.255         On-link        127.0.0.1    331
  127.255.255.255  255.255.255.255         On-link        127.0.0.1    331
       172.16.0.0    255.255.255.0         On-link      172.16.0.40    271
      172.16.0.40  255.255.255.255         On-link      172.16.0.40    271
     172.16.0.255  255.255.255.255         On-link      172.16.0.40    271
        224.0.0.0        240.0.0.0         On-link        127.0.0.1    331
        224.0.0.0        240.0.0.0         On-link      172.16.0.40    271
  255.255.255.255  255.255.255.255         On-link        127.0.0.1    331
  255.255.255.255  255.255.255.255         On-link      172.16.0.40    271
===========================================================================
Persistent Routes:
  Network Address          Netmask  Gateway Address  Metric
          0.0.0.0          0.0.0.0       172.16.0.1  Default
===========================================================================

IPv6 Route Table
===========================================================================
Active Routes:
 If Metric Network Destination      Gateway
  1    331 ::1/128                  On-link
  3    271 2001:ab1:442e:1323::/64  On-link
  3    271 2001:ab1:442e:1323::1/128
                                    On-link
```

Figure 5-21
The `route print` command

This command shows a list of network adapters (or interfaces) on the local computer, including the MAC address and name of each. Then, the IPv4 route table is displayed. You will notice several networking connections. The Network Destination column tells you where the computer is trying to connect to. The Netmask is the subnet mask for that particular Network Destination. The Gateway is the IP address of the host that is used to gain access to the remote network. The Interface is the IP address of the network adapter that is making the connection to the other network. The Metric column specifies an integer between 1 and 9999; this metric is associated with the speed of the connection, the number of hops across networks, and so on. Normally, the lowest metric is selected for connections to other networks. This is not an issue if the computer (often a router) only has two or three connections.

If a packet is destined to any system on the 10.254.254.0 subnet, as shown on the second line, the packets will be forwarded to 10.254.254.112. The 0.0.0.0 network destination is the default gateway. If there is no matching route as listed in lines 2 through 12, the packets will be sent to the default gateway via the specified interface.

Single IP addresses will also get a route line item, as you can see in the third line. The local loopback network (127.0.0.0) and the actual local loopback IP address (127.0.0.1) also get route line items, and so on.

There is also an IPv6 route table if you are running IPv6. This table shows link-local and global unicast address line items.

3. Now, you will add and remove routes. Adding a router requires syntax similar to the `netsh` command you used to add IP addresses. In the following portion of this exercise, you will add a fictitious route using your local IP address as the interface that makes the connection to the remote network. Execute **`route add 192.168.1.0 mask 255.255.255.0 [LocalIPAddress]`**. An example of this is shown in Figure 5-22.

Figure 5-22

The `route add` command

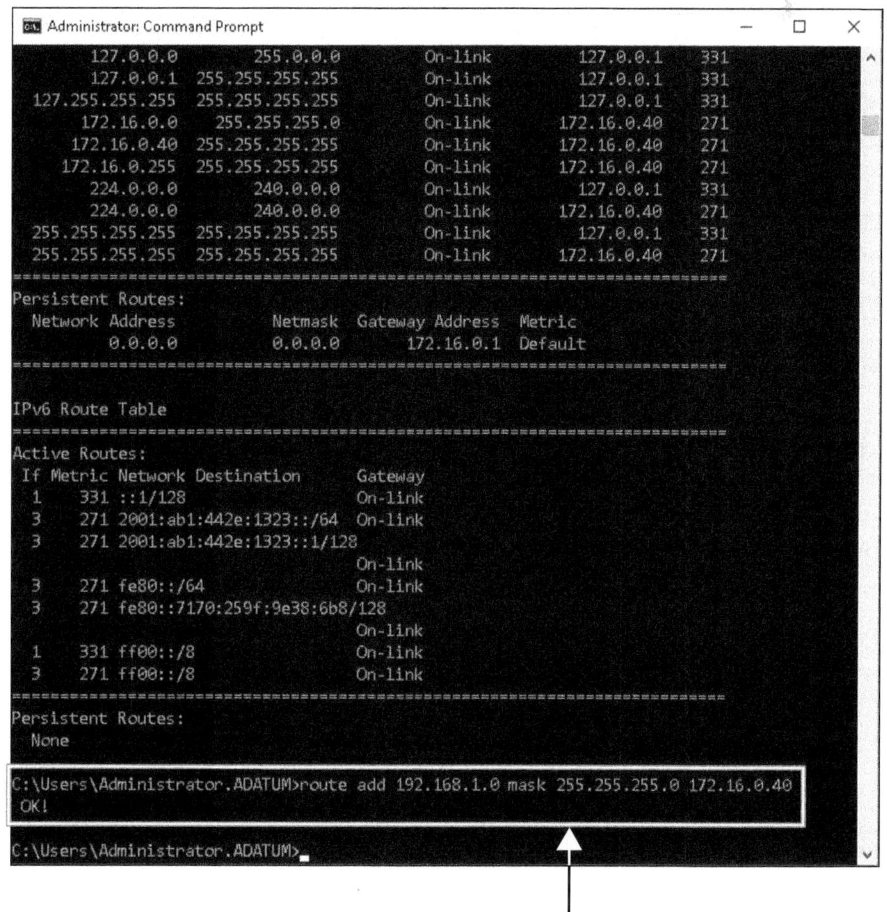

The network you are attempting to connect to is 192.168.1.0 and it has a default Class C subnet mask of 255.255.255.0. The word *mask* takes the place of *subnet mask*. Then, you use your local IP address, in this case 10.254.254.112, to connect to the remote network. After you press Enter, a simple OK! message appears. This means that the route has been added to the local routing table.

4. Execute the **route print** command. The new route in the IPv4 route table is shown in Figure 5-23.

Figure 5-23

The `route print` command with a new route

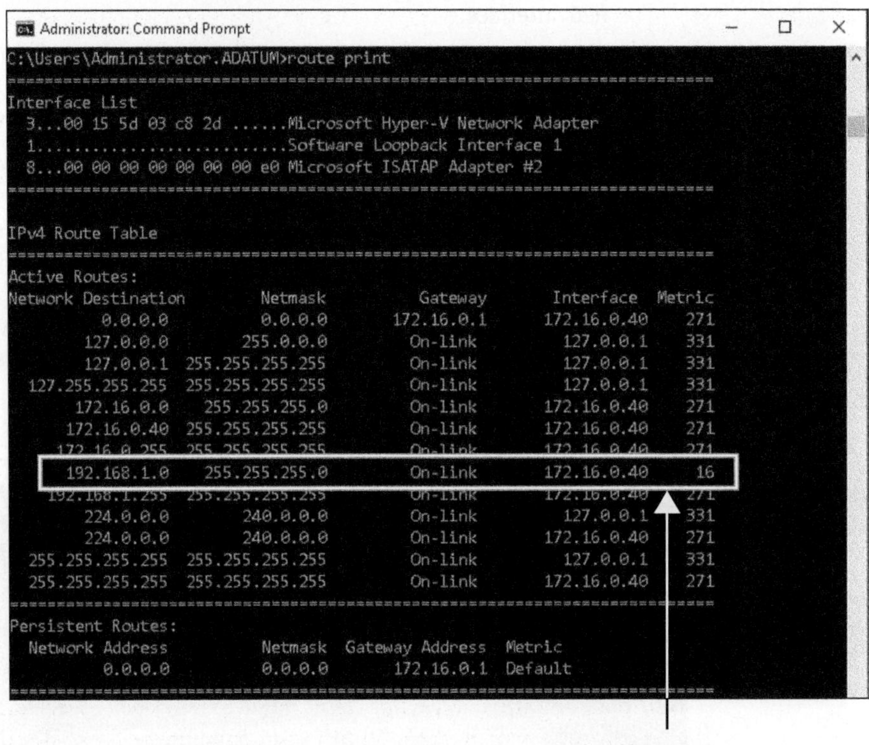

The new route is created for the network address: 192.168.1.0 as well as the broadcast address: 192.168.1.255.

5. Execute the **route delete 192.168.1.0 mask 255.255.255.0** command. This should remove the route you added previously. You could also remove all added routes with one command: **route -f**. But be careful with this command. Depending on the operating system and protocols used, and the network configuration, this could stop all network connections.

6. Execute **route print** and view the results. If you start to have any issues with your routing table, consider stopping and restarting TCP/IP, or restarting the computer. By the way, TCP/IP can be reset in the command line by typing the command: **netsh int ip reset c:\resetlog.txt**.

Generally, these added routes will be lost if TCP/IP or the computer is restarted. But routes can also be added in a persistent manner by using the `-p` option. The *p* stands for persistent; it preserves the route within the registry even if TCP/IP is restarted.

Again, the idea behind routing is to make connections to remote networks. Let's illustrate this with some network documentation, as shown in Figure 5-24.

Figure 5-24

Routing documentation

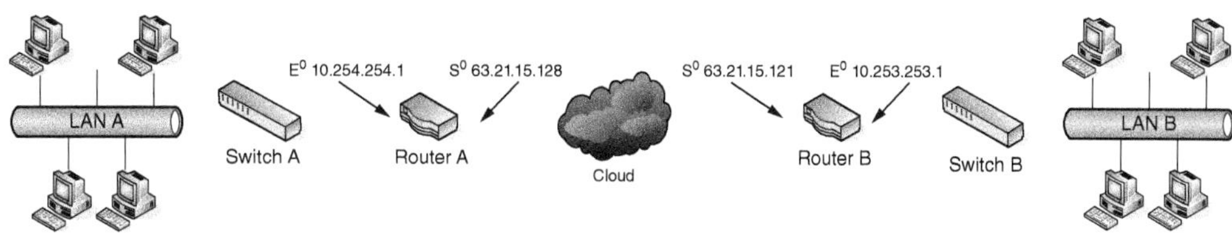

There are two LANs, LAN A and LAN B. By default, computers on these LANs would not be able to talk to each other because they are separated by routers and the "cloud" (whatever "the cloud" happens to be). To allow the computers on each LAN to talk to each other, a specific route would have to be created on each LAN's router. Each router has a LAN address (known as E^0) and a WAN address (known as S^0). These are also known as private and public addresses, respectively. Let's say that the subnet mask used on both LANs is 255.255.255.0, just like the CIDR setup we have been using. On router A, we would need the following syntax:

```
Route add 10.253.253.0 mask 255.255.255.0 63.21.15.121
```

This makes the connection to the 10.253.253.0 network utilizing the LAN B router's public address. This address is labeled as S^0 or the first serial connection, which are used to connect to different networks.

On router B, we would need the following syntax:

```
Route add 10.254.254.0 mask 255.255.255.0 63.21.15.128
```

This makes the connection to the 10.254.254.0 network utilizing the LAN A router's public address.

Once these two connections have been made, communications should be possible between the two LANs.

Now, if the routers are Windows servers, some additional configuration would be necessary prior to adding these route line items. Each server would need to be equipped with two network adapters, making them multihomed computers. Then, Routing and Remote Access would have to be configured to allow for IP forwarding. (Alternate software such as ISA could also be used.) Then, the route line items could be added.

If you were using conventional black box routers or appliances, TCP/IP protocols, such as RIP and OSPF, would be employed to streamline and automate the process:

- ***Routing Information Protocol (RIP)*** is a distance vector protocol that uses algorithms to decipher which route to send data packets.
- ***Open Shortest Path First (OSPF)*** is a link-state protocol that monitors the network for routers that have a change in their link-state, meaning whether they were turned off or on or restarted.
- ***Border Gateway Protocol (BGP)*** is a standardized exterior gateway protocol/distance vector protocol, which is often used with the Internet.

MORE INFORMATION

You'll learn more about routing protocols in Lesson 7.

Using net

In the next exercise, you will work with the `net` command. Although not really considered part of the TCP/IP command set, the ***net*** command can display all kinds of important networking data and allow you to configure various networking options such as services.

USE THE NET COMMAND

GET READY. To use the `net` command, perform the following steps.

1. Execute the **`net`** command and view the results. You will see options such as `view`, `user`, `session`, `start`, and `stop`. Each of these options can help you to analyze networking configurations and to make modifications.
2. Execute **`net view`** to show the computers on your immediate network, be it a workgroup or a domain. Each computer listed is preceded by a double backslash. This indicates a ***Universal Naming Convention (UNC)***. The UNC can be used when mapping drives and connecting to computers for other reasons.
3. Execute the **`net time \\[localcomputer]`** command. For example, **`net time \\lon-svr2`** is shown in Figure 5-25, displaying the current time of the computer. This command can also be used to synchronize time to other computers or time servers.

Figure 5-25

The `net time` command

4. Execute **`net user`** to display the user accounts on the computer.
5. Execute **`net stop themes`** to stop the themes service, which controls your desktop themes.
6. Execute **`net start themes`** to restart the service.

This only scratches the surface of what the `net` command can do. It can be very useful to network administrators. Examine some of the other options by typing `net` followed by the option and then /?, for example, `net time /?`.

Table 5-1 provides the descriptions of the TCP/IP commands covered in this lesson.

Table 5-1

Summary of TCP/IP Commands

Command	Description
Ipconfig	The ipconfig command displays information pertaining to your network adapter, namely TCP/IP configurations.
Ping	Ping is used to test the existence of other hosts on the network.
Netstat	The netstat command is used to display active TCP (or UDP) connections.
Nbtstat	Nbtstat displays NetBIOS over TCP/IP statistics for local and remote computers.
Tracert	The tracert command shows paths to a destination on another network. It does this by pinging each step along the way three times.
Pathping	Pathping is similar to tracert, but also computes the degree of packet loss.
NSLookup	Nslookup displays information about DNS names and their corresponding IP addresses, and can be used to diagnose DNS servers.
FTP	FTP is the File Transfer Protocol. It is an Application layer protocol as well as an application. The FTP command is used in the Command Prompt window to connect to FTP servers.
Telnet	Telnet is used to take control of a remote computer via the command line.
Netsh	Netsh is a built-in command-line scripting utility that enables you to display and modify network configurations of the local computer.
Route	Route enables you to display and make changes to the local IP routing table of the computer.

SKILL SUMMARY

In this lesson, you learned:

- The Command Prompt window is the Microsoft version of a command-line interface (CLI). Just about anything you can accomplish in the GUI can also be done in the Command Prompt window, and when it comes to TCP/IP commands, the Command Prompt window can be even more effective.
- Ipconfig and ping are some of the best friends to a network administrator. These basic TCP/IP commands can help to analyze and troubleshoot networking issues that might occur. They also offer a certain amount of configurative ability as well as the ability to create performance baselines.
- Nslookup displays information about DNS names and their corresponding IP addresses and can be used to diagnose DNS servers. An Internet connection is required.
- Netstat and nbtstat commands both show statistics of the network connection, but netstat centers on the local computer, whereas nbtstat can also show statistics for remote machines.

- To show network paths, you would use the `tracert` and `pathping` commands.
- Windows PowerShell is a command-line interface used mainly by IT professionals to run cmdlets (pronounced command-lets), complete background jobs (processes or programs that run in the background without a user interface), and run scripts to perform administrative tasks.
- The `net` command can display all kinds of important networking data and allow you to configure various networking options such as services.

■ Knowledge Assessment

Multiple Choice

Select the correct answer for each of the following questions.

1. When troubleshooting a network connectivity problem, the following command results appear. Which of the following commands generated these results?

```
Request timed out.
Request timed out.
Request timed out.
Request timed out.
Packets: Sent = 4, Received = 0, Lost = 4 (100% loss),
```

   a. `ipconfig`
   b. `netstat`
   c. `ping`
   d. `nbtstat`

2. Which of the following commands should be used to find the MAC address of a Windows computer?

   a. `ipconfig`
   b. `ipconfig /all`
   c. `ipconfig /release`
   d. `ipconfig /flushdns`

3. The administrators at Proseware, Inc., need to decipher the command results listed below. Which command generated these results?

```
Active Connections
  Proto  Local Address          Foreign Address        State
  TCP    0.0.0.0:80             0.0.0.0:0              LISTENING
  TCP    0.0.0.0:135            0.0.0.0:0              LISTENING
  TCP    0.0.0.0:445            0.0.0.0:0              LISTENING
  TCP    10.254.254.205:139     0.0.0.0:0              LISTENING
  TCP    127.0.0.1:2804         127.0.0.1:49159        ESTABLISHED
```

```
UDP    0.0.0.0:123           *:*
UDP    0.0.0.0:500           *:*
UDP    0.0.0.0:2190          *:*
UDP    0.0.0.0:3702          *:*
UDP    0.0.0.0:3702          *:*
UDP    0.0.0.0:4500          *:*
UDP    0.0.0.0:62038         *:*
UDP    10.254.254.205:137    *:*
UDP    10.254.254.205:138    *:*
```

a. `netstat`
b. `nbtstat`
c. `netstat -an`
d. `nbtstat -an`

4. Which type of table is this?

Network Destination	Netmask	Gateway	Interface
0.0.0.0	0.0.0.0	10.254.254.1	10.254.254.205
10.254.254.0	255.255.255.0	On-link	10.254.254.205
10.254.254.205	255.255.255.255		10.254.254.205
127.0.0.0	255.0.0.0	On-link	127.0.0.1

a. ARP table
b. DNS table
c. Local ARP table
d. Local routing table

5. Which of the following commands should be used to continuously ping a computer?

a. `ping -n`
b. `ping -t`
c. `ping -l`
d. `ping 127.0.0.1`

6. When troubleshooting a computer that cannot obtain the proper IP address from a DHCP server, which of the following commands should be used first?

a. `ipconfig /release`
b. `ipconfig /renew`
c. `ipconfig /displaydns`
d. `ipconfig /source=dhcp`

7. The following results appear in the Command Prompt window. Which command generated these results?

```
Resolved By Broadcast     = 0
Resolved By Name Server   = 0
Registered By Broadcast   = 9
Registered By Name Server = 0
```

a. `nbtstat -r`
b. `nbtstat -RR`
c. `nbtstat -R`
d. `nbtstat -s`

8. A computer can ping other computers but it cannot connect to websites. Examine the following `ipconfig` results and select the best explanation as to why this has occurred.

```
IPv4 Address. . . . . . . . . . . : 10.254.254.1
Subnet Mask . . . . . . . . . . . : 255.255.255.0
Default Gateway . . . . . . . . . : 10.254.254.255
DNS Servers . . . . . . . . . . . : 127.0.0.1
```

a. The subnet mask is incorrect.
b. The IP address is incorrect.
c. The default gateway is incorrect.
d. The DNS server is incorrect.

9. A user cannot connect to the 192.168.1.0 network. Review the following `ipconfig` results and select the best explanation as to why this has occurred.

```
Windows IP Configuration
    Host Name . . . . . . . . . . . . : Computer1
    Primary Dns Suffix . . . . . . . :
    Node Type . . . . . . . . . . . . : Hybrid
    IP Routing Enabled . . . . . . . . : No
    WINS Proxy Enabled . . . . . . . . : No
Ethernet adapter lan:
    Connection-specific DNS Suffix . . :
    Description . . . . . . . . . . . : Intel(R) 82566DC-2 Gigabit
    Network Connection
    Physical Address . . . . . . . . . : 00-1C-C0-A1-55-16
    DHCP Enabled . . . . . . . . . . . : No
    Autoconfiguration Enabled . . . . : Yes
    IPv4 Address . . . . . . . . . . . : 10.254.254.105(Preferred)
    Subnet Mask . . . . . . . . . . . : 255.255.255.0
    Default Gateway . . . . . . . . . : 10.254.254.1
    DNS Servers . . . . . . . . . . . : 10.255.254.1
```

a. The MAC address is incorrect.
b. The DNS server address is incorrect.
c. The default gateway address is incorrect.
d. The IP address is incorrect.

10. When troubleshooting a network connectivity problem, the following command results appear. Which command was used to acquire these results?

```
1     15 ms     19 ms     19 ms   10.21.80.1
2     12 ms     22 ms     12 ms   208.59.252.1
```

```
3    152 ms    216 ms    149 ms  207.172.15.38
4     14 ms     24 ms     37 ms  207.172.19.222
5     21 ms     16 ms     25 ms  207.172.19.103
6     17 ms     23 ms     30 ms  207.172.9.126
7     15 ms     14 ms     15 ms  72.14.238.232
8     15 ms     35 ms     18 ms  209.85.241.148
9     30 ms     23 ms     44 ms  66.249.91.104
```

a. `ipconfig`
b. `netstat`
c. `tracert`
d. `pathping`

Fill in the Blank

Fill in the correct answer in the blank space provided.

1. The _____ command was used to retrieve the following results:

```
Reply from 10.254.254.1: bytes=32 time=1ms TTL=64
Reply from 10.254.254.1: bytes=32 time<1ms TTL=64
Reply from 10.254.254.1: bytes=32 time<1ms TTL=64
Reply from 10.254.254.1: bytes=32 time<1ms TTL=64
Reply from 10.254.254.1: bytes=32 time<1ms TTL=64
Reply from 10.254.254.1: bytes=32 time<1ms TTL=64
Reply from 10.254.254.1: bytes=32 time<1ms TTL=64
Reply from 10.254.254.1: bytes=32 time<1ms TTL=64
Reply from 10.254.254.1: bytes=32 time<1ms TTL=64
Reply from 10.254.254.1: bytes=32 time<1ms TTL=64
```

2. A coworker is unable to finish troubleshooting a computer he was working on. Before leaving, he tells you that the following results took nearly five minutes to acquire and he requests that you *not* delete them. The screen that displays the following results was produced by the _____ command:

```
C:\Windows\system32>pathping msn.com
Tracing route to msn.com [13.82.28.61]
over a maximum of 30 hops:
  0  Pat10.hsd1.ca.comcast.net. [192.168.3.101]
  1  DARK2WING3DUCK [192.168.3.1]
  2  10.0.0.1
  3  96.120.14.61
  4  ae214-rur01.sacramento.ca.ccal.comcast.net [68.87.212.193]
  5  ae-2-ar01.sacramento.ca.ccal.comcast.net [162.151.18.133]
```

```
  6  be-33667-cr01.9greatoaks.ca.ibone.comcast.net [68.86.93.25]
  7  hu-0-12-0-5-pe01.9greatoaks.ca.ibone.comcast.net
     [68.86.87.102]
  8  50.242.151.142
  9  be-67-0.ibr01.bay.ntwk.msn.net [104.44.9.183]
 10  be-5-0.ibr01.was02.ntwk.msn.net [104.44.4.200]
 11  ae62-0.bl2-96c-1a.ntwk.msn.net [104.44.8.171]
 12     *        *        *
Computing statistics for 275 seconds...
            Source to Here   This Node/Link
Hop  RTT    Lost/Sent = Pct  Lost/Sent = Pct  Address
  0
   Pat10.hsd1.ca.comcast.net. [192.168.3.101]
                                0/ 100 =  0%   |
  1    0ms     0/ 100 =  0%    0/ 100 =  0%  DARK2WING3DUCK
   [192.168.3.1]
                                0/ 100 =  0%   |
  2    1ms     0/ 100 =  0%    0/ 100 =  0%  10.0.0.1
                                0/ 100 =  0%   |
  3   11ms     0/ 100 =  0%    0/ 100 =  0%  96.120.14.61
                                0/ 100 =  0%   |
  4   12ms     0/ 100 =  0%    0/ 100 =  0%  ae214-
   rur01.sacramento.ca.ccal.comcast.net [68.87.212.193]
                                0/ 100 =  0%   |
  5   12ms     0/ 100 =  0%    0/ 100 =  0%  ae-2-
   ar01.sacramento.ca.ccal.comcast.net [162.151.18.133]
                                0/ 100 =  0%   |
  6   16ms     0/ 100 =  0%    0/ 100 =  0%  be-33667-
   cr01.9greatoaks.ca.ibone.comcast.net [68.86.93.25]
                                0/ 100 =  0%   |
  7   14ms     0/ 100 =  0%    0/ 100 =  0%  hu-0-12-0-5-
   pe01.9greatoaks.ca.ibone.comcast.net [68.86.87.102]
                                0/ 100 =  0%   |
  8   15ms     0/ 100 =  0%    0/ 100 =  0%  50.242.151.142
                                0/ 100 =  0%   |
  9  ---     100/ 100 =100%  100/ 100 =100%  be-67-
   0.ibr01.bay.ntwk.msn.net [104.44.9.183]
                                0/ 100 =  0%   |
```

```
10   ---        100/ 100 =100%    100/ 100 =100%  be-5-
   0.ibr01.was02.ntwk.msn.net [104.44.4.200]
                                  0/ 100 =   0%   |
11   85ms       0/ 100 =   0%     0/ 100 =   0%  ae62-0.b12-96c-
   1a.ntwk.msn.net [104.44.8.171]
Trace complete.
C:\Windows\system32>
```

3. The IP address 192.168.1.1 needs to be added to the network adapter via the command line. It also needs to have a gateway address of 192.168.1.100. The command that needs to be executed in the Windows PowerShell command window is ______.
4. An administrator is troubleshooting a computer that is making strange connections to the Internet all on its own. The ______ command will show the network sessions to various computers on the Internet.
5. A manager wants to download manuals from an FTP site. He wants to do it via the command line. The ______ command will allow him to accomplish this.
6. A coworker typed the ______ command to find out the IP address of a domain name, as shown in the following results:

```
DNS request timed out.
    timeout was 2 seconds.
Server:  UnKnown
Address:  10.254.254.1

Non-authoritative answer:
Name:    google.com
Address:  66.249.91.104
```

7. An administrator is troubleshooting a server and decides to refresh the NetBIOS names. She types the ______ command to yield the following results:

```
The NetBIOS names registered by this computer have been refreshed.
```

8. An administrator is simulating network traffic to a remote host. The following are the results of the ______ command:

```
Reply from 10.254.254.1: bytes=1500 time=2ms TTL=64
Reply from 10.254.254.1: bytes=1500 time<1ms TTL=64
Reply from 10.254.254.1: bytes=1500 time<1ms TTL=64
Reply from 10.254.254.1: bytes=1500 time<1ms TTL=64
Ping statistics for 10.254.254.1:
    Packets: Sent = 4, Received = 4, Lost = 0 (0% loss),
Approximate round trip times in milli-seconds:
    Minimum = 0ms, Maximum = 2ms, Average = 0ms
```

9. The DNS cache of a computer needs to be emptied and reconnected to the nearest DNS server. To do this, the ______ commands should be executed.

10. You are hired to troubleshoot a client's network. The client is using the following IP network scheme:

IP network: 10.254.254.0
Subnet mask: 255.255.255.0

The client cannot access the 10.253.253.0 network. On the server, which is also acting as the router between the two networks, you execute the _____ command, which shows the following results. The reason the client cannot access the 10.253.253.0 network is because _____.

Network Destination	Netmask	Gateway	Interface
0.0.0.0	0.0.0.0	10.254.254.1	10.254.254.205
10.254.254.0	255.255.255.0	On-link	10.254.254.205
10.254.254.205	255.255.255.255		10.254.254.205
127.0.0.0	255.0.0.0	On-link	127.0.0.1

Business Case Scenarios

Scenario 5-1: Connecting to an FTP Server

Proseware, Inc., requires that you download several files from an FTP server. Details follow:

Server name: ftp.proseware.com

File names: manual1.txt, manual2.txt, manual3.txt, manual4.txt

List the commands you should use in the command line to connect to the fictitious FTP server and download the files.

Scenario 5-2: Troubleshooting TCP/IP Results

Proseware, Inc., cannot connect a particular computer to the 10.253.253.0 network, either to the 10.253.253.1 router or any other host on that network.

One of their technicians managed to get the following results within two different command-line windows:

Results #1:

```
IPv4 Address . . . . . . . . . . . : 10.254.254.205
Subnet Mask . . . . . . . . . . . : 255.255.255.0
Default Gateway . . . . . . . . . : 10.254.254.1
```

Results #2:

```
Pinging 10.253.253.1 with 32 bytes of data:
Request timed out.
Request timed out.
Request timed out.
Request timed out.
Packets: Sent = 4, Received = 0, Lost = 4 (100% loss),
```

1. Which commands were issued?
2. Describe the problem.
3. Describe how to resolve this problem.

Scenario 5-3: Documenting a Basic Wide Area Network

A client wants you to design a basic WAN with two LANs that can communicate with each other. They would like the following configuration:

LAN A

- 192.168.1.0 network
- 255.255.255.0 subnet mask
- A router with the following configurations
  a. LAN address: 192.168.1.250
  b. WAN address: 18.52.197.1

LAN B

- 192.168.2.0 network
- 255.255.255.0 subnet mask
- A router with the following configurations
  a. LAN address: 192.168.2.199
  b. WAN address: 18.52.197.2

Create network documentation that shows the LANs, their central connecting device such as a switch, and the router. Then, show the command syntax you would use in the command line to make the routed connections between the LANs.

Scenario 5-4: Using Advanced Ping

Proseware, Inc., wants you to set up a baseline to a server. You decide to implement the `ping` command and its various options.

1. Which syntax is used to set up daily ping tests to a server with the IP address 10.254.254.1 that will consist of 1,000 ICMP echoes?
2. Which syntax is used to set up daily ping tests to a server with the same IP address that will consist of 100 1,500-byte ICMP packets?

Describe how to configure these so that they run every day and are outputted to a text file.

Workplace Ready

TCP/IP Command Table

TCP/IP commands are a huge part of a network administrator's life. The ability to use them quickly and efficiently is based on the knowledge of the user. Memorization of the commands, and especially the options of the commands, is imperative. Appropriate and effective usage of the Command Prompt window is also vital.

Research the commands listed after the table and create your own table that describes them and each of their options (for example, `ping -t`). In the table, include a column that describes why the command (and its option) would be used.

For example:

`Ping`	`-t`	Pings a remote computer continuously	Used to determine long-term connectivity. Works well with cabling tests.
`Ipconfig`	`/all`	Shows in-depth information about a network adapter	Can help to find details such as the MAC address, DNS server, and so on.

`ftp`

`ipconfig`

`nbtstat`

`net` command

`netstat`

`nslookup`

`pathping`

`ping`

`route`

`telnet`

`tracert`

You will note that navigation in Windows can be slightly different in the various versions. Once you are finished assembling the table, spend some time working with each of the commands on as many of the following operating systems that you can access:

- Windows 7
- Windows 10
- Windows Server 2012 R2 or 2016

Working with Networking Services

LESSON 6

OBJECTIVE DOMAIN MATRIX

Skills/Concepts	Objective Domain Description	Objective Domain Number
Setting Up Common Networking Services	Understand networking services	3.5
Introducing Remote Administration	Understand networking services	3.5
Defining More Networking Services	Understand networking services	3.5
	Understand wide area networks (WANs)	1.3
Defining Name Resolution Techniques	Understand names resolution	3.4

KEY TERMS

acknowledge
authentication header (AH)
discovery
Domain Name System (DNS)
DORA
Dynamic Host Configuration Protocol (DHCP)
Encapsulating Security Payload (ESP)
Internet Protocol Security (IPsec)
offering
Remote Access Service (RAS)
Remote Assistance
Remote Desktop Protocol (RDP)
Remote Desktop Services
RemoteApp
request
Routing and Remote Access Service (RRAS)
security association (SA)
Terminal Services
Windows Internet Naming Service (WINS)

A network engineer loves networking services. Services, such as DHCP and DNS, busy at work are the equivalent of the beautiful sound of the hammer to a building contractor. These services are what make the networking world go 'round.

Proseware, Inc., expects you, as the network engineer, to set up a smart, efficient set of networking services, including DHCP, DNS, Terminal Services, and even WINS for its older devices.

It is important to understand how to configure servers to run the services and how to configure clients to connect appropriately to those services. This should be understood from a theoretical standpoint as well as a practical one. Testing, troubleshooting, and performance baselining are all important aspects of network services as well.

In this lesson, you will learn how to install and configure DHCP, DNS, WINS, and Terminal Services, and we'll discuss other technologies, such as RAS and IPsec. By mastering these skills and concepts, you will gain another level of experience on your way to becoming a network engineer.

■ Setting Up Common Networking Services

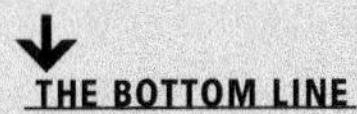

Networking services, such as DHCP and Terminal Services, are common in Microsoft networking environments. These help to automate processes that would otherwise be done manually by a network administrator. They also allow greater connectivity for a much broader group of computing solutions.

This section demonstrates the basics of DHCP and Terminal Services in action. Some of the popular network services are shown in Table 6-1.

Table 6-1

Summary of Networking Services

COMMAND	DESCRIPTION
DHCP	Short for the Dynamic Host Configuration Protocol. It allows properly configured client computers to obtain IP addresses automatically from a DHCP server.
Terminal Services	A type of thin client terminal server computing. It allows client computers to connect to and take control of a server. Thin client computers *and* PCs can connect to servers running Terminal Services/Remote Desktop Services.
Routing and Remote Access Service	A network service in Windows Server 2008 and higher. It allows an administrator to configure dial-up remote access servers, VPN servers, IP routing, and NAT.
IPsec	A protocol within the TCP/IP suite that encrypts and authenticates IP packets. It is designed to secure any application traffic because it resides on the Network layer.
DNS	A worldwide service that resolves host names to IP addresses. This facilitates proper communication between computers. A hierarchy of DNS servers communicates with each other in an effort to teach each other their name resolutions.
WINS	A service that resolves NetBIOS names to IP addresses. It is the Microsoft version of the NetBIOS Name Service (NBNS) combined with a name server.

Working with the Dynamic Host Configuration Protocol (DHCP)

The Dynamic Host Configuration Protocol (DHCP) sends IP information to clients automatically, making configuration of IP on the network easier and automated. It uses a four-step process known as DORA when disseminating IP addresses. DHCP uses ports 67 and 68.

CERTIFICATION READY
How is a DHCP network set up?
Objective 3.5

To better understand how to work with DHCP on the server and on the client side, it is necessary to discuss how DHCP works.

Dynamic Host Configuration Protocol (DHCP) allows properly configured client computers to obtain IP addresses automatically from a DHCP server. This is done so that a network administrator does not have to manually configure IP addresses on all of the computers on the network individually. The DHCP server takes care of this task quickly and automatically. This protocol reduces the amount of system administration, allowing devices to be added to the network with little or no manual intervention.

The IP information obtained might include:

- IP addresses
- Subnet masks
- Gateway addresses
- DNS server addresses
- Other advanced options

A server or appliance runs the DHCP service and is configured to send the IP information to the clients. Usually, it is client computers that benefit from this service; however, sometimes servers also obtain IP information automatically. This depends on the type of server, and as far as DHCP goes, the server acquiring the IP address automatically also becomes a client. For example, a file server may host files, but may also be a client of a DHCP server. There are a few types of hosts that can be excluded from the scope of DHCP, including routers, firewalls, and some servers such as domain controllers. The beauty of a DHCP device is that it is fast, efficient, and should not cause an IP conflict.

Let's talk about how DHCP works. DHCP sessions use a four-step process known as ***DORA***. The four steps are:

- ***Discovery***: The client computer broadcasts out to the network in order to find a DHCP server.
- ***Offering***: The DHCP server sends out a unicast "offering" of an IP address to the client computer.
- ***Request***: The client broadcasts to all servers that it has accepted the offer.
- ***Acknowledge***: The DHCP server sends a final unicast to the client, including the IP information that the client will use.

Normally, when a computer first tries to obtain an IP address, it goes through all four of the stages. However, if a client already has an address and wants to renew it (within certain time parameters), only the last two steps are necessary. For example, if the client computer ran the `ipconfig/release` and `ipconfig/renew` commands, only the request and acknowledge steps would occur. This is because the computer retains information about the IP address within the registry. If the IP address's lease hasn't run out, the information can be taken directly from the client's registry, and as long as the server agrees to the computer reusing the address, everything will work the same as it did previously.

Let's discuss the DHCP ports. DHCP works on two ports, port 67 and port 68. Servers run inbound port 67 to listen to client requests in order to hand out IP addresses. Clients run inbound port 68 to accept the data from the server.

In the following exercise, you will learn how to configure DHCP on the server and on the client side. You will be using Windows Server 2016 as the DHCP server. This server will have a static IP address assigned to its network adapter. Installing a DHCP server consists of the following:

- Installing the DHCP service
- Authorizing the server
- Configuring an IP scope
- Activating the scope
- Configuring advanced IP options (optional)

CONFIGURE DHCP

GET READY. To configure DHCP on the server and on the client side, perform the following steps.

1. Go to your Windows server. As previously mentioned, you are using a Windows Server 2016 computer as your DHCP server. Configure the DHCP server statically with the IP address: 192.168.1.100.
2. Install and configure the DHCP service.
   a. Go to the Server Manager console. You can get to this in various ways, for example by clicking **Start > Server Manager.**
   b. Click **Manage > Add Roles and Features.**
   c. In the Add Roles and Features Wizard, on the Before You Begin page, click **Next.**
   d. On the Installation Type page, the Role-based or feature-based installation option is already selected. Click **Next.**
   e. On the Server Selection page, select the server you want to install the DHCP Server on and then click **Next.**
   f. On the Server Roles page, select the **DHCP Server** option. When you are prompted to add features that are required for DHCP Server, click **Add Features.** Then, click **Next.**
   g. On the Features page, click **Next.**
   h. On the DHCP Server page, click **Next.**
   i. On the Confirmation page, click **Install.**
   j. On the Results page, click the **Complete DHCP configuration** option.
   k. In the DHCP Post-Install Configuration Wizard, on the Description page, click **Next.**
   l. On the Authorization page, in the User Name text box, type the user name of a domain administrator using the ***<domainname>*|*<username>*** format, and click **Commit.**
   m. On the Summary page, click **Close.**
   n. Back on the Results page, click **Close.**

3. Create and activate a DHCP scope:
   a. In Server Manager, click **Tools > DHCP**.
   b. In the DHCP console, expand the server node and click the **IPv4** node, as shown in Figure 6-1.

Figure 6-1

Adding a DHCP scope

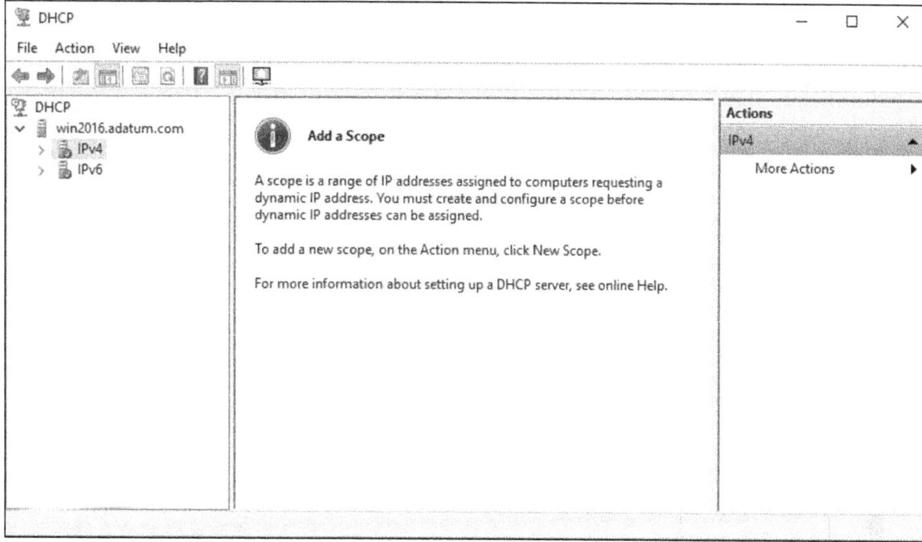

   c. A scope is a range of IP addresses that can be handed out to clients. Right-click the **IPv4** node and choose **New Scope**.
   d. In the New Scope Wizard, on the Welcome page, click **Next**.
   e. On the Scope Name page, in the Name text box, type a descriptive name, such as **Proseware Scope1**, and click **Next**.
   f. On the IP Address Range page (as shown in Figure 6-2), type the following and click **Next**:

      Start IP address: 192.168.1.150

      End IP address: 192.168.1.199

      Length: 24

      Subnet mask: 255.255.255.0
   g. On the Add Exclusions and Delay page, click **Next**.
   h. The lease will specify the amount of time a client will own the IP address when assigned. The default lease duration is 8 days. On the Lease Duration page, click **Next**.
   i. On the Configure DHCP Options page, click **Next**.
   j. On the Router (Default Gateway) page, in the IP address text box, type **192.168.1.1** and then click **Add**. Click **Next**.
   k. On the Domain Name and DNS Servers page, click **Next**.
   l. On the WINS Servers page, click **Next**.
   m. On the Activate Scope page, the Yes, I want to activate this scope now option is already selected. Click **Next**.
   n. On the Completing the New Scope Wizard page, click **Finish**.

      At this point, the DHCP server is ready to hand out IP addresses to client computers.

Figure 6-2

Specifying IP address range

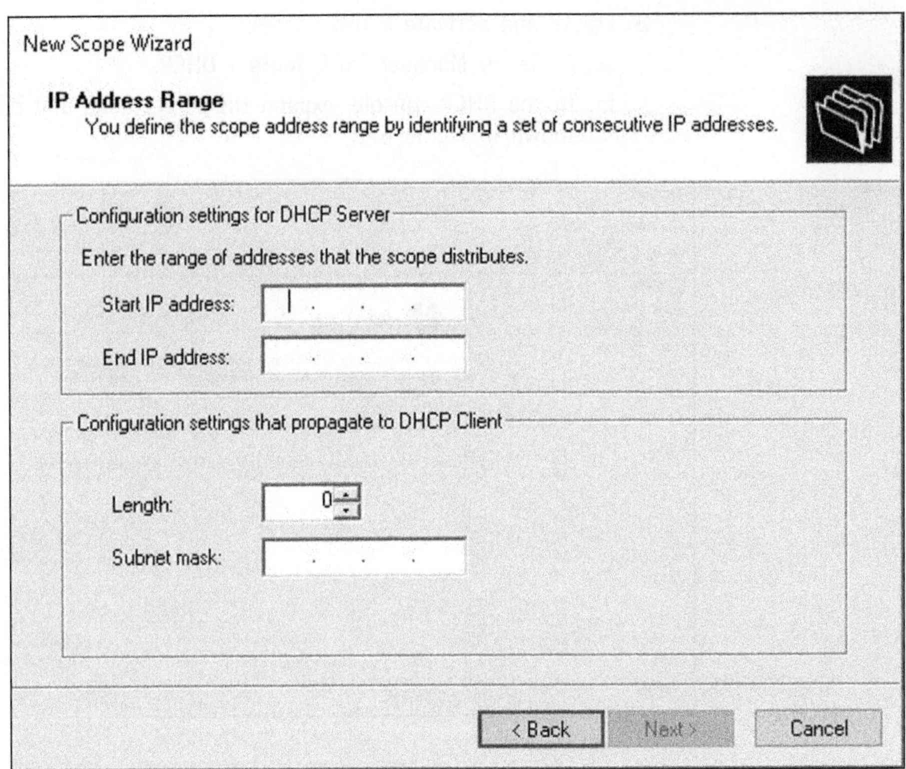

4. Go to a Windows client computer and obtain an IP address automatically:
   a. Access the IPv4 Properties dialog box for the wired network adapter.
   b. Select the **Obtain an IP address automatically** radio button.
   c. Click **OK** for all dialog boxes.
   d. Open the Command Prompt window and execute **ipconfig /all**. You should obtain an IP address automatically from the list of IP addresses in the DHCP server's IP scope. Most likely, it will be the first one on the list: 192.168.1.150.
   e. If you cannot obtain an IP address, check your configuration settings on the server. Also, on the client, you can try to execute **ipconfig /release** and **ipconfig /renew** to retry obtaining an IP address. In some cases, you might obtain an IP address from another DHCP device or server. If this is the case, remove that device from the network. If you see your client has obtained an address on the 169.254.0.0 network, then APIPA has intervened and self-assigned an IP address. See the next exercise about how to disable APIPA.
   f. Test your new IP address by pinging the IP address of the DHCP server and another client on the network. Disable any firewalls that might block pings.
5. When you are finished, return the client computers to normal. If necessary, access the server and stop the DHCP service.

Sometimes, APIPA can get in the way of a client obtaining an IP address properly, for example, if a client attempts to obtain an IP address from a DHCP server, but the DHCP server is too busy. At that point, APIPA self-assigns an IP address to the client computer, and the computer is stuck with that address until the `ipconfig/release` and `/renew` commands are run from the command line. Depending on the version of Windows and the configuration, this still might not be enough. When you see an IP address of 169.254.x.x, you know that the client has self-assigned an IP address with the help of APIPA. This shouldn't happen often, but you never know, so let's show how to disable APIPA in the Registry.

DISABLE APIPA

GET READY. To disable APIPA in the registry, perform the following steps.

1. Access the registry by pressing **Windows+R** on the keyboard and typing **regedit.exe**.
2. Navigate the following path:

   Computer > HKEY_LOCAL_MACHINE > SYSTEM > CurrentControlSet > Services > Tcpip > Parameters > Interfaces
3. In the Interfaces subkey, find the network adapter that you want to disable APIPA on. The best way to do this is to find out the current IP address of the network adapter with the `ipconfig` command, then locate that adapter in the registry by searching through each of the interfaces one at a time and examining the IPAddress entry.
4. Right-click the right pane and choose **New > DWORD**.
5. Name the new dword **ipautoconfigurationenabled**.
6. Then, make sure the entry is set to 0. This is the disabled setting. An example of this is shown in Figure 6-3.

Figure 6-3

Disabling APIPA

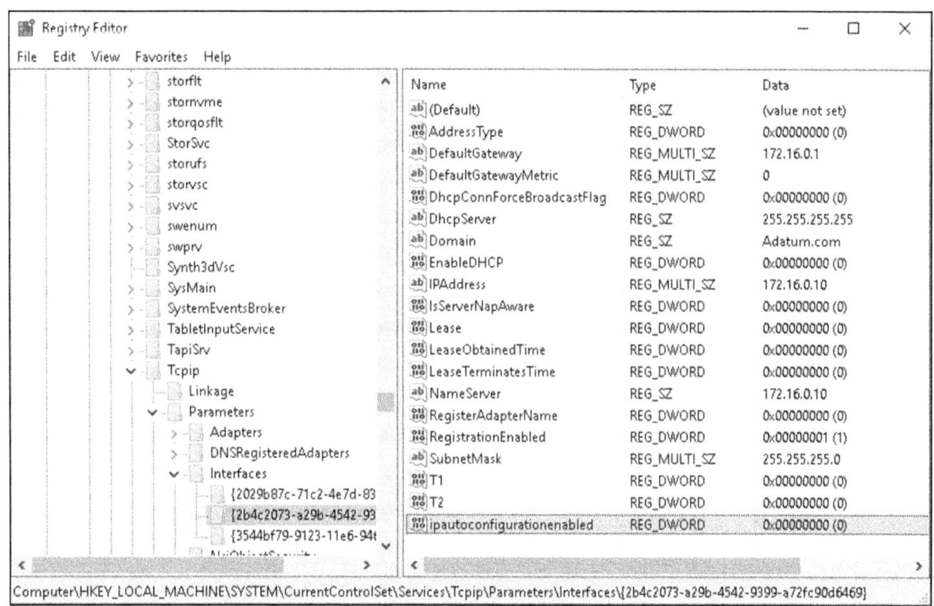

Once APIPA is disabled, it will not interfere with the client's network adapter attempting to obtain an IP address. However, this does not ensure that the client receives an IP address. Always verify that the DHCP server is configured properly and connected to the network.

■ Introducing Remote Administration

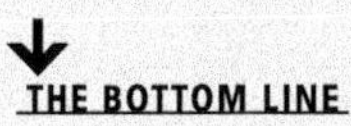

THE BOTTOM LINE

With early networks, users utilized dumb terminals (systems consisting of a monitor and keyboard without a processor) to connect to a mainframe. Later, computers could use Telnet to connect to a server and execute commands at a command prompt. Terminal Services was relabeled as ***Remote Desktop Services***, starting with Window Server 2008 R2. Remote Desktop Services is one of the components of Microsoft Windows that allows a user to access applications and data on a remote computer over a network.

CERTIFICATION READY
Which tool allows you to access a machine remotely, including programs, the desktop, and the command prompt?
Objective 3.5

By default, Windows servers are configured to use Remote Desktop for Administration licensing mode, which supports up to two remote sessions. These sessions are meant for an administrator to log on to the computer directly, so that the server can be managed remotely. However, if you want to run applications that require more than the standard two remote sessions, you need to first load and configure the computer running Windows Server as a Remote Desktop Session Host server role. You also need an RD licensing manager to keep track of the licenses used, and you must purchase and install terminal server licenses.

To access a computer running Remote Desktop Services, you would use Remote Desktop Connections to access a computer's graphical user interface (including the desktop, Start menu, and programs) just as if you were sitting in front of the computer. See Figure 6-4. Two technologies that allow you to remotely access a computer's desktop are Remote Desktop and ***Remote Assistance*** over TCP port 3389. Both are based on the ***Remote Desktop Protocol***, which provides a user with a graphical interface to connect to another computer over a network connection.

Figure 6-4

Accessing another computer via Remote Desktop Connection

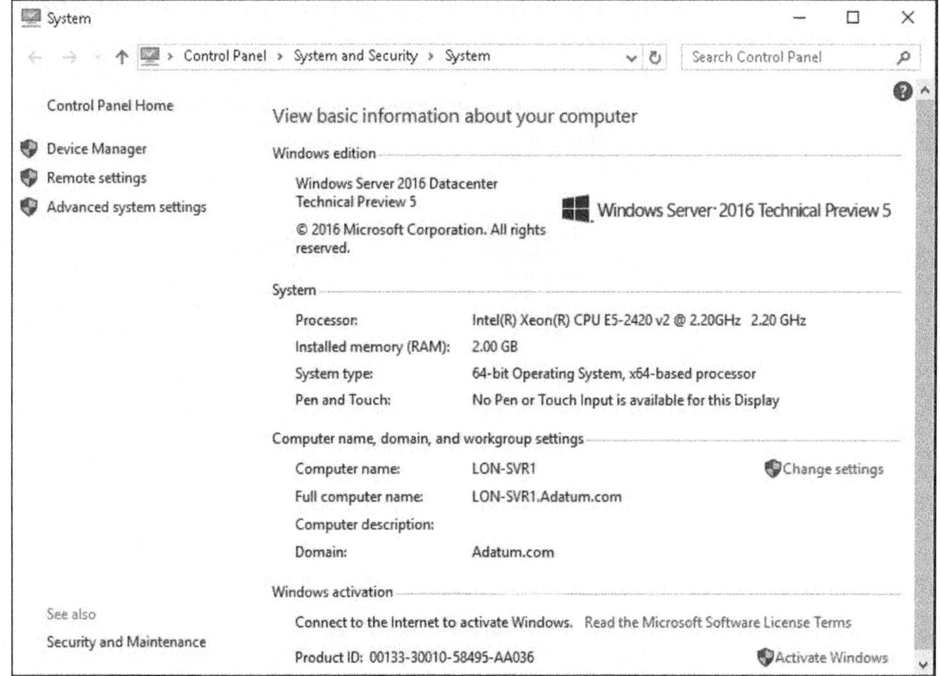

To connect to a remote computer:

- The computer must be turned on.
- It must have a network connection.
- Remote Desktop must be enabled in the System Properties.
- You must have permission to connect (be a member of the administrators group or the Remote Desktop Users group).

ENABLE REMOTE DESKTOP

GET READY. To enable Remote Desktop on Windows 10, perform the following steps.

1. Right-click **Start** and choose **System.**
2. In the Control Panel System window, click **Remote Settings.** If you are prompted to confirm that you want to continue, click **Yes.**

3. On the Remote Settings tab, select one of the following options:
   - **Allow remote connections to this computer**
   - **Don't allow remote connections to this computer**
4. If you are prompted for an administrator password or confirmation, type the password or provide confirmation.
5. Click **Select Users.** If you are enabling Remote Desktop for your current user account, your name will automatically be added to this list of remote users and you can skip the next two steps.
6. In the Remote Desktop Users dialog box, click **Add.** This adds users to the Remote Desktop Users group.
7. In the Select Users dialog box, type the user's name and then click **OK.**

ACCESS REMOTE DESKTOP

GET READY. To start Remote Desktop on the computer you want to work from, perform the following steps.

1. Open Remote Desktop Connection by clicking **Start**, typing **Remote Desktop**, and then clicking **Remote Desktop Connection.** (Or you can execute the **mstsc.exe** command.)
2. In the Computer text box, type the name of the computer that you want to connect to and then click **Connect.** (You can type the IP address—instead of typing the computer name—if you would like.)

For more advanced options before the connection, click the Show Options button. See Figure 6-5.

Figure 6-5

Configuring Remote Desktop Connections

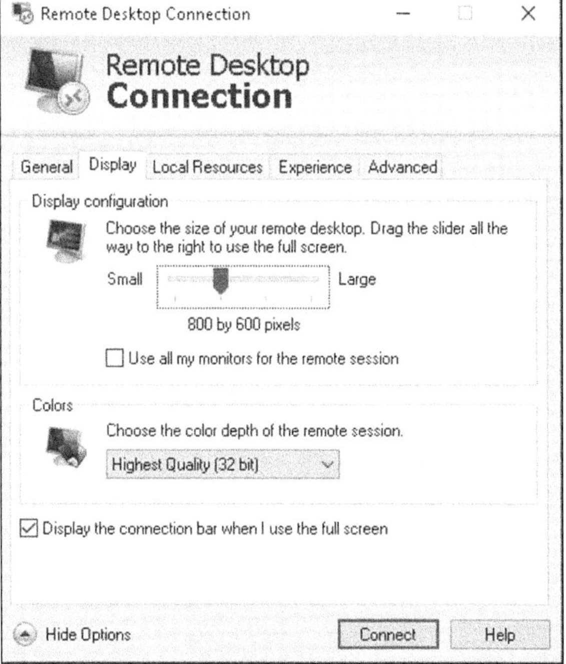

On occasion, you might need to connect to a server with the administrative session by using the `mstsc.exe /admin` command. This becomes particularly useful when the terminal server or Remote Desktop Services has exceeded the maximum number of allowed connections or when you get a black screen after you RDP to a system, assuming the system has not crashed.

RemoteApp (or TS RemoteApp) is a special mode of Remote Desktop Services that allows you to run an application in its own window instead of opening a session with Remote Desktop Connection. For the most part, the application looks like a normal application running on your local computer, but in reality, it is running remotely on a server. A RemoteApp can be packaged either as an .rdp file or distributed via an .msi Windows Installer package.

Besides using a VPN tunnel, you can use a Remote Desktop Gateway (RD Gateway) role service to enable authorized remote users to connect to resources on an internal private network over the Internet using a Remote Desktop Connection (RDC) client. RD Gateway uses the Remote Desktop Protocol (RDP) over HTTPS to establish a secure, encrypted connection between remote users on the Internet and the internal network resources on which their productivity applications run.

■ Defining More Networking Services

Remote Access Service (RAS) is the grouping of different hardware and software platforms to allow for remote access to another computer or network device. Originally used with dial-up services, Microsoft RAS has morphed into RRAS (Routing and Remote Access Service). This powerful service allows clients to connect remotely to a central network using dial-up and high-speed Internet connections. It also allows connectivity through VPNs. IPsec is an encrypting and authenticating protocol that helps to secure VPNs and other types of network transactions.

CERTIFICATION READY
How would you define RRAS?
Objective 3.5

Defining RRAS

Microsoft RRAS is built in to Windows Server and offers a variety of functions, including dial-in service and the ability to create virtual private networks.

CERTIFICATION READY
Which Windows Server role provides dial-up support?
Objective 1.3

Routing and Remote Access Service (RRAS) is a network service in Windows servers, including Windows Server 2012, Windows Server 2012 R2, and Windows Server 2016. It allows an administrator to configure dial-up remote access servers, VPN servers, IP routing, and NAT.

Early data communication utilize a direct dial-up connection. This is illustrated in Figure 6-6. Although this allowed for connectivity, it was often slow and suffered from noisy lines and dropped lines.

Now, the standard is to utilize a virtual private network (VPN). With VPNs, the inherent power of the Internet is exploited and direct IP connections are made from clients to a VPN server or router. Dial-up connections via modems that connect to the Internet are still supported, but more commonly high-speed connections such as DSL, cable, and fiber optic are the weapons of choice. An example of a VPN is shown in Figure 6-7.

Figure 6-6
Illustration of a dial-up connection

Figure 6-7

Illustration of a VPN connection

To provide RAS, Microsoft includes Routing and Remote Access Service , which provides the following functionality:

- A virtual private network (VPN) gateway where clients can connect to an organization's private network using the Internet
- The ability to connect two private networks using a VPN connection via the Internet
- A dial-up remote access server, which enables users to connect to a private network using a modem
- Network Address Translation (NAT), which enables multiple users to share a single public network address
- Routing functionality, which can connect subnets and control where packets are forwarded based on the destination address
- Basic firewall functionality and the ability to allow or disallow packets based on addresses of source, destination, and/or protocols

An early method to connect to an organization's network was over an analog phone line or ISDN line using a modem. Because the modem creates a dedicated connection to the server, the connection does not typically need to be encrypted. However, by today's networking standards and bandwidth requirements, the phone and ISDN system do not have the bandwidth needed. Therefore, this method typically is not used today.

Before you can use RRAS, you need to first add the Remote Access role. Then, you need to initially configure RRAS so that you can specify which options are available with it.

To install the Remote Access role, you use Server Manager to install the proper role. Because the remote access computer is used to connect an organization's internal private network with the Internet, the server should have two network cards.

INSTALL THE REMOTE ACCESS ROLE

GET READY. To install the Remote Access role, perform the following steps.

1. Log on to a server running Windows Server 2016 as **adatum\administrator** with the password of **Pa$$w0rd.**
2. Click **Start** and then click **Server Manager.**
3. At the top of Server Manager, click **Manage > Add Roles and Features.** The Add Roles and Feature Wizard opens.
4. On the Before You Begin page, click **Next.**
5. Click **Role-based or feature-based installation** and then click **Next.**
6. Click **Select a server from the server pool**, click the name of the desired server, and then click **Next.**
7. On the Server Roles page, scroll down and click **Remote Access**, and then click **Next.**

8. On the Features page, click **Next.**
9. On the Remote Access page, click **Next.**
10. On the Role Services page, click **Routing** and click **Next.**
11. When you are prompted to add features required for routing, click **Add Features.** DirectAccess and VPN (RAS) will automatically be selected.
12. Back on the Role Services page, click **Next.**
13. On the Confirmation page, click **Install.**
14. When the installation is complete, click **Close.**

After you install RRAS, you need to enable the server and configure RRAS. When you start the RRAS Setup Wizard, you can use the wizard to automatically configure RRAS for specific applications or configure the service manually.

The wizard offers five basic options for configuring RRAS:

- **Remote access (dial-up or VPN):** Sets up the server to accept incoming remote access connections (dial-up or VPN)
- **Network Address Translation (NAT):** Sets up the server to provide NAT services to clients on the private network that need to access the Internet
- **Virtual private network (VPN) access and NAT:** Sets up the server to support incoming VPN connections and to provide NAT services
- **Secure connection between two private networks:** Sets up a demand-dial or persistent connection between two private networks
- **Custom configuration:** Enables you to choose individual services, including NAT, LAN routing, and VPN access

CONFIGURE ROUTING

GET READY. To configure routing on Windows Server 2016, perform the following steps.

1. On the server running Windows Server 2016, in Server Manager, click **Tools > Routing and Remote Access.** The Routing and Remote Access console opens.
2. Right-click the server and choose **Configure and Enable Routing and Remote Access.**
3. In the Routing and Remote Access Server Setup Wizard, click **Next.**
4. On the Configuration page (as shown in Figure 6-8), select **Custom configuration** and then click **Next.**
5. On the Custom Configuration page, select **LAN routing** and then click **Next.**
6. On the Completing the Routing and Remote Access Server Setup Wizard page, click **Finish.**
7. When the Routing and Remote Access Service is ready to use, click the **Start service** button.

Figure 6-8
Configuring Routing and Remote Access

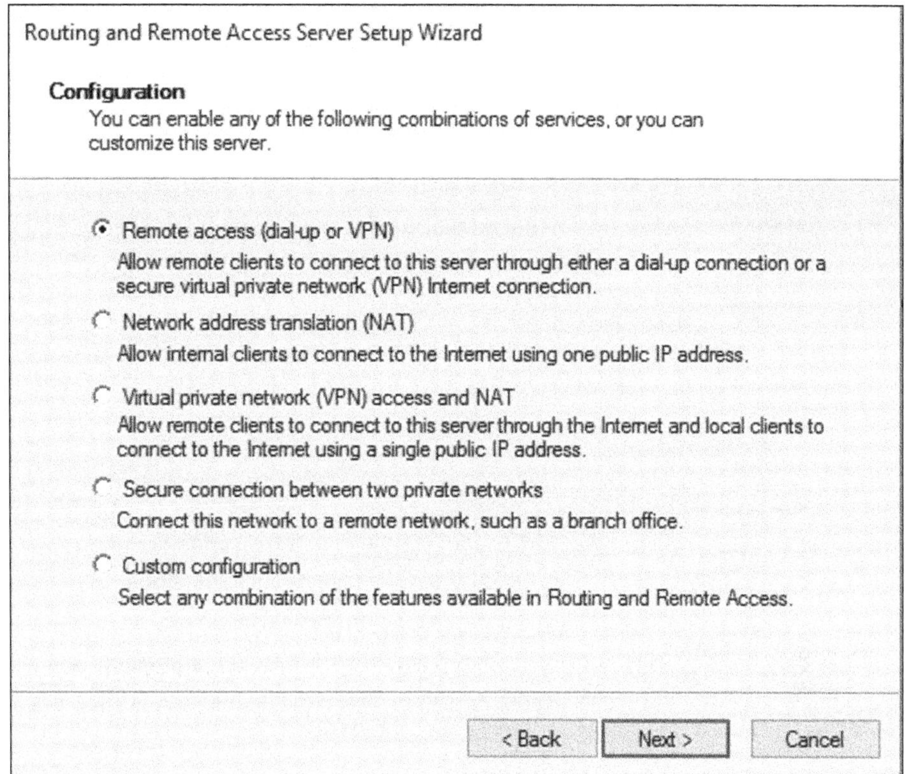

You might also want to disable RRAS in case you will be using other services that might conflict with it in the future. To do this, in the MMC, right-click the server and choose Disable.

Defining IPsec

Internet Protocol Security (IPsec) is a protocol within the TCP/IP suite that encrypts and authenticates IP packets. It is designed to secure any application traffic because it resides on the Network layer (or Internet layer as TCP/IP programmers refer to it).

CERTIFICATION READY
Which technology is built in to IPv6 to encrypt data transmitted over a network?
Objective 3.5

IPsec is used in conjunction with virtual private networks and is an integral part of IPv6. There are three main protocols that IPsec uses to perform its necessary functions:

- ***Security association (SA)*:** This generates the encryption and authentication keys that are to be used by IPsec.
- ***Authentication header (AH)*:** This provides connectionless integrity and the authentication of data. It also provides protection versus replay attacks.
- ***Encapsulating Security Payload (ESP)*:** This provides the same services as AH but also provides confidentiality when sending data.

The particular IPsec protocol to be used is determined by the application utilizing IPsec. You will learn more about IPsec when we delve into VPNs in Lesson 8.

■ Defining Name Resolution Techniques

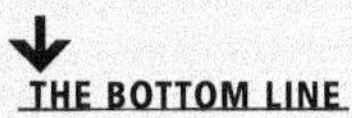

Computers work best when communicating by IP address. But humans work best when they communicate with words. Therein lies the purpose of name resolution. Names can be resolved or translated to IP addresses by services such as DNS and WINS.

Defining DNS

The ***Domain Name System (DNS)*** is a worldwide service that resolves host names to IP addresses. This facilitates proper communication between computers.

CERTIFICATION READY
What is the most popular form of name resolution?
Objective 3.4

A hierarchy of DNS servers communicates with each other to teach each other their name resolutions. DNS servers are also implemented in today's LANs, for example, Microsoft domains, although DNS can be used on any operating system that runs TCP/IP. The LAN DNS servers do the same thing as their Internet counterparts, just on a smaller scale—although sometimes not so small! DNS servers use inbound port 53 to accept name resolution requests. Microsoft DNS servers run the DNS service and clients can connect to and use that service as long as their IP Properties pages are configured properly.

INSTALL DNS AND CREATE A ZONE

GET READY. To install DNS on Windows Server 2016, perform the following steps.

1. Click **Start** and then click **Server Manager.**
2. At the top of Server Manager, click **Manage > Add Roles and Features.**
3. On the Before You Begin page, click **Next.**
4. Click **Role-based or feature-based installation** and then click **Next.**
5. Click **Select a server from the server pool**, click the name of the server to install DNS to, and then click **Next.**
6. Click **DNS Server.**
7. In the Add Roles and Features Wizard dialog box, click **Add Features** and then click **Next.**
8. On the Select Features page, click **Next.**
9. On the DNS Server page, click **Next.**
10. On the Confirm Installation Selections page, click the **Install** button.
11. When the installation is complete, click **Close.**
12. Open **Server Manager.**
13. Open the DNS Manager console by clicking **Tools > DNS.**
14. If necessary, expand the DNS Manager console to a full-screen view.
15. Expand the server so that you can see the Forward Lookup Zones and Reverse Lookup Zones folders, as shown in Figure 6-9.

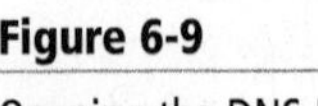

Figure 6-9
Opening the DNS Manager console

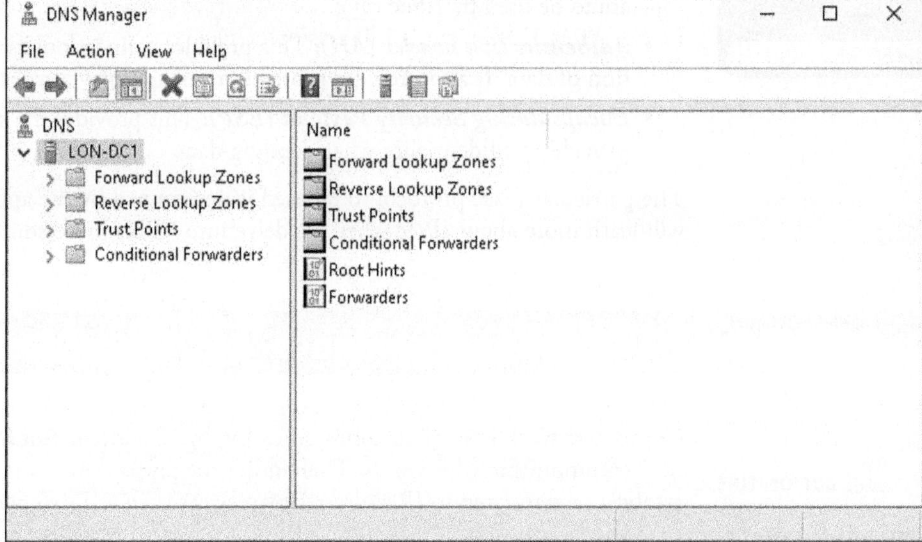

16. Click, then right-click **Forward Lookup Zones** and choose **New Zone.**
17. On the Welcome to the New Zone Wizard page, click **Next.**
18. On the Zone Type page, select the **Primary zone** radio button (see Figure 6-10). Deselect the **Store the zone in Active Directory** check box and then click **Next.**

Figure 6-10

Selecting the zone type

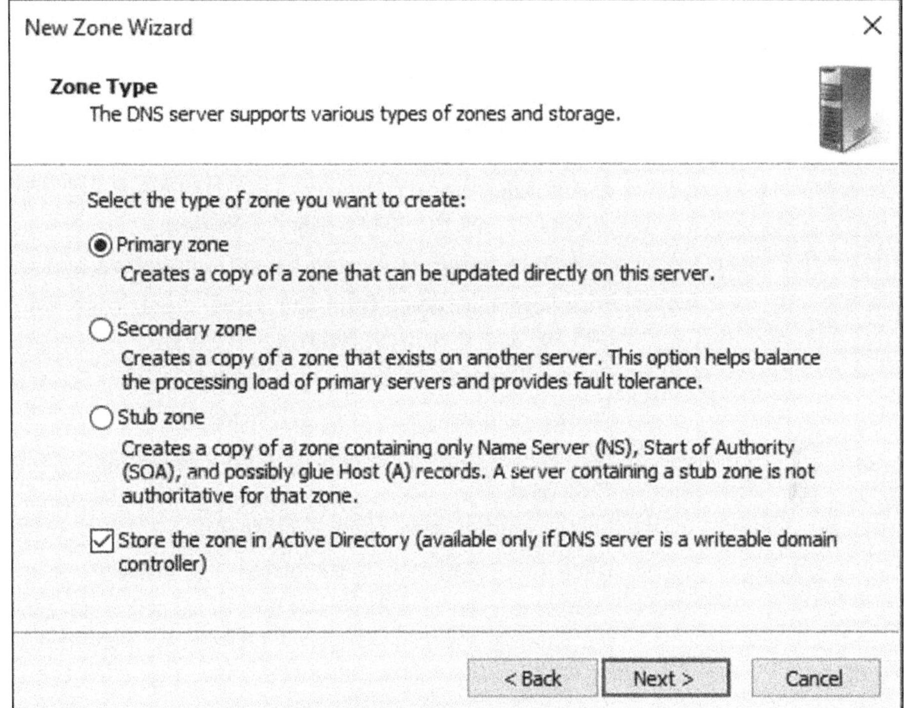

19. On the Zone Name page, in the Zone name text box, type the name of the domain, such as **contoso.com**, and then click **Next.**
20. On the Zone File page, ensure that the **Create a new file with this file name** radio button is selected and then click **Next.**
21. On the Dynamic Update page, ensure that the **Do not allow dynamic updates** radio button is selected and then click **Next.**
22. On the Completing the New Zone Wizard page, click **Finish.**

You should now have a zone called contoso.com inside of the Forward Lookup Zones folder. This is where DNS records will be stored, such as host names and their corresponding IP addresses. Some zones allow for these records to be created automatically, for example in a domain. Otherwise, records can be added manually. If client computers want to use this DNS server, their IP Properties pages need to be updated by adding the IP address of the server to the preferred or alternate DNS server field.

Defining WINS

The ***Windows Internet Naming Service (WINS)*** is a service that resolves NetBIOS names to IP addresses. It is the Microsoft version of the NetBIOS Name Service (NBNS) combined with a name server. A Windows computer name, for example Computer1, can be a host name and interact with DNS, and/or a NetBIOS name, either working alone or in concert with a WINS server.

CERTIFICATION READY
Which legacy name resolution method was used to resolve computer names to IP addresses?
Objective 3.4

Most companies opt to use DNS, but sometimes you will find WINS-enabled devices and WINS servers. This could be due to design of less common devices or the age of the device. Whereas DNS can have hosts added statically or dynamically, WINS only works in a dynamic fashion. No configuration of a WINS server is necessary once it is installed other than database replication.

INSTALL WINS

GET READY. To install WINS on Windows Server 2016, perform the following steps.

1. Click **Start** and then click **Server Manager.**
2. At the top of Server Manager, click **Manage** > **Add Roles and Features.**
3. On the Before You Begin page, click **Next.**
4. Click **Role-based or feature-based installation** and then click **Next.**
5. Click **Select a server from the server pool**, click the name of the server to install DNS to, and then click **Next.**
6. On the Server Roles page, click **Next.**
7. On the Features page, click **WINS Server.**
8. In the Add Roles and Features Wizard dialog box, click **Add Features** and then click **Next.**
9. On the Confirmation page, click **Install.**
10. When the installation is complete, click **Close.**
11. To have the WINS server take care of name resolution for Windows clients, go to the Internet Protocol Version 4 (TCP/IPv4) Properties dialog box of the client computer, click the **Advanced** button, and then click the **WINS** tab. From there, one or more WINS servers can be added.

SKILL SUMMARY

IN THIS LESSON, YOU LEARNED:

- DHCP is the Dynamic Host Configuration Protocol. It sends IP information to clients automatically, making configuration of IP on the network easier and automated. It uses a four-step process known as DORA when disseminating IP addresses. It uses ports 67 and 68.
- Sometimes, APIPA can get in the way of a client obtaining an IP address properly, for example, if a client attempts to obtain an IP address from a DHCP server, but the DHCP server is too busy. At that point, APIPA self-assigns an IP address to the client computer, and the computer is stuck with that address until the `ipconfig/release` and `/renew` commands are run from the command line. Depending on the version of Windows and the configuration, this still might not be enough. If you see an IP address of 169.254.x.x, you know that the client has self-assigned an IP address with the help of APIPA.
- With early networks, users utilized dumb terminals (systems consisting of a monitor and keyboard without a processor) to connect to a mainframe. Later, computers could use Telnet to connect to a server and execute commands at a command prompt. Terminal Services was relabeled as Remote Desktop Services, starting with Window Server 2008 R2. Remote Desktop Services is one of the components of Microsoft Windows that allows a user to access applications and data on a remote computer over a network.

- Remote Access Service (RAS) is the grouping of different hardware and software platforms to allow for remote access to another computer or network device. Originally used with dial-up services, Microsoft RAS has morphed into Routing and Remote Access Service (RRAS). This powerful service allows clients to connect remotely to a central network using dial-up and high-speed Internet connections. It also allows connectivity through VPNs. IPsec is an encrypting and authenticating protocol that helps to secure VPNs and other types of network transactions.
- The Domain Name System (DNS) is a worldwide service that resolves host names to IP addresses. This facilitates proper communication between computers. A hierarchy of DNS servers communicates with each other in an effort to teach each other their name resolutions. DNS servers are also implemented in today's LANs, for example Microsoft domains, although DNS can be used on any operating system that runs TCP/IP.

■ Knowledge Assessment

Multiple Choice

Select the correct answer for each of the following questions.

1. When configuring IP addresses via DHCP, the Windows client fails to broadcast to all servers that it has accepted an IP address offer. Which step is this in the four-step DHCP process?
   a. Discovery
   b. Offering
   c. Request
   d. Acknowledge
2. As an administrator at Proseware, Inc., you are in charge of setting up a DHCP server to hand out IP addresses and other IP-related information. Which of the following cannot be obtained from a DHCP server?
   a. IP address
   b. MAC address
   c. DNS server address
   d. Gateway address
3. Administrators at Proseware, Inc., want to scan servers for DHCP activity. Which ports should they be looking for?
   a. 53 and 54
   b. 80 and 443
   c. 20 and 21
   d. 67 and 68
4. A coworker asks for help in analyzing a problem with a DHCP server. The server's scope has been created and the IP range appears to be valid. Yet no clients are obtaining IP addresses. Which of the following could be the reason for this?
   a. The server was not authorized.
   b. The scope was not activated.
   c. The scope was not authorized.
   d. The server is down.

5. You want to set up a computer to acquire an IP address from a newly configured DHCP server. Which of the following is the best command to use?
   a. `ping -n`
   b. `ipconfig /renew`
   c. `ipconfig /release`
   d. `ping -renew`

6. A computer cannot obtain the proper IP address from a DHCP server. After running `ipconfig`, the address 169.254.25.53 shows up in the results. Which service is assigning the IP address to the client?
   a. DHCP
   b. WINS
   c. APIPA
   d. DNS

7. After scanning the ports of a server, it is found that port 3389 is open. Which of the following can be deduced from this?
   a. The WINS service is running.
   b. The DNS service is running.
   c. Terminal Services is running.
   d. RRAS is running.

8. Which of the following is the proper tool to use to take control of a server remotely from within the GUI of the client OS?
   a. Remote Desktop
   b. Telnet
   c. FTP
   d. SSH

9. A client wants to install a VPN server. Which of the following services should be chosen to accomplish this?
   a. DNS
   b. RRAS
   c. WINS
   d. IPsec

10. Which of the following protocols generates encryption and authentication keys that are used by IPsec?
    a. ESP
    b. AH
    c. SA
    d. IPv6

11. Which command is used to connect to a server with an administrative session?
    a. `mstsc.exe /AD`
    b. `mstsc.exe /a`
    c. `mstsc.exe /console`
    d. `mstsc.exe /admin`

12. In the Remote Desktop Connection options, which tab is used to access local drives on the remote computer?
    a. General
    b. Display
    c. Local Resources
    d. Advanced

Fill in the Blank

Fill in the correct answer in the blank space provided.

1. The _____ service resolves host names to IP addresses.
2. The _____ service resolves NetBIOS names to IP addresses.
3. The _____ step in the DHCP four-step process is when a client broadcasts out to the network in order to find a DHCP server.
4. When renewing a DHCP-assigned IP address, usually _____ steps of the DORA process are involved.
5. To install the DHCP service on a Windows Server 2016 computer, _____ should be used.
6. By default, wired DHCP leases last for _____ days.
7. The _____ and _____ commands are useful when troubleshooting a client that is having difficulty obtaining an IP address from a DHCP server.
8. A client that has obtained an IP address of 169.254.10.175 is getting the IP address from _____.
9. _____ enables clients to connect to and take control of a server.
10. _____ take the place of direct dial-up connections by using the inherent power of the Internet.

■ Business Case Scenarios

Scenario 6-1: Selecting the Appropriate Services

A client wants you to install a service or services that will allow her to do the following:

1. Enable NetBIOS name to IP address resolution.
2. Allow virtual connectivity to the LAN from remote clients in a secure manner.

Which two services will enable this functionality?

Scenario 6-2: Selecting the Appropriate Services

The ABC Company wants you to install a service or services that will allow the company to do the following:

1. Enable host name to IP address resolution internally in the company.
2. Enable client computers to obtain IP information automatically.
3. Allow administrators to access servers to control them remotely.

Which three services will enable this functionality?

Scenario 6-3: Setting Up a DHCP Server

Proseware, Inc., requires that you set up a DHCP server on a D-Link DIR-655 router. Details follow for the IP configuration:

- **IP scope:** 10.254.254.1–10.254.254.199
- **DHCP lease time:** 480 minutes

- **Always broadcast:** Enabled
- **NetBIOS announcement:** Enabled
- **NetBIOS node type:** Broadcast only
- **Primary WINS address:** 10.254.254.250

Access the DIR-655 emulator at the following link and configure the DHCP server appropriately: http://support.dlink.com/emulators/dir655/133NA/login.html

Scenario 6-4: Setting Up a New DHCP and Migrating Old Computers

Proseware, Inc., currently uses the 192.168.1.0 Class C network. The company currently has 225 computers. Administration wants to add another 200 new computers and install a new DHCP server. Specifically, they want you to:

1. Select a classful IP network number that can support their total number of computers, old and new.
2. Obtain new addresses from the new DHCP server on the original 225 computers.

Describe your recommendations for each solution.

Scenario 6-5: Managing Remote Connections

As an administrator for the Contoso Corporation, you manage various accounting applications that are executed directly on a server. You have configured the server to allow up to five remote connections. Describe how to enable remote users to access those applications as if they were sitting in front of their computers at their desks in the office while still being able to access their files on their local machines.

✳ Workplace Ready

DHCP Is Everywhere!

IP addresses obtained from a DHCP server can be found everywhere. Most computers on a LAN get their IP information, including IP address, subnet mask, gateway address, DNS server address, and more, from a DHCP server. Home users' computers usually get their IP information from the DHCP server in their four-port SOHO router. And the router gets its WAN address from an Internet service provider (ISP). Equipment such as gaming consoles and digital video recorders also get dynamically assigned IPs. PDAs, some cell phones, and other handheld computers and handheld gaming equipment are also in the DHCP group.

Take a look around your house, work, school, library, and so on and make a list of devices and computers that obtain IP addresses automatically from a DHCP server. Then, research on the Internet and try to find out who the major ISPs are that hand out IP addresses and what IP network numbers they use.

Understanding Wide Area Networks

LESSON 7

OBJECTIVE DOMAIN MATRIX

Skills/Concepts	Objective Domain Description	Objective Domain Number
Understanding Routing	Understand routers	2.2
Understanding Quality of Service (QoS)	Understand routers	2.2
Defining Common WAN Technologies and Connections	Understand wide area networks (WANs)	1.3

KEY TERMS

Asynchronous Transfer Mode (ATM)
Basic Rate ISDN (BRI)
broadband cable
Committed Information Rate (CIR)
converged network
CSU/DSU
Digital Subscriber Line (DSL)
dynamic routing
E1
E3
Fiber Distributed Data Interface (FDDI)
Frame Relay
header
hops
Integrated Services Digital Network (ISDN)
Interior Gateway Routing Protocol (IGRP)
leased lines
packet switching
Packet Switching Exchanges (PSEs)
permanent virtual circuits (PVCs)
POTS/PSTN
Primary Rate ISDN (PRI)
Quality of Service (QoS)
SONET
static routing
synchronous
T1
T3
T-carrier
trailer
virtual circuit
X.25

Your client Proseware, Inc., needs to expand its network. You have previously set up local area networks for the company, but now Proseware, Inc., desires a wide area network with all the routers necessary to make those connections.

You must provide several wide area networking options along with the different types of routers that will work best for each of those options. The skills required for this task include the ability to document wide area networks and the know-how to install various networking services and protocols.

Of course, to develop these skills, a lot of knowledge is required, so this lesson defines the most common WAN technologies available and increases your understanding of routing protocols and routing devices.

■ Understanding Routing

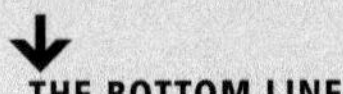

THE BOTTOM LINE

Routing is the process of moving data across networks or internetworks between hosts or between routers themselves. Information is transmitted according to the IP networks and individual IP addresses of the hosts in question. A router is in charge of maintaining tables of information about other routers on the network or internetwork. It also utilizes several different TCP/IP protocols to transfer the data and to discover other routers. IP routing is the most common kind of routing as TCP/IP is the most common protocol suite. IP routing occurs on the Network layer of the OSI model.

Identifying Static and Dynamic Routing

A static route is one that has been manually configured. A dynamic route is one that has been implemented dynamically with special routing protocols. In this section, you will configure RRAS statically and add the Routing Information Protocol (RIP) to allow for dynamic routing.

CERTIFICATION READY
How can you identify the difference between static and dynamic routing?
Objective 2.2

Static routing is when a router has been manually configured. For example, when a routing entry is manually entered into the routing table with the `route add` command, it is known as static routing. We demonstrated a basic example of this in Lesson 5. An example of a static router is a Windows Server 2016 computer with two network adapters and IP routing (IP forwarding) enabled, as shown in Lesson 6. This is a very basic type of router that does not change with the network and is not fault tolerant. Statically entered routes do not "know" what is happening on the network; they cannot sense new routers or the modified state of a router. There is a lot of maintenance required with a static router. Because of all this, a better solution is to utilize dynamic routing.

Dynamic routing is implemented by dynamically configuring routing tables. This is done with dynamic routing protocols, such as RIP and OSPF, as mentioned in Lesson 5. Both of these are part of the TCP/IP suite of protocols and they work on Layer 3 of the OSI model. It is important to be able to distinguish between routable protocols and routing protocols. An example of a routable protocol is TCP/IP; a nonroutable protocol example is NetBEUI. An example of a routing protocol is RIP. Let's talk about RIP and some other routing protocols in a little more depth:

- *Routing Information Protocol (RIP)* is a dynamic protocol that uses distance-vector routing algorithms to decipher which route to send data packets. In packet-switched networks, a distance-vector routing protocol uses the Bellman-Ford algorithm to calculate where and how data will be transmitted. The protocol calculates the direction or interface that packets should be forwarded to as well as the distance from the destination. RIPv1 and RIPv2 are common among today's networks.

- *Open Shortest Path First (OSPF)* is a link-state protocol that monitors the network for routers that have a change in their link-state, meaning whether they were turned off or on or restarted. This is perhaps the most commonly used interior gateway protocol in large networks. Interior gateway protocols are used to determine connections between autonomous systems.
- ***Interior Gateway Routing Protocol (IGRP)*** is a proprietary protocol used in large networks to overcome the limitations of RIP.
- *Border Gateway Protocol (BGP)* is a core routing protocol that bases routing decisions on the network path and rules.

A directly connected network is a network that is directly attached to one of the router interfaces. The routing table includes the network address, subnet mask interface type, and number of the network. A remote network is a network that is not directly connected to the router. Remote networks are added to the routing table using either a dynamic routing protocol or by configuring static routes.

When it comes to larger networks and the Internet, routing tables can become very cumbersome. A router requires a lot of fast and efficient memory to handle these routing tables. Older routers simply cannot cope with the number of entries, and some protocols such as BGP might not work properly on these older routers. Because the Internet is growing so quickly, ISPs collectively utilize CIDR to keep the size of the routing tables down. Network congestion is also an issue as well as load-balancing. Depending on the scenario, you might need to use newer routers with more memory and faster network connections, and you need to consider carefully which protocols you use. Generally, though, a small to midsized company can make do with RIP. Let's show this in action.

CONFIGURE ROUTING

GET READY. To configure RIP on Windows Server 2016, perform the following steps.

1. On a server with Routing and Remote Access installed, click **Start** and click **Server Manager**.
2. Click **Tools > Routing and Remote Access.**
3. Right-click the server and choose **Configure and Enable Routing and Remote Access.**
4. In the Routing and Remote Access Server Setup Wizard, click **Next.**
5. On the Configuration page, click **Custom configuration** and click **Next.**
6. On the Custom Configuration page, click **LAN routing** and click **Next.**
7. On the Completing the Routing and Remote Access Server Setup Wizard page, click **Finish.**
8. When you are prompted to start the service, click **Start service.**
9. Expand the server node and expand **IPv4.**
10. Right-click the **General** tab and choose **New Routing Protocol.** The New Routing Protocol dialog box opens (see Figure 7-1).
11. Click **RIP Version 2 for Internet Protocol.**
12. Click **OK** to close the New Routing Protocol dialog box. A RIP node appears under IPv4.

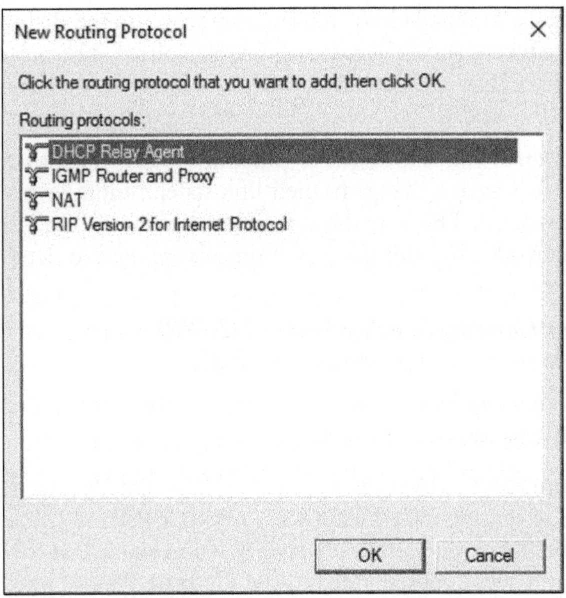

Figure 7-1

Specifying a new routing protocol

13. Right-click **RIP** and choose **New Interface.** The New Interface for RIP Version 2 for Internet Protocol dialog box opens.
14. Select the interface that you want to use RIP on.
15. Click **OK** to close the New Interface for RIP Version 2 for Internet Protocol dialog box. The RIP Properties dialog box opens (see Figure 7-2).

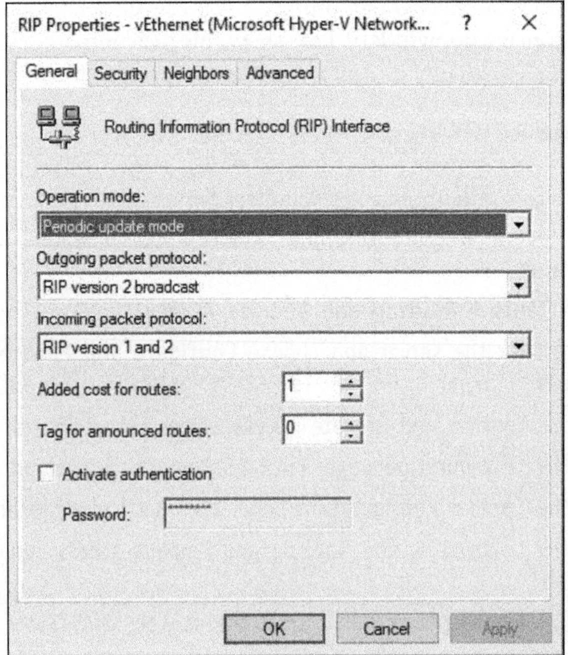

Figure 7-2

Configuring the RIP Properties

16. Click **OK** to close the RIP Properties dialog box.

RIP can now take care of what we previously did with static routes in previous lessons. Keep in mind that for much bigger networks, other protocols will be more desirable.

Understanding Quality of Service (QoS)

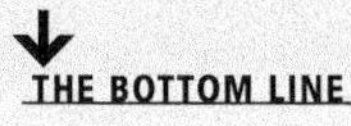

THE BOTTOM LINE

Today, most networks are a ***converged network***, which means that the network supports telephone, video, and data communications on a single network. Whereas a traditional network would only have carried data packets—such as when you open a file from a shared folder, access a website over the Internet, or retrieve email—a converged network also supports voice, video, and other time-sensitive packets. ***Quality of Service (QoS)*** is an industry-wide set of standards and mechanisms that ensure high-quality performance for critical and time-sensitive applications on shared networks.

CERTIFICATION READY
Can you define Quality of Service (QoS)?
Objective 2.2

Quality of Service refers to the network's ability to use maximum bandwidth while reducing latency, error rates, and downtime. When accessing a shared folder or a normal web page, the data packets are fed to your computer and you can read the shared file or web page after a reasonable short period of time. However, when you access a real-time application, such as a video or voice call over a packet-switched network, you need dedicated bandwidth to make sure the application runs smoothly.

Some of the problems found with packet-switched networks include:

- **Low throughput:** Some applications need more bandwidth than other applications.
- **Dropped packets and errors:** If a data load gets corrupted (such as from noise or interference), or the router buffers are already full, packets will be dropped.
- **Latency:** If a packet gets held up in long queues, or it takes a less direct route to avoid congestion, packets may be delayed. Excessive latency can cause real-time applications to be unusable, such as when audio and videos do not play properly.
- **Jitter:** The time variation when packets leave one system and reach another affect the flow of real-time data. When listening to audio or video recordings, the sound or video might pause and stop frequently.
- **Out-of-order delivery:** When packets take different routes, packets could experience different delays. As a result, the packets arrive in a different order than they were sent.

QoS can provide the following benefits:

- Give administrative control over how the network resources use the network.
- Ensure that time-sensitive and mission-critical applications have the necessary network bandwidth while allowing other applications to also access the network.
- Reduce cost by using the existing network infrastructure, thereby delaying or reducing the need for upgrades and replacement.
- Improve user experience.

QoS works by classification and queuing. Classification identifies and marks traffic so that network devices know how to identify and prioritize data as it traverses a network. Queues provide a holding place for packets so that they can send the packets when necessary, based on the QoS policy. If the queues fill up, the queues overflow and drop traffic.

QoS policies are used to classify and identify traffic. These policies are defined by the following:

- **Shaping by application:** When you shape by application, you categorize specific types of network traffic and assign that category a bandwidth limit.
- **Shaping network traffic per user:** When you shape by network traffic per user, you delegate certain bandwidth to a user.

- **Priority shaping:** When you shape by priority, you define the relative importance or priority of different types of traffic.

When you define a QoS policy, you define one of the following:

- Best-Effort
- Integrated Services (IntServ)
- Differentiated Services (DiffServ)

Without a QoS policy, each network device treats all data equally and provides resources on a first-come, first-served basis. Policies define the amount of bandwidth reserved or a limit for a specified data type. You can also define a Best-Effort policy, which is based on a first in, first out (FIFO) fashion.

Integrated services require devices to communicate using a special protocol, to reserve bandwidth for specific applications. Of course, all devices must support the same protocol. Differentiated services add tags to individual packets, which marks them with a requested priority. DiffServ requires a smaller load than IntServ, and is the preferred technology used today.

■ Defining Common WAN Technologies and Connections

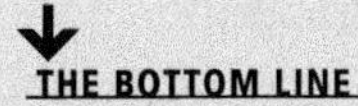

Wide area networks connect multiple local area networks together. If an organization wants to have a wide area connection to another office, administrators need to decide on a networking service and the speed that they want to connect at. Budgeting plays a big role in these types of decisions.

Defining Packet Switching

Packet switching is the moving of data packets over switched wide area networks. Types of packet switching services include X.25 and Frame Relay. This section defines those two types of services.

CERTIFICATION READY
What are the primary differences between Frame Relay and T1 connections?
Objective 1.3

Most WANs utilize some type of packet switching technology. Let's discuss the technology world before packet switching and talk about why packet switching is a far superior solution.

Packet switching services include X.25 and Frame Relay. Before packet switching, there were direct dial-up connections and other archaic forms of communication. Some of the problems associated with these include the following:

- Until the early 1970s, data transfer was analog with much static and noise. It was also primarily asynchronous and conducted by dial-up modems.
- Data transfer could be as much as 40% overhead and only 60% actual information. Overhead included the allowance for noise, error checking, flagging, stop/start bits, parity, and so forth.
- Longer data transfers could be disconnected for many reasons, including:
    - Poor connection
    - Network degradation
    - Loss of circuits
- If there was a disconnection, the entire message (file) would have to be re-sent, usually after the person dialed out again.

DEFINING X.25

Then, packet switching arrived. The ***X.25*** communications protocol was one of the first implementations of packet switching and it is still in use today.

Packet switching was originally created to break down large messages into smaller, more manageable segments for transmission over the WAN. Basically, a source computer sends its message over the LAN to the hardware/software component known as the router. The router then breaks down the file into more manageable pieces (known as packets). Every packet gets a portion of the original message. Every packet also gets a segmentation number and address information. The packet is then transmitted over the physical link to the switching system (Telco), which picks a wire for transmission from the header information of the packet. This establishes a virtual connection or virtual circuit. Next, packets are reassembled at the receiving router.

The X.25 packet switching steps are as follows:

1. A computer proceeds as usual through the OSI model over the LAN. It sends data to the router.
2. Data (as the message) is gathered by the router, but it then disassembles the entire lot into jumbled packets. The router is known as a PAD (packet assembler/disassembler). Packets are then sent by the PAD to a ***CSU/DSU*** (high-speed digital data interchange device) as serial information. The CSU/DSU is the equivalent of the modem for the entire LAN. It is known as the data communications equipment (DCE). In this scenario, the PAD (or router) is known as the data terminating equipment (DTE).
3. Packets are sent by the CSU/DSU to the demarcation point (demarc) in the office or company. Often, the CSU/DSU is the demarc, otherwise known as the point where your responsibility as an administrator ends and the telecommunications or data communications provider's responsibility begins. The demarc could also be a network interface device or simple networking jack.

   Figure 7-3 illustrates the process up to this point.

Figure 7-3

X.25 packet switching process

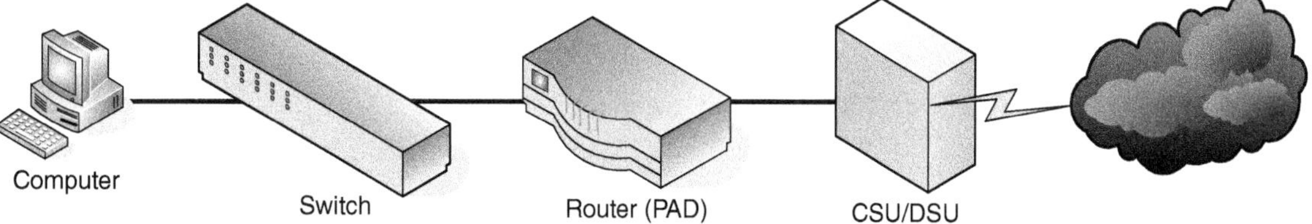

4. This then leads to the central office of the phone company, which provides the X.25 service.
5. The central office (CO) picks a wire and transmits to the switching office, which then continues to the power lines, and so on. When the central office does this, it is known as a virtual circuit. The information then ends up at the receiving central office, which sends the data over another virtual circuit to the appropriate line that leads to the other office.
6. The area between both demarcation points is known as the "cloud," which leads to the demarcation point (demarc), CSU/DSU, and the receiving router (PAD). The receiving PAD buffers the information, checks it, recounts it, and puts the packets in sequence.
7. It then sends the packets over the LAN in regular OSI model fashion to the receiving and intended computer.

The *cloud* is the area of the telephone company's infrastructure that is between the demarcation point of your office and the receiving office. All central offices, switching offices, telephone poles, and lines are part of the cloud.

The cloud is represented in Figure 7-4.

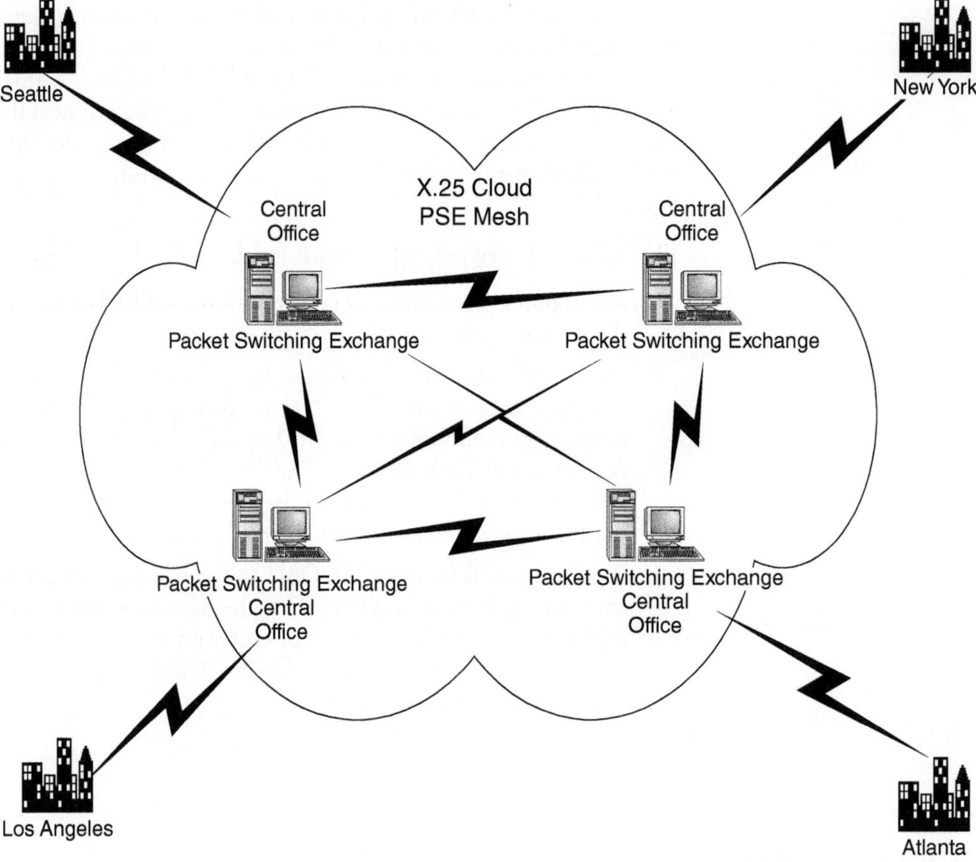

Figure 7-4
X.25 cloud

Here are some of the characteristics of X.25:

- X.25 is usually digital.
- X.25 is usually synchronous, which means that the connection is controlled by a clocking circuit so that both X.25 devices know when to transmit data without having collisions.
- X.25 usually has a 56-Kbps or 64-Kbps maximum speed.
- X.25 is known as variable-length packet switching.
- A PAD decides which circuit the information is going to take as part of the virtual circuit concept.
- Usually packets have 128 bytes of actual data.
- Some configurations go up to 512 bytes.

Now, let's cover the X.25 components. Basically, an X.25 packet is made up of overhead and data. Overhead is the packet's header and trailer information combined. If someone asks what the *two* parts of a packet are, you would answer the overhead and the data. If someone asked about the *three* parts of a packet, you would say the header, the data, and the trailer. Overhead is not message data. It is information sent as additional electrical impulses, but it is not part of the original message.

The ***header*** information includes items such as the packet flag, HDLC (High-Level Data Link Control), a from address, information with error detection, and so on. Figure 7-5 illustrates an entire X.25 packet. The ***trailer*** includes a couple of bits that tell the receiving device that it has reached the end of the packet. It may also contain some type of error checking.

Figure 7-5

X.25 packet

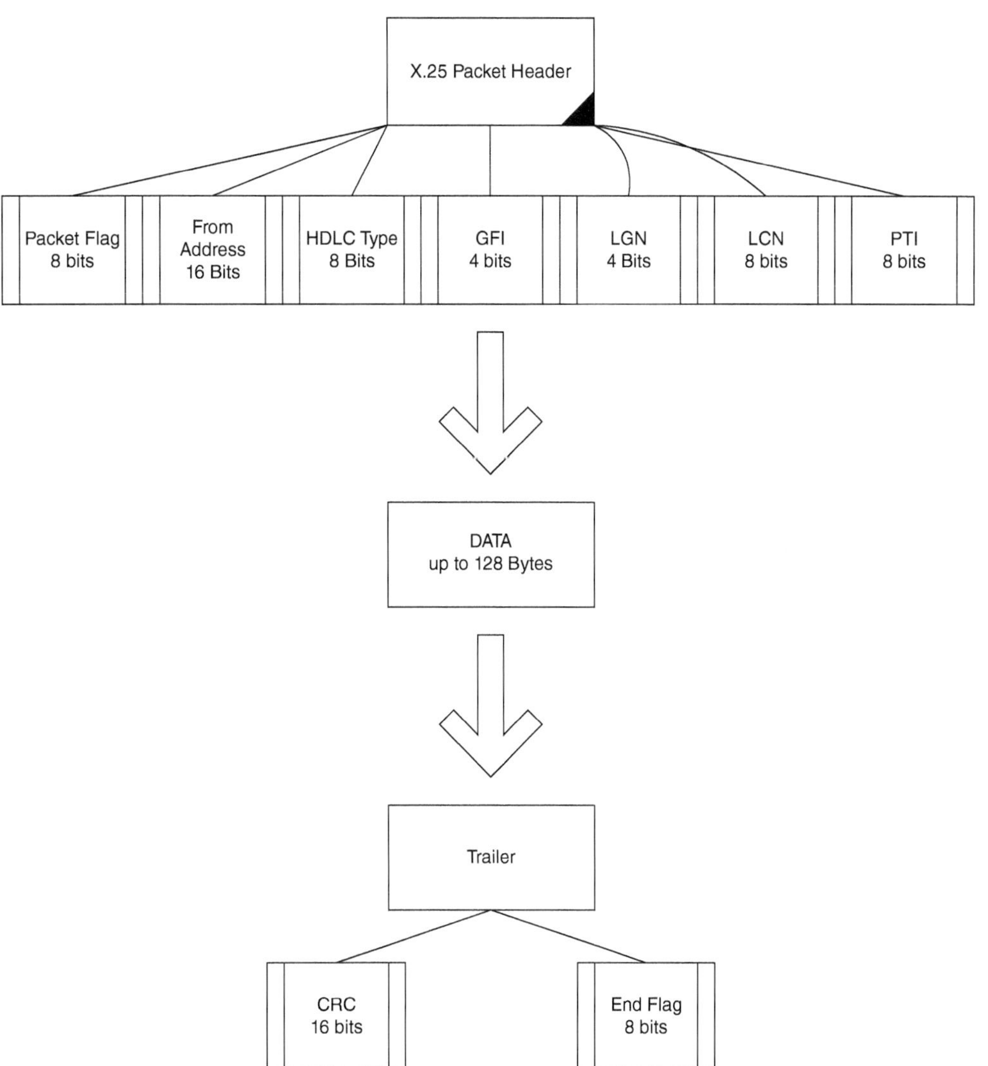

Generally, an X.25 packet will be a maximum of 128 bytes, but remember that a packet's data can be up to 512 bytes and is always of variable length. Some packets have no data at all; they are informational only to the X.25 system.

Let's move onto ***Packet Switching Exchanges (PSEs)*** and switching to virtual circuits. PSEs are located in the central offices just inside the cloud and are really mega switching computers that handle huge amounts of packets and decide which circuit (out of tens of thousands) that the packet will take. Often, these PSEs are UNIX powered. Immense amounts of processing power are needed for the task of sending X.25 packets.

The PSE reads the address and framing information of the packet and then *routes* it in the correct direction. This is another example of the fact that computers can be routers as well; in fact, they are the original routers. They act as routers because they can determine multiple paths for the packet. The PSE chooses a circuit (out of thousands) that is used least, is most direct, or is most available. The PSE then orders a leased line from the Local Exchange Carrier (LEC). It uses this line as the circuit for the packets. In the early days, this was an analog line (2,400 bps). Now, it is a digital line, usually at the speed of 64 kbps. It is also ***synchronous***, which means that there is a clocking circuit that controls the timing of communications between the different routers.

Remember, the PSE has thousands of circuits to choose from. These are known as a circuit set. The chances of the entire message of packets taking one circuit are slim because so many different users and companies are utilizing the bandwidth. For example, a typical message of 10 packets could be spread over five circuits. Because multiple circuits are being used and not just one, the entire circuit set is known as the ***virtual circuit.***

There could be several PSE stops along the way. These PSEs are also PADs. They disassemble and reassemble the packets. These stops are also known as ***hops***. For every hop along the way, the PSE buffers the packets into RAM and holds them there until the next PSE along the way gets the packets and acknowledges them. This way, if a packet is lost between two PSEs, the first will resend. At the receiving office, the PAD (router) reassembles the packets and the overhead (header and trailer) is discarded. The router then sends the information in the regular OSI format to the receiving computer on the LAN.

X.25 has several advantages compared with dial-up analog lines:

- If any data fails, X.25 automatically recovers and resends. This is assuming that there are circuits available in the virtual circuit. If this is not the case and all of the circuits are being used by others, then other arrangements are made. There is a TTL (Time To Live) for the packets to be buffered in the PSE, but if a virtual circuit is not available past the TTL, the PSE notifies the previous PSE or sending router.
- X.25 allows shared access among multiple users on the LAN. They share access through the LAN via the router and the CSU/DSU out to a 64-kbps line. They share access as opposed to each user having a separate dial-up line.
- X.25 has full error and flow control.
- There is also protection from intermediate link failure. It is not completely fault tolerant, but is 70% effective. This is because of the virtual circuit, whereas on a dial-up line, you are using the same circuit to move a file through the whole transfer. If that circuit is lost, the whole message must be re-sent.
- Pricing is per shared packet sent, not per minute.
- X.25 is a synchronous, digital transmission. Digital is inherently better and faster because there is less noise, and the information does not have to be converted from analog to digital and back. So, there is less overhead in this form of conversion.
- There is less *overhead* per file. For dial-up, it could be as much as 40% overhead per file, but with X.25, it could be as little as 8% overhead.

X.25 is considered legacy technology, which has been replaced by less complex and faster technologies. However, X.25 may be found in niche and legacy applications.

DEFINING FRAME RELAY

Frame Relay is an advancement over X.25 packet switching. It is a newer form of packet switching designed for faster connections. The packets are now referred to as *frames*. Like X.25, it uses transmission links only when needed. It also uses a virtual circuit, but one that is more advanced. Frame Relay created the "virtual network," which resides in the cloud. Many customers use the same groups of wires or circuits, which is known as shared circuits. Like private connections (T1, etc.), Frame Relay transmits very quickly. It might use a T1 connection but not in a private manner. The T1 is a trunk carrier, a physical connection that has a data transfer rate of 1.544 Mbps. Unlike X.25, much less processing is needed in Frame Relay. Inside the switches or PSEs, much overhead is eliminated. The network only looks at the address in the frame. Unlike dedicated T1 private connections, it uses a public leased line.

Frame Relay was created to take advantage of the low-error, high-performance digital infrastructure now in place. It is a much simpler network compared with a private line network.

Figure 7-6 illustrates an example of a T1 mesh network. Connections are between each city. This is conceptually similar to the mesh topology.

Figure 7-6

T1 mesh network

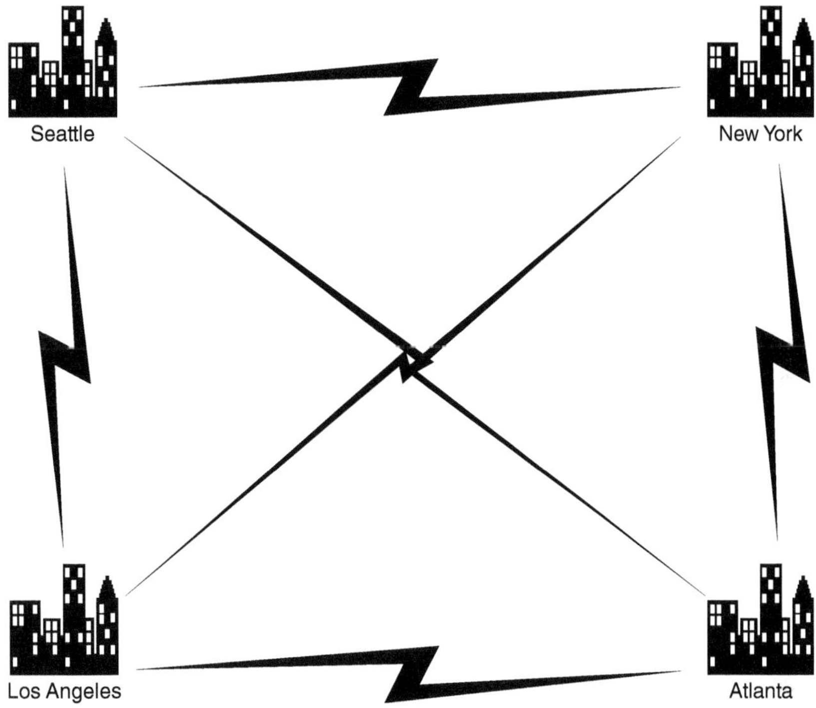

Figure 7-7 illustrates an example of a Frame Relay WAN. Only one connection is needed to the cloud per city.

Disadvantages of Frame Relay are speed and privacy in comparison with a private T1 internetwork. Advantages are much less cost and less equipment.

Let's discuss some of the characteristics of Frame Relay. Multiple sessions can run simultaneously on the same link. These connections to the cloud are known as permanent logical links or ***permanent virtual circuits (PVCs)***, not to be confused with the plastic casing on a Cat5 cable. The PVC links the sites together in the cloud and this is accomplished, once again, by the PSE (Packet Switching Exchange). This is just like a private T1 network, but here the bandwidth is shared at each PVC and with other customers as well. Fewer routers, CSU/DSUs, as well as multiplexors are needed per site. A PVC is always available, so the call setup time of X.25 is eliminated. Constant fine-tuning that is normally needed in private mesh T1 networks is not needed.

CERTIFICATION READY
What are the advantages and disadvantages of leased lines over packet-switched lines?
Objective 1.3

Like any communications, you must purchase the service from an Internet Services or telecommunications provider. These services are known as ***leased lines***. With Frame Relay, you must commit to a certain amount of information over time. This is the ***Committed Information Rate (CIR)***. The CIR is assigned to each PVC that services the organization's account. Because this transmission is full-duplex, there can be two CIRs for each PVC.

Figure 7-7
Frame Relay network

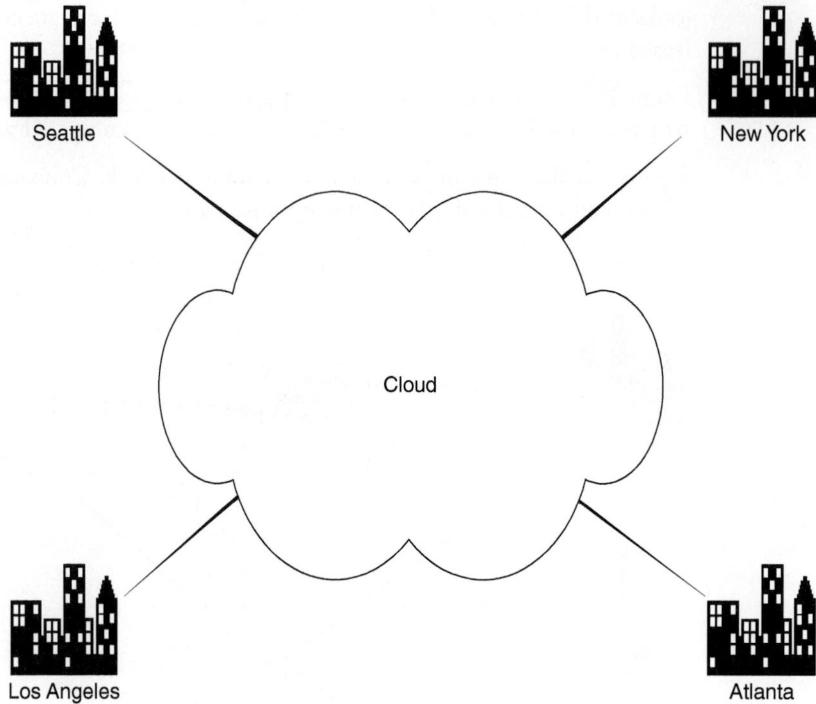

Besides the CIR, there is also Burst Rate (Br), which is equal to the CIR, and Burst Excess Rate (Be), which is 50% above the Br.

Example:

CIR = 128 Kbps
Br = 128 Kbps beyond CIR
Be = 64 Kbps beyond Br

Burst Rates are for two seconds max. The aggregate throughput in this example is 320 Kbps. If you purchase a 128-Kbps Frame Relay leased line, then you get temporary 320 Kbps. You save money and you get the bandwidth when you need it. The frame format in Frame Relay consists of the following:

- **Flag:** Usually 126 or 127 (01111110 or 01111111 in binary). Marks the beginning and end of the frame.
- **DLCI:** Data Link Control ID. 1,024 LCNs (Logical Channel Numbers) Max. Marks the PVC Addressing Scheme.
- **FECN:** Forward Explicit Congestion Notification.
- **BECN:** Backward Explicit Congestion Notification.
- **CR:** Command Response Rate. Usually not in Frame Relay.
- **EA:** Extension bit. If 0, it extends the DLCI address to the address extension in the optional fourth byte.
- **DE:** Discard Eligibility Bit. Denotes if a frame is eligible or if the CIRs are congested.
- **2nd EA:** If this is 1, it ends the DLCI.
- **FCS:** Frame Check Sequence. This is 2 bytes of error checking very similar to the CRC.

TAKE NOTE*

FECN and BECN are for congested CIRs and order of priority.

Figure 7-8 illustrates the components of a frame in Frame Relay.

Figure 7-8

Frame Relay frame

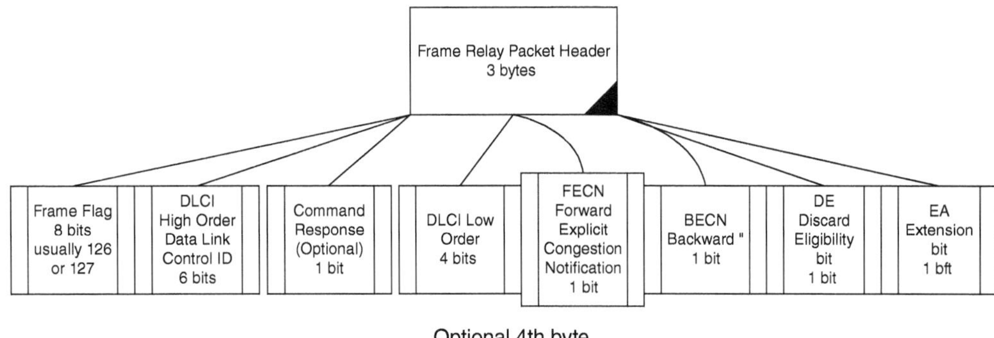

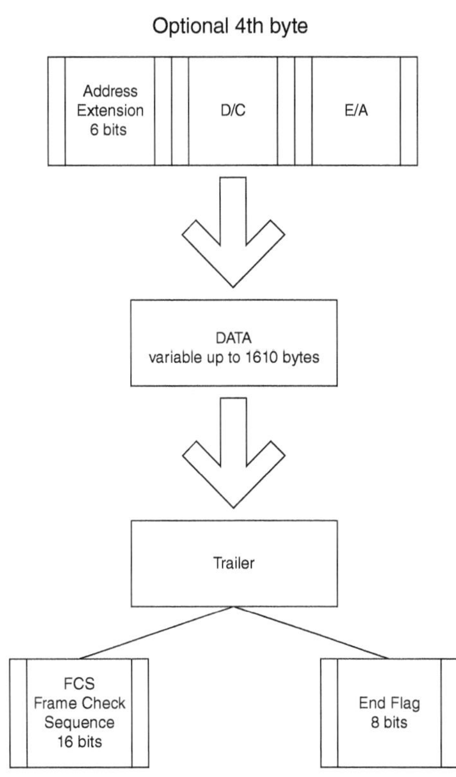

TAKE NOTE*

Circuit switching is another WAN switching method in which a dedicated physical circuit through a carrier network is established, maintained, and terminated for each communication session. Used extensively in telephone company networks, it operates much like a normal telephone call. Circuit switching is used in PSTN data connections.

Defining T-Carriers

T-carriers are interfaces implemented in midsize and large organizations that carry data at high speeds, generally 1.544 MB/s or higher. This section defines a few of the common T-carrier lines.

CERTIFICATION READY
What are the differences between T1 lines and E1 lines?
Objective 1.3

A ***T-carrier*** or telecommunications carrier system is a cabling and interface system designed to carry data at high speeds. The most common of these is the T1. The basic data transfer rate of the T-carrier system is 64 Kbps. This is known as DS0, which is the digital signaling scheme. Correspondingly, DS1 would be the digital signaling scheme for the T1 carrier. The two most common T-carrier systems are:

- ***T1:*** Actual Trunk carrier circuit that is brought into a company. It can run as a dedicated high-speed link or can have other shared technologies run on top of it like Frame

Relay and ISDN. It is considered 1.544 Mbps, but only 1.536 Mbps of that is for data. The remaining 8 Kbps is for T1 trimming/overhead. The 1.536 Mbps is broken into 24 equal 64-Kbps channels and can be used with a multiplexor.

- ***T3*:** Trunk Carrier 3. This is considered as the equivalent of 28 T1s. This is 44.736 Mbps, which uses 672 64-Kbps B channels. This comes to the company as 224 wires or thereabouts and must be punched down to a DSX or like device.

T1 and T3 are names used in the United States. In Japan, they are also known as J1/J3. Europe has a similar carrier system designated as ***E1*** and ***E3***. However, the E1 has 32 channels/2.048 Mbps and E3 has 512 channels at 34.368 Mbps. Table 7-1 shows common carrier systems.

Different services can run on a T-carrier system. It might be Frame Relay, ISDN, or other services. Otherwise, the T-carrier can be a dedicated private connection between LANs to form a completely private WAN.

Figure 7-9 shows an illustration of a typical T1 connection and service.

Figure 7-9

Typical T1 configuration with Frame Relay

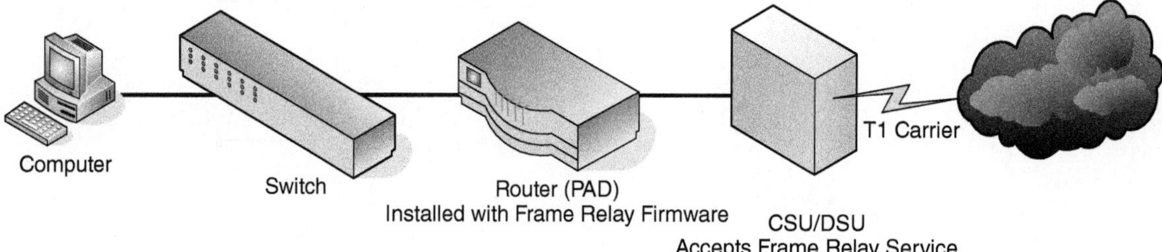

Table 7-1 summarizes the main types of T-carrier systems and their equivalents.

Table 7-1

Common T-Carriers, Their Speeds, and Equivalents

Carrier System	United States	Japan	Europe
Level 0–DS0	64 Kbps	64 Kbps	64 Kbps
Level 1–DS1	1.544 Mbps—T1	1.544 Mbps—J1	2.048 Mbps—E1
Level 3–DS3	44.736 Mbps—T3	32.064 Mbps—J3	34.368 Mbps—E3
Level 4–DS4	274.176 Mbps—T4	97.728 Mbps—J4	139.264 Mbps—E4

Defining Other WAN Technologies and Internet Connectivity

Although Frame Relay and T-carriers are very common WAN connectivity technologies, there are other types of connections that a company might opt for, such as ISDN, ATM, SONET, cable, or DSL. This section defines those other WAN technologies, which is summarized in Table 7-2.

Table 7-2

Summary WAN Technologies and Connections

WAN Technology	Description
X.25	One of the first implementations of packet switching. Usually 64 Kbps with a 128-byte payload per packet.
Frame Relay	The advancement of X.25 packet switching. It is a newer form of packet switching designed for faster connections.
T-carrier	A cabling and interface system designed to carry data at high speeds. The most common of these is T1.
ISDN	A digital technology developed to combat the limitations of PSTN. Users who have ISDN can send data, talk on the phone, and fax simultaneously from one line.
ATM	A cell-based switching technology as opposed to a packet switching technology. The cells are a fixed length, normally 53 octets.
SONET	The abbreviation for Synchronous Optical NETwork. It transfers multiple digital bit streams over optical fibers.
FDDI	A standard for transmitting data on optical fiber cables at a rate of around 100 Mbps.
DSL	A family of technologies that provide data transmissions over local telephone networks.
Broadband cable	A high-speed cable Internet allowing for connections up to 5 to 7 Mbps.
POTS/PSTN	Plain Old Telephone System/Public Switched Telephone Network.

CERTIFICATION READY
What is the difference between BRI and PRI?
Objective 1.3

The ***Integrated Services Digital Network (ISDN)*** is a digital technology developed to combat the limitations of PSTN. Users who have ISDN can send data, talk on the phone, and fax simultaneously from one line. ISDN can be broken down into two major categories:

- ***Basic Rate ISDN (BRI)*:** 128 Kbps with two equal B channels at 64 Kbps each for data, and one 16-Kbps D channel for timing. Generally, devices that connect to BRI lines can handle eight simultaneous connections to the Internet.
- ***Primary Rate ISDN (PRI)*:** 1.536 Mbps, runs on a T1 circuit. PRI has 23 equal 64-Kbps B channels for data and one 64-Kbps D channel for timing.

Many companies still use this for videoconferencing or as a fault-tolerant secondary Internet access connection. Videoconferencing requires a PRI line because BRI does not have enough bandwidth. Today, BRI is difficult to find because it has been mostly replaced by DSL and cable connections.

Asynchronous Transfer Mode (ATM) is a cell-based switching technology as opposed to a packet switching technology. The cells are a fixed length, normally 53 octets (or 53 8-bit bytes). It is used as a backbone for ISDN.

OCx is the standard for data throughput on ***SONET*** connections. SONET is an abbreviation for Synchronous Optical NETwork. It transfers multiple digital bit streams over optical fibers. The rates shown in Table 7-3 are known as synchronous transport signal rates.

Table 7-3

Synchronous Transport Signal Rates

OC Level	Transmission Rate
OC-1	51.84 Mbps
OC-3	155.52 Mbps
OC-12	622.08 Mbps
OC-24	1.244 Gbps
OC-48	2.488 Gbps
OC-192	9.953 Gbps

Fiber Distributed Data Interface (FDDI) is a standard for transmitting data on optical fiber cables at a rate of around 100 Mbps. It uses the ring topology.

Digital Subscriber Line (DSL) is a family of technologies that provide data transmissions over local telephone networks. Variations of DSL include:

- **xDSL:** xDSL is the standard for the various Digital Subscriber Lines.
- **ADSL (Asymmetrical Digital Subscriber Lines):** ADSL can run on your home telephone line so that you can talk on the phone and access the Internet at the same time. However, some versions limit you to 28,800 bps upload speed, and the download is variable spiking as high as 7 Mbps. It is usually not as fast as cable Internet.
- **SDSL (Symmetrical Digital Subscriber Line):** SDSL is installed (usually to companies) as a separate line and is more expensive. SDSL data transfer rates can be purchased at 384 K, 768 K, 1.1 M, and 1.5 M. The upload and download speeds are the same, or symmetrical!

Broadband cable is used for cable Internet and cable TV. Higher speed than DSL, broadband cable can usually get up to an average of 5 to 7 Mbps, although the serial connection has the theoretical ability to go to 18 Mbps. DSLreports.com commonly shows people connecting with cable at 10 Mbps.

POTS/PSTN is the Plain Old Telephone System/Public Switched Telephone Network. This is what we use today for our regular phone line and it's been around since the forties. It is now digital at the switching office and some central offices, but there are analog lines to the home.

SKILL SUMMARY

In this lesson, you learned:

- Static routing is when a router has been manually configured. For example, when a routing entry is manually entered in to the routing table with the `route add` command, it is known as static routing.
- Dynamic routing is implemented by dynamically configuring routing tables. This is done with dynamic routing protocols, such as RIP and OSPF.
- Today, most networks are converged, which means that the network supports telephone, video, and data communications on a single network. Whereas a traditional network would only have carried data packets—such as when you open a file from a shared folder, access a website over the Internet, or retrieve email—a converged network also supports voice, video, and other time-sensitive packets. Quality of Service (QoS) is an industry-wide

set of standards and mechanisms that ensure high-quality performance for critical and time-sensitive applications on shared networks.

- Wide area networks connect multiple local area networks together. If an organization wants to have a wide area connection to another office, administrators need to decide on a networking service and the speed that they want to connect at. Budgeting plays a big role in these types of decisions.
- Although Frame Relay and T-carriers are very common WAN connectivity technologies, there are other types of connections that a company might opt for, such as ISDN, ATM, SONET, cable, or DSL.

Knowledge Assessment

Multiple Choice

Select the correct answer for each of the following questions.

1. You have been hired as an administrator to install several routing protocols to a group of routers. Which one of the following is *not* an example of a dynamic routing protocol?
   a. RIP
   b. IGRP
   c. RRAS
   d. OSPF
2. A server running Windows Server 2016 needs to have the latest version of RIP installed. Which version of RIP should be selected?
   a. Version 1
   b. Version 2
   c. Version 3
   d. RIP does not have any versions.
3. Proseware, Inc., needs to install a PAD (router) that will enable a packet-switched connection to the Internet. Which of the following is an example of packet switching technology?
   a. T1
   b. Frame Relay
   c. 802.1X
   d. ATM
4. Which of the following is the best tool to use for installing a NAT server?
   a. DNS
   b. RIP
   c. ATM
   d. RRAS
5. The IT director wants to install a new demarc device. Which of the following is he referring to? (Choose the best answer.)
   a. A router
   b. A CSU/DSU
   c. A switch
   d. A server

6. As an administrator, you have been asked to troubleshoot a wide area networking technology that has a maximum data transfer rate of 64 Kbps. Which technology will you be troubleshooting?
   a. Frame Relay
   b. ATM
   c. X.25
   d. SONET
7. Which of the following devices is a PAD most similar to?
   a. Hub
   b. Switch
   c. Router
   d. CSU/DSU
8. Which of the following is the total speed or throughput of a T1 line?
   a. 1.536 Mbps
   b. 1.544 Mbps
   c. 1.5 Mbps
   d. 15.35 Mbps
9. A customer wants to install an ISDN line for videoconferencing. Which of the following should be installed?
   a. BRI
   b. ATM
   c. PRI
   d. OC3
10. A small business wants to ensure that its DSL Internet connection uploads and downloads the same amount of information per second. Which type of DSL should be installed?
    a. xDSL
    b. ADSL
    c. SDSL
    d. DSL Lite
11. Which of the following is used to ensure that time-sensitive packets are delivered promptly?
    a. Remote Assistance
    b. VPN Reconnect
    c. Quality of Service
    d. Connection Manager

Fill in the Blank

Fill in the correct answer in the blank space provided.

1. It is a requirement to install a routing protocol that monitors the network for routers that have changed their link state. The _____ protocol provides the ability to accomplish this.
2. The _____ is a protocol that bases routing decisions on the network path and rules.
3. RIPv2 needs to be installed to enable dynamic routing. This should be installed in the _____ snap-in.
4. A customer requires a high-speed packet switching alternative to X.25. _____ should be installed.

5. X.25 connections utilize a clocking circuit. This makes them _____.

6. While analyzing Frame Relay frames, it is found that a message consisting of 10 separate packets was sent over five different circuits. These five circuits together form a _____ circuit.

7. A company just purchased a leased line that runs the Frame Relay service. The standard data rate for this service is known as _____.

8. A client wants to upgrade her remote users from dial-up to a faster service. However, cable Internet and DSL are not available in their respective areas. Another valid alternative is to use _____.

9. A customer wants a WAN technology that does not use variable-length packets but instead uses fixed-length cells. _____ is the recommended solution.

10. A client with eight computers needs a cost-effective Internet solution that can transmit 128 Kbps. _____ is the recommended solution.

■ Business Case Scenarios

Scenario 7-1: Selecting the Appropriate Service and Protocol

A client wants you to install a service that will allow network connections from a Windows Server 2016. The client wants you to select a well-known routing protocol that utilizes distance-vector algorithms. Describe your recommended solution.

Scenario 7-2: Selecting the Appropriate WAN Technology

The ABC Company wants you to install a WAN technology that will allow high-speed access to its satellite office. Administrators want it to be a private, dedicated connection. Which technology should be used?

Scenario 7-3: Recommending the Right Service

Proseware, Inc., requires that you set up an extremely fast wide area connection that can communicate at 2.4 Gbps over fiber-optic lines. Which service should be used?

Scenario 7-4: Setting Up Routes to Other Networks

Proseware, Inc., wants you to set up several routes to other networks. They provide you with the following documentation:

Route #1:

- **Network:** 192.168.1.0
- **Subnet mask:** 255.255.255.0
- **Gateway:** 65.43.18.1

Route #2:

- **Network:** 10.10.1.0
- **Subnet mask:** 255.255.255.0
- **Gateway:** 128.52.67.101

Route #3:

- **Network:** 172.16.0.0
- **Subnet mask:** 255.255.0.0
- **Gateway:** 84.51.23.132

Access the DIR-655 emulator at the following link and configure the routing options appropriately: http://support.dlink.com/emulators/dir655/133NA/login.html. Capture a screen shot showing your results.

Workplace Ready

Find the Path—with Routing

IP routing is one of the most important pieces of TCP/IP. Without it, companies would not be able to communicate; home offices wouldn't be able to get on the Internet. In short, the world would come crashing down. IP routing (also known as IP forwarding) makes the connection between a router's two or more network adapters on different IP networks. There are many types of routers that allow connections from one network to another.

Research the Internet for different types of routers, from SOHO four-port routers to business-level routers to enterprise routers that an ISP would use. Make a list of your findings, including manufacturer, model, price, and, if possible, who uses them. Try to find at least three routers for each of the following categories:

- Small Office/Home Office (SOHO)
- Business level (small to midsize business)
- Enterprise level

Analyze your findings and state your case for the best router in each category. Back up your case with pricing, functionality, speed, and amount of routes and data transactions each device can handle.

Defining Network Infrastructures and Network Security

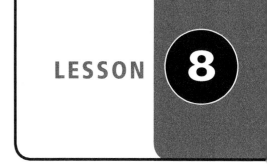

OBJECTIVE DOMAIN MATRIX

Skills/Concepts	Objective Domain Description	Objective Domain Number
Understanding Networks Outside the LAN	Understand the concepts of the Internet, intranet, and extranet	1.1
Configuring VPN Connections and Authentication	Understand the concepts of the Internet, intranet, and extranet	1.1
Understanding Security Devices and Zones	Understand the concepts of the Internet, intranet, and extranet	1.1
Putting It All Together	(None)	(None)

KEY TERMS

3-leg perimeter configuration
application-level gateway (ALG)
back-to-back configuration
caching proxy
Challenge Handshake Authentication Protocol (CHAP)
circuit-level gateway
Connection Manager (CM)
Connection Manager Administration Kit (CMAK)
Extensible Authentication Protocol (EAP-MS-CHAPv2)
extranet
firewalls
Internet
Internet content filter
Internet Key Exchange version 2 (IKEv2)
intranet
IP proxy
Layer 2 Tunneling Protocol over IPsec (L2TP/IPsec)
Microsoft CHAP version 2 (MS-CHAPv2)
NAT filtering
network intrusion detection system (NIDS)
network intrusion prevention system (NIPS)
packet filtering
Password Authentication Protocol (PAP)
Point-to-Point Tunneling Protocol (PPTP)
Protected Extensible Authentication Protocol (PEAP)
proxy server
Secure Socket Tunneling Protocol (SSTP)
stateful packet inspection (SPI)
virtual private network (VPN)
VPN Reconnect
Web 2.0
World Wide Web (WWW)

Proseware, Inc., is a growing, dynamic company that not only needs fast connections on the LAN and WAN, but also requires various network infrastructures so that they can communicate properly with customers, sister organizations, and partners.

As the network engineer, you are in charge of setting up secure connections for remote users and clients. You are also responsible for the private connectivity to partners' websites and other corporate networks.

By using network infrastructure concepts, such as VPNs, intranets, and extranets, and by utilizing security devices, such as firewalls and proxy servers, you can develop a secure method of connecting everything together while limiting access to only those who require it.

■ Understanding Networks Outside the LAN

The biggest wide area network of them all is the Internet. Obviously, it is well-known as the World Wide Web, but it is not as well-known for other services that reside on the Internet, or the inner workings of the Internet.

THE BOTTOM LINE

Other technologies, such as intranets and extranets, enable organizations to communicate with and share data with other organizations in a secure manner using the inherent properties of the Internet but in a privatized way. Virtual private networks often come into play when it comes to intranets and extranets. They are used to create secure connections that can cross over public networks.

Defining the Internet

The Internet is the largest WAN in the world. It is a public domain available to everyone in the United States, and is available to most other countries as well. This section defines the Internet and the way it functions.

CERTIFICATION READY
How do you define the Internet?
Objective 1.1

The ***Internet*** is a worldwide system of connected computer networks. The computers that connect to the Internet use the TCP/IP protocol suite. It is estimated that there are 2 billion users of the Internet, and an estimated 650 million computers connect to the Internet, although it is difficult to estimate this due to NAT and other similar services. The origins of the Internet can be traced back to the United States' ARPANET, which was developed for government security purposes; however, this was a disjointed group of networks using deprecated or nonuniform protocols. By using TCP/IP to join different types of networks together, the true Internet was born.

The Internet is not controlled by any one governing body except in two technical aspects. First, the IP classification system is defined by the IANA (Internet Assigned Numbers Authority). Second, DNS is defined by the Internet Engineering Task Force (IETF). Otherwise, the Internet is "controlled" by various ISPs and network providers depending on the location. How the Internet is accessed is defined by these companies.

Companies use the Internet for many reasons, including:

- To communicate messages such as email
- To gather information, often through the usage of web pages

- To share information, often using a web server
- For e-commerce
- To collaborate with other companies, organizations, and users

Individuals use the Internet for the above reasons as well as for social networking, shopping, file sharing, and for gaming and other multimedia use.

Though the World Wide Web is a big part of the Internet, it is not the entire Internet. However, users often use the terms interchangeably. The Internet is the entire data communications system that connects the world, including hardware and software. The ***Word Wide Web (WWW)*** is an enormous system of interlinked hypertext documents that are accessed with a web browser. Standards for how documents are created and interlinked are defined by the World Wide Web Consortium. Currently, the World Wide Web is in a stage known as ***Web 2.0*** (with Web 3.0 just under way). Web 2.0 is an interactive type of web experience compared with the previous version 1.0. Web 2.0 allows users to interact with each other and act as contributors to the website as well. When most people access the Internet, they do it through a web browser, but there are many other tools that can be used to access the Internet, including instant messaging programs, FTP clients, third-party media programs, and much more.

Defining Intranets and Extranets

Intranets and extranets are used by organizations to share data with select individuals. Whereas an intranet is used by an organization to share data with its employees, an extranet is used to share data with sister companies or other partnered organizations.

CERTIFICATION READY
How do you define intranets and extranets?
Objective 1.1

An ***intranet*** is a private computer network or single website that an organization implements in order to share data with employees around the world. User authentication is necessary before a person can access the information in the intranet; this keeps the general public out, as long as the intranet is properly secured.

Generally, a company refers to an intranet as its private website, or the portion of its website that is private. But intranets use all of the inherent technologies of the Internet. TCP/IP protocols, such as HTTP and FTP, and email protocols, such as POP3 and SMTP, are all utilized in the same way that they are on the Internet. Again, the only difference is this is a privatized version of the Internet, and any company can have one.

An ***extranet*** is similar to an intranet except that it is extended to users outside the company, and possibly to entire organizations that are separate from, or lateral to, the company. If a company needs to do business with a specific organization, it might be beneficial to set up an extranet in order to facilitate the sharing of information. User authentication is still necessary, and the extranet is not open to the general public.

Figure 8-1 illustrates an intranet and extranet. Intranets and extranets can be connected to by simply logging on to a website or by using a virtual private network.

Configuring VPN Connections and Authentication

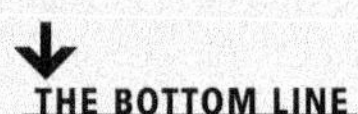

A ***virtual private network (VPN)*** is a private network that uses a public network (for example, the Internet) to connect remote sites and users. The VPN makes it appear to computers, on each end of the connection, as if they are actually connected to the same network. This point-to-point connection is emulated by encapsulating the packet in an IP header. The information in the header is used to route the information between the two VPN endpoints.

Figure 8-1

Illustration of intranet and extranet

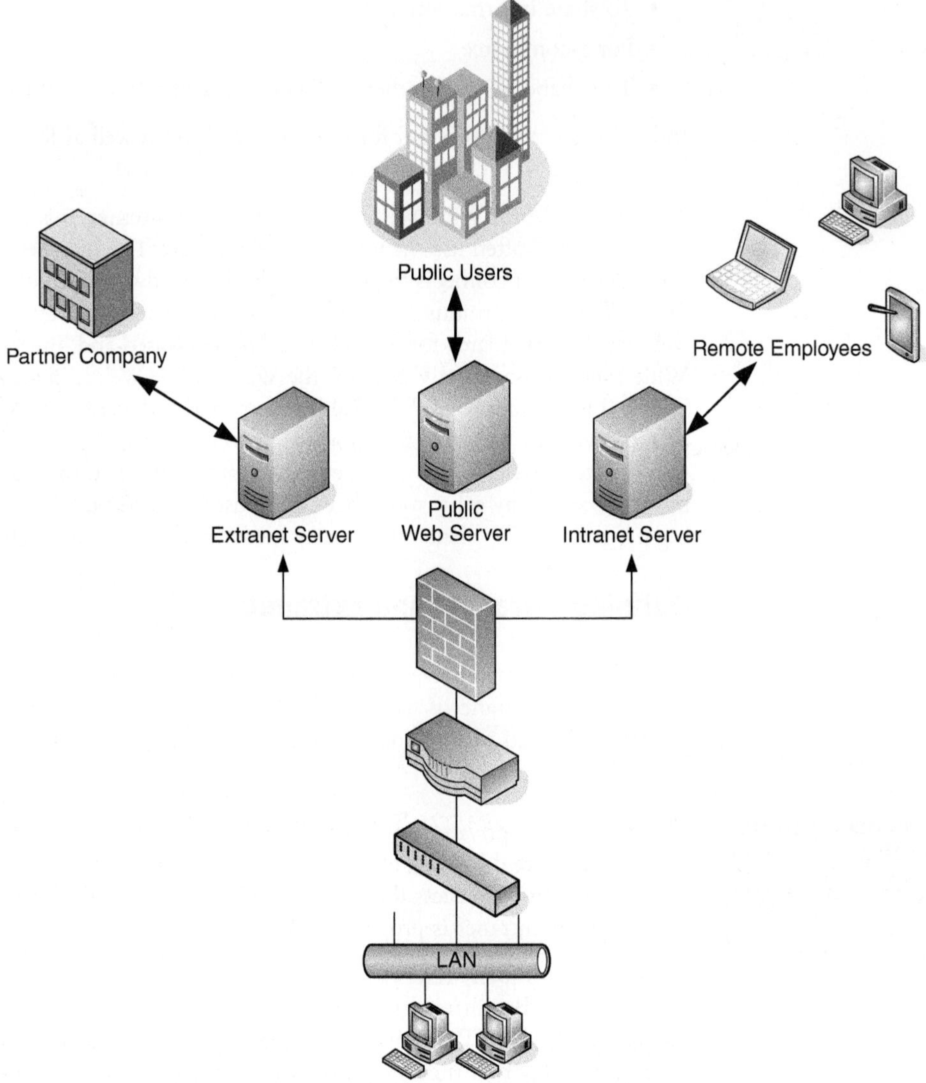

CERTIFICATION READY
How would you define and configure a VPN?
Objective 1.1

Tunneling protocols, authentication protocols, and encryption levels applied to the VPN connections determine the level of VPN security you have available. For a VPN to work, both the client and server need to utilize the same protocols. Overall, VPNs can provide the following capabilities:

- Data encryption (confidentiality)
- Authentication
- Data integrity, which ensures the packets are not modified while in transit
- Nonrepudiation, which guarantees the packets came from the claimed source at a specific time

The VPN uses the concept of tunneling (see Figure 8-2) to establish and maintain a logical network connection.

Figure 8-2
VPN tunnel

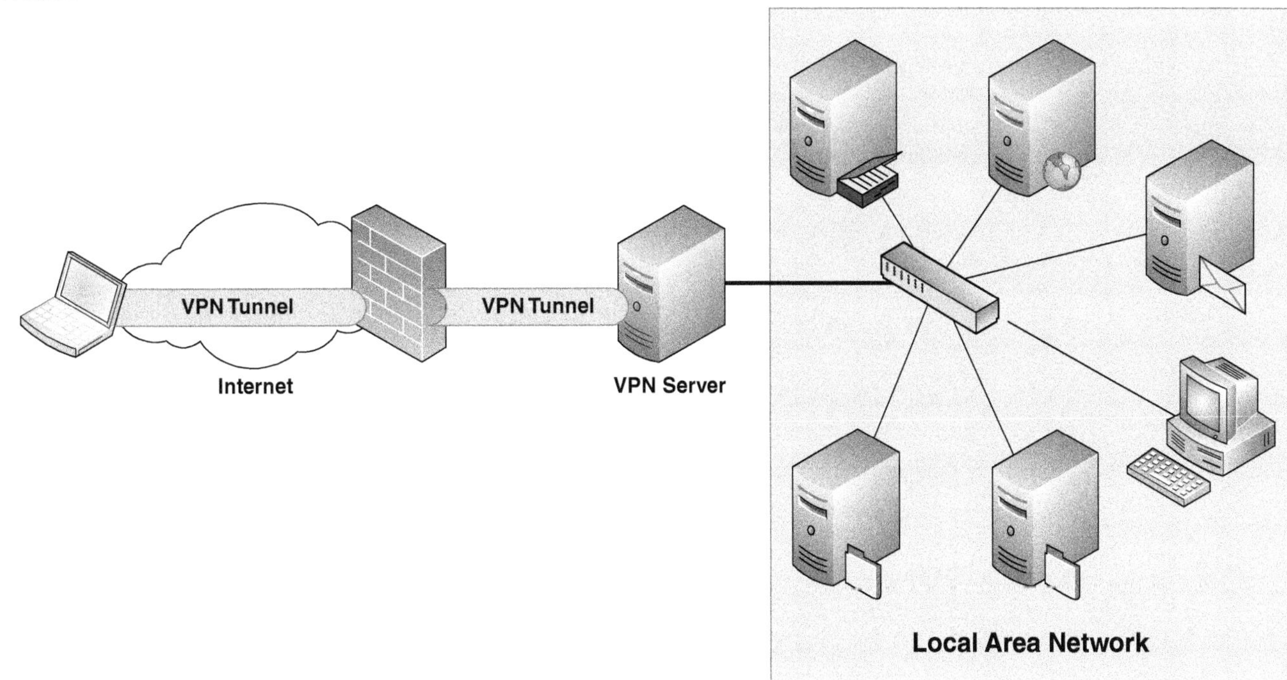

Selecting Types of VPN Protocols

There are four types of VPN tunneling protocols that are available in Windows 10. They include Point-to-Point Tunneling Protocol (PPTP), Layer 2 Tunneling Protocol over IPsec (L2TP/IPsec), Secure Socket Tunneling Protocol (SSTP), and VPN Reconnect (or IKEv2).

Point-to-Point Tunneling Protocol (PPTP) has widespread support with nearly all versions of Windows. It uses the Microsoft Point-to-Point Encryption (MPPE) protocol with RC4 (128-bit key) to protect data that is in transit. Although not as secure as L2TP/IPsec (discussed later), it can provide a reasonably secure option for remote access and site-to-site VPNs when used in combination with an authentication protocol, such as MS-CHAPv2.

PPTP provides confidentiality, meaning that it prevents the data from being viewed, but it does not provide data integrity. In other words, it does not protect the packet from being intercepted and modified. PPTP does not implement nonrepudiation, since there is no mechanisms used to ensure the data is truly sent by the authorized person.

TAKE NOTE*

PPTP is typically used for remote access and site-to-site VPNs, works with IPv4, and uses Network Address Translation (NAT), which is supported via PPTP-enabled NAT routers. It uses PPP for user authentication and RC4 for data confidentiality.

Whereas PPTP supports authentication of the user only, ***Layer 2 Tunneling Protocol over IPsec (L2TP/IPsec)*** requires that the computers also mutually authenticate themselves to each other. The computer-to-computer authentication takes place before the user is authenticated.

L2TP provides a support mechanism for pre-shared keys, digital certificates, or Kerberos for mutual authentication. Pre-shared keys are basically passwords and should only be used in test networks when you don't want to set up a public key infrastructure (PKI). Digital certificates, which are stored in a format that cannot be modified, offer a more secure option. They are issued by certificate authorities that you trust. Kerberos is the native authentication protocol for Windows Server 2003 and later and provides the easiest way to secure VPN connections in a domain-based environment. It provides mutual authentication, anti-replay, and nonrepudiation just like digital certificates.

Kerberos can only be used when both computers involved in the L2TP tunnel are in the same forest. L2TP uses IPsec to encrypt the Point-to-Point Protocol (PPP) packets. L2TP/IPsec provides data confidentiality and data integrity as well as proof that an authorized individual sent the message.

TAKE NOTE*

L2TP with IPsec is typically used for remote access and site-to-site VPNs, works over IPv4 and IPv6, and supports Network Address Translation. It uses IPsec with 3DES (168-bit key) and uses UDP ports (500, 1701, 4500). It uses IPsec for machine authentication followed by PPP for user authentication.

Secure Socket Tunneling Protocol (SSTP) improved upon the PPTP and L2TP/IPsec VPN tunneling protocols. It works by sending PPP or L2TP traffic through an SSL 3.0 channel.

The SSTP protocol uses SSL and TCP port 443 to relay traffic. By using TCP port 443, it works in network environments where other VPN protocols might be blocked when traversing firewalls, Network Address Translation (NAT) devices, and web proxies. SSTP uses a 2,048-bit certificate for authentication and implements stronger encryption, which makes it the most secure VPN protocol.

IKEv2 consists of the following protocols: IPsec Tunnel Mode, IKEv2, Encapsulating Security Payload (ESP), and MOBIKE. IKEv2 is used by IPsec for key negotiations, ESP is used for securing the packet transmissions, and MOBIKE (Mobility and Multihoming Protocol) is used for switching tunnel endpoints. MOBIKE ensures that if there is a break in connectivity, the user can continue without restarting the connection.

TAKE NOTE*

SSTP is supported by Windows Vista SP1 and later client operating systems, and Windows Server 2008 and later server operating systems. It is designed for remote access VPNs; works over IPv4 and IPv6 networks; and traverses NAT, firewalls, and web proxies. It uses a generic port that is rarely blocked by firewalls. It uses PPP for user authentication and RC4/AES for data confidentiality.

VPN Reconnect, also known as ***Internet Key Exchange version 2 (IKEv2)***, is a feature introduced with Routing and Remote Access Service (RRAS) in Windows Server 2008 R2 and Windows 7. It is designed to provide users with consistent VPN connectivity and automatically reestablishes a VPN when users temporarily lose their Internet connection.

VPN Reconnect was designed for those remote workers who are sitting in the coffee shop, waiting at the airport for their next plane to arrive, trying to submit that last expense report from their hotel room, or working anywhere Internet connections are less than optimal.

It differs from other VPN protocols in that it will not drop the VPN tunnel that is associated with the session. Instead, it keeps the connection alive for 30 minutes by default after it's been dropped. This allows you to reconnect automatically without having to go through the process of selecting your VPN connection and authenticating yourself all over again.

TAKE NOTE*

VPN Reconnect is designed for remote access VPNs. It works well over IPv4 and IPv6 networks and traverses NAT. It also supports user or machine authentication via IKEv2 and uses 3DES and AES for data confidentiality. IKEv2 uses UDP port 500.

When selecting the appropriate VPN protocol to use, you must take into consideration operating systems, authentication requirements, and limitations. Therefore, you should consider the following:

- Operating systems that you will be using and their ability to traverse firewalls, NAT devices, and web proxies

- Authentication requirements (for computers as well as users)
- Implementations: site-to-site VPN or a remote access VPN

In most situations, using VPN Reconnect (IKEv2) will provide you the best option for security and uninterrupted VPN connectivity. You can then use SSTP for your VPN solution as a fallback mechanism.

Selecting Authentication for VPN Connections

During a VPN connection, the user must be authenticated to prove who is logging on. Therefore, you need to choose the most secure form of authentication that can be deployed to your remote users.

Authentication for VPN connections takes one of the following forms:

- User-level authentication by using Point-to-Point Protocol (PPP) authentication. User-level authentication is usually user name and password. With a VPN connection, if the VPN server authenticates, the VPN client attempts the connection using a PPP user-level authentication method and verifies that the VPN client has the appropriate authorization. If the method uses mutual authentication, the VPN client also authenticates the VPN server. By using mutual authentication, clients are ensured that the client does not communicate with a rogue server masquerading as a VPN server.
- Computer-level authentication by using IKE to exchange either computer certificates or a pre-shared key. Microsoft recommends using computer-certificate authentication because it is a much stronger authentication method. Computer-level authentication is performed only for L2TP/IPsec connections.

When using VPNs, Windows 10 supports the following forms of authentication:

- ***Password Authentication Protocol (PAP)*:** A basic authentication method that uses plaintext (unencrypted passwords). PAP is the least secure authentication and is not recommended.
- ***Challenge Handshake Authentication Protocol (CHAP)*:** A challenge-response authentication that uses the industry standard MD5 hashing scheme to encrypt the response. CHAP was an industry standard for years and is still quite popular.
- ***Microsoft CHAP version 2 (MS-CHAPv2)*:** A mature authentication method that provides two-way authentication (mutual authentication). MS-CHAPv2 provides stronger security than CHAP. Finally, MS-CHAPv2 is the only authentication protocol that Windows Server 2016 provides that allows you to change an expired password during the connection process.
- ***Extensible Authentication Protocol (EAP-MS-CHAPv2)*:** A universal authentication framework that allows third-party vendors to develop custom authentication schemes, including retinal scans, voice recognition, fingerprint identifications, smart cards, Kerberos, and digital certificates. It also provides a mutual authentication method that supports password-based user or computer authentication.
- ***Protected Extensible Authentication Protocol (PEAP)*:** An authentication method that encapsulates the EAP with an encrypted and authenticated Transport Layer Security (TLS) tunnel.

It is always best to use EAP-MS-CHAPv2 or MS-CHAPv2 whenever possible. However, Windows 10 will be able to negotiate MSCHAP v2, EAP-MS-CHAPv2, and PEAP with MSCHAPv2.

Creating a VPN Connection Using the Create a VPN Connection Wizard

Windows 10 provides a simple Getting Started Wizard—also known as the Get Connected Wizard (GCW) and Create a VPN Connection Wizard—that helps make the setup and configuration of a VPN connection quick and simple for end users.

To make the process of setting up a VPN profile and connecting to a VPN much simpler in Windows 10, you can use the Getting Started Wizard.

The Getting Started Wizard requires that you enter the server information and then it auto-discovers the authentication methods and tunneling protocols during the initial connection process.

CREATE A VPN CONNECTION USING THE GETTING STARTED WIZARD

GET READY. To create a VPN using the Getting Started Wizard, perform the following steps.

1. Right-click **Start** and choose **Control Panel.**
2. In the Search Control Panel, type **VPN** and press **Enter.** From the search results, click **Set up a virtual private network (VPN) connection.**
3. In the Create a VPN Connection Wizard (as shown in Figure 8-3), in the Internet address text box, type a domain name (such as **vpn.adatum.com**) or IP address. In the Destination name text box, type a label that will identify the VPN connection. Click **Create.**

Figure 8-3

Creating a VPN connection

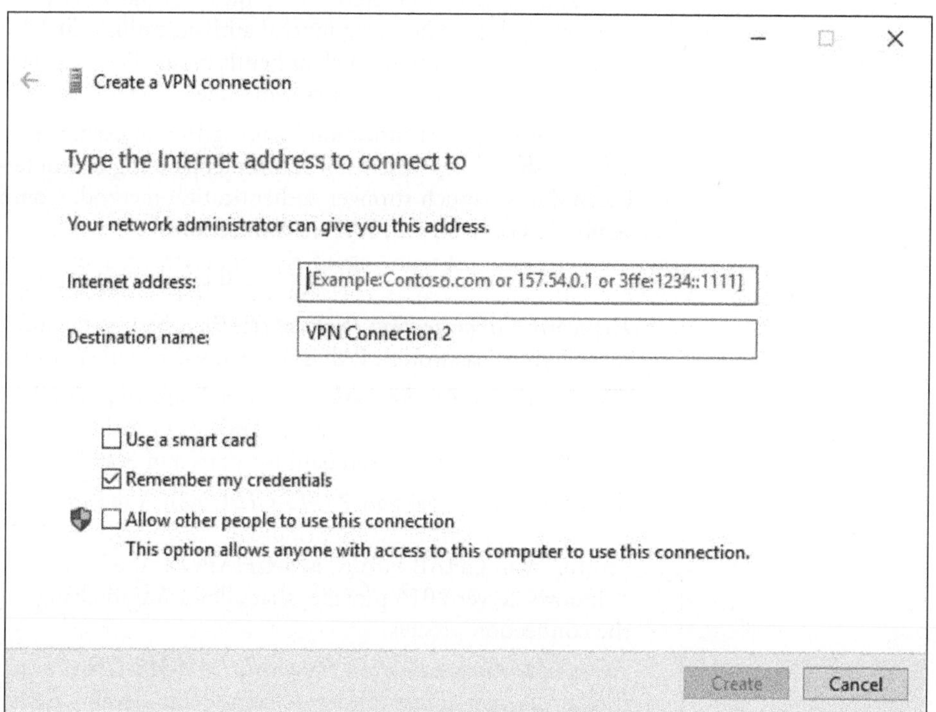

4. Right-click the **network status** icon on the taskbar and choose **Open Network and Sharing Center.**
5. In the Network and Sharing Center, click **Change adapter settings.**
6. In the Network Connections window, right-click the **VPN connection** and choose **Properties.**
7. Click the **Security** tab, as shown in Figure 8-4.

   The Security tab allows you to specify the VPN protocol—Point-to-Point Tunneling Protocol (PPTP), Layer 2 Tunneling Protocol over IPsec (L2TP/IPsec), Secure Socket Tunneling Protocol (SSTP), and IKEv2—and the authentication method.
8. Click **OK** to close the VPN Connection Properties dialog box.

Figure 8-4

Configuring VPN security settings

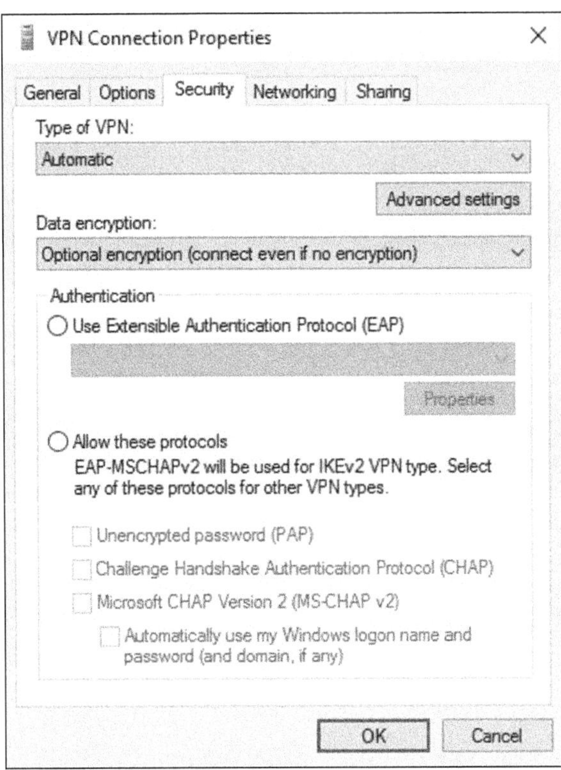

To connect to the remote network using the VPN connection, click the network status icon on the taskbar and then click the VPN connection that you just created. In the Network & Internet window, click VPN Connection (as shown in Figure 8-5) and then click Connect. You will then be prompted to provide a user name and password. Click OK.

Figure 8-5

Connecting to a VPN connection

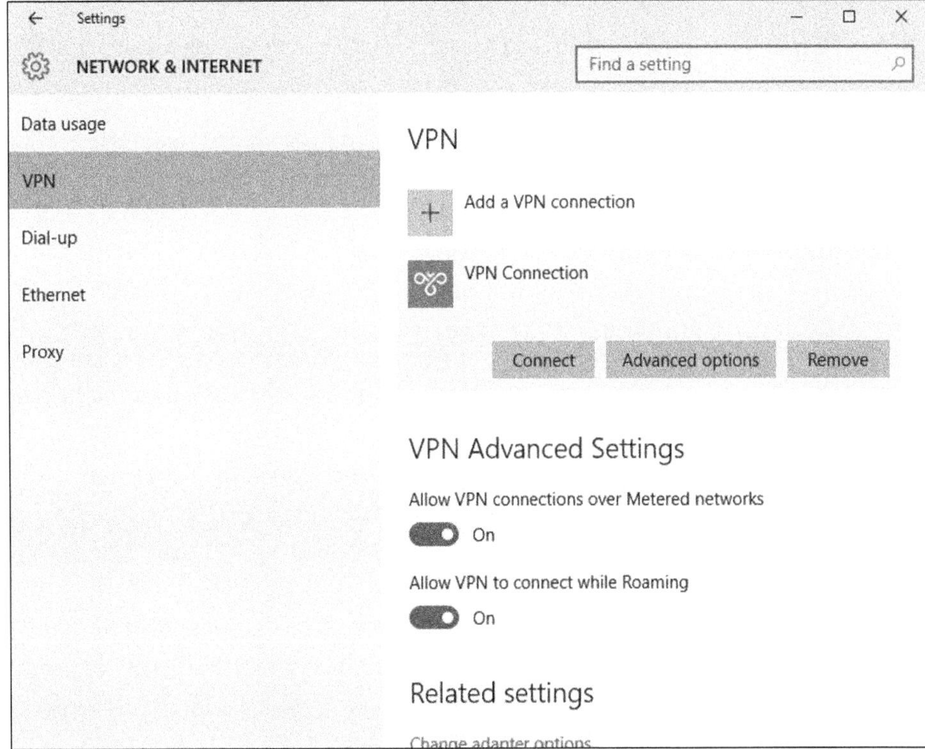

Creating a VPN Connection Using Windows 10 Settings

Windows 10 VPN connections can also be configured by opening the Windows 10 Settings and clicking Network & Internet > VPN. From the VPN page, you can add a VPN connection, connect to a current VPN connection, specify a VPN connection over metered networks, allow a VPN to connect while roaming, and select other advanced options, as shown in Figure 8-6.

Figure 8-6

Managing connections in Windows 10 Settings

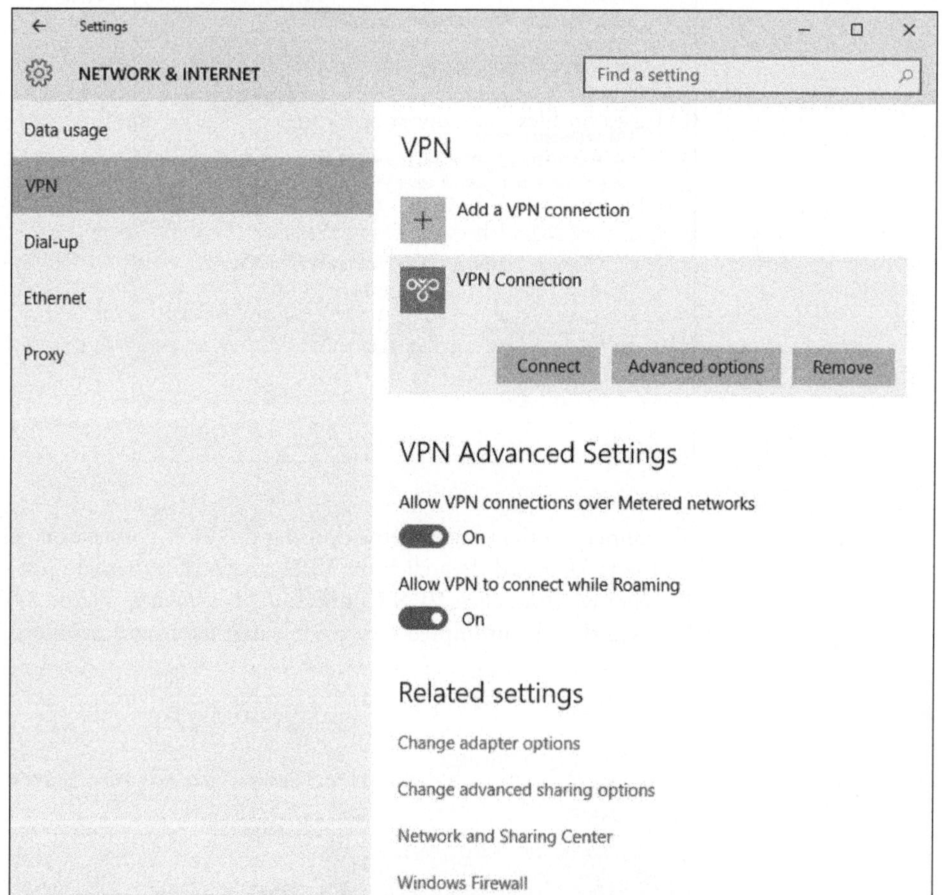

CREATE A VPN CONNECTION USING WINDOWS 10 SETTINGS

GET READY. To create a VPN using the Windows 10 Settings, perform the following steps.

1. On Win10A, log on as **adatum\administrator** with the password of **Pa$$w0rd.**
2. Click **Start** and then click **Settings.**
3. On the Settings page, click **Network & Internet.** Click **VPN.**
4. Click **Add a VPN connection.**
5. On the Add a VPN Connection page, in the VPN provider, select **Windows (built-in).**
6. In the Connection name text box, type **MyVPN2.**
7. In the Server name or address text box, type **vpn.adatum.com.**
8. In the VPN type drop-down menu, select the appropriate VPN protocol, such as **L2TP/IPsec with pre-shared key.**

9. In the Pre-shared key text box, type **Pa$$w0rd**.
10. For the Type of sign-in info option, User name and password is already selected. Click **Save**.

Using Connection Manager (CM) and the Connection Manager Administration Kit (CMAK)

Connection Manager (CM) is a client network connection tool that helps administrators to simplify the management of their remote connections.

CM uses profiles that consist of settings that allow connections from the local computer to a remote network.

The ***Connection Manager Administration Kit (CMAK)*** is used to create and customize the profiles for CM and to distribute them to users. The profile, once completed, contains all the settings necessary for the user to connect, including the IP address of the VPN server.

VPN devices can also come in the form of appliances and routers. For example, the D-Link DIR-655 router we have used previously can be set up to accept incoming VPN connections with the PPTP or L2TP protocols.

SHOW VPN FUNCTIONALITY ON A ROUTER

GET READY. To demonstrate VPN functionality on a router, perform the following steps.

1. Access the D-Link DIR-655 router at the following link: http://support.dlink.com/emulators/dir655/133NA/login.html
2. Log on (no password is required).
3. At the top of the screen, click the **Setup** link.
4. Click the **Manual Internet Connection** setup button.
5. In the Internet Connection Type drop-down menu, select **PPTP (Username /Password)**. This modifies the rest of the details of the page. Note that you can also select **L2TP** from this list.
6. Scroll down to PPTP Internet Connection Type.
7. From here, you need to select either static or dynamic IP. If you have received a static IP address from your ISP, select the **Static IP** radio button and enter the IP information. If you are receiving a dynamic IP from the ISP, select the **Dynamic IP** radio button. This grays out the PPTP IP Address, PPTP Subnet Mask, and PPTP Gateway IP Address fields.

   At this point, you can have the router forward PPTP requests to a server, for example the VPN server set up in the previous exercise. Or, you could simply enter a user name and password.
8. Enter a user name and password. Then, verify the password.
9. Save the configuration. This doesn't really save any information because it is an emulator, but this would work the same way on an actual router. At this point, external users would not be able to connect to your network without a user name, password, and VPN adapter utilizing PPTP.
10. Log off the DIR-655 router.

This is one way for small offices and home offices to create a sort of intranet of their own. By only accepting secure connections from users who know the proper user name and password, you weed out the public Internet users. This, in addition to security devices and zones on the perimeter of your network, can help to keep your data safe.

■ Understanding Security Devices and Zones

THE BOTTOM LINE

Security devices such as firewalls are the main defense for a company's networks, whether they are LANs, WANs, intranets, or extranets. Perimeter security zones such as demilitarized zones help to keep certain information open to specific users or to the public, while keeping the rest of an organization's data secret.

Defining Firewalls and Other Perimeter Security Devices

Firewalls are used to protect a network from malicious attack and unwanted intrusion. It is the most commonly used security device in an organization's perimeter.

CERTIFICATION READY
What is a DMZ and how is it related to the internal network and the Internet?
Objective 1.1

Firewalls are primarily used to protect one network from another. They are often the first line of defense in network security. There are several types of firewalls; some run as software on server computers, some as stand-alone dedicated appliances, and some that work as just one function of many on a single device. They are commonly implemented between the LAN and the Internet, as shown in Figure 8-7.

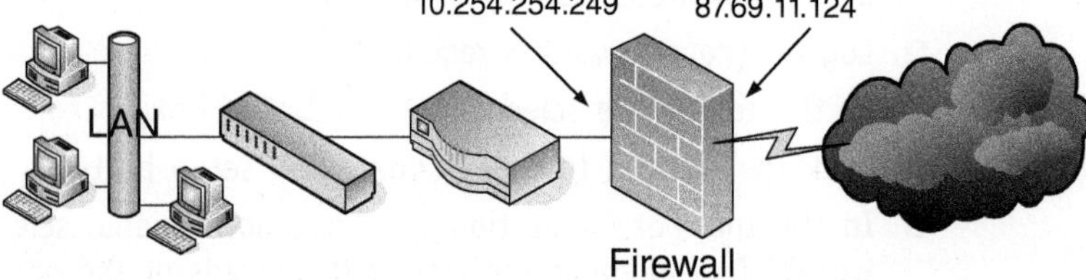

Figure 8-7
Example of a firewall

Generally, there will be one firewall with the network and all devices and computers residing "behind" it. By the way, if a device is "behind" the firewall, it is also considered to be "after" the firewall, and if the device is "in front of" the firewall, it is also known as being "before" the firewall.

Figure 8-7 shows that the firewall has a local address of 10.254.254.249, which connects it to the LAN. It also has an Internet address of 87.69.11.124, which allows connectivity for the entire LAN to the Internet. It also hides the LAN IP addresses. By default, the IP address 87.69.11.124 should be completely shielded. This means that all inbound ports are effectively closed and will not allow incoming traffic, unless a LAN computer initiates a session with another system on the Internet. Regardless, you should check this with third-party applications such as Nmap or with a web-based port scanning utility like ShieldsUP! We will show these in upcoming exercises. If any ports are open, or unshielded, they should be addressed immediately. Then, the firewall should be rescanned for vulnerabilities.

TAKE NOTE*
Scan whatever firewall you are running with Nmap or an online scanner, such as ShieldsUP!

A lot of today's firewalls have two types of firewall technologies built in to them: SPI and NAT. However, there are a couple other types of firewall methodologies that you should be aware of:

- ***Packet filtering*** inspects each packet that passes through the firewall and accepts or rejects it based on a set of rules. There are two types: stateless packet inspection and

stateful packet inspection (SPI). A stateless packet filter, also known as pure packet filtering, does not retain memory of packets that have passed through the firewall. Due to this, a stateless packet filter can be vulnerable to IP spoofing attacks. But a firewall running stateful packet inspection is normally not vulnerable to this because it keeps track of the state of network connections by examining the header in each packet. It is able to distinguish between legitimate and illegitimate packets. This function operates at the Network layer of the OSI model.

- ***NAT filtering,*** also known as NAT endpoint filtering, filters traffic per ports (TCP or UDP). This can be done in three ways: by way of basic endpoint connections, by matching incoming traffic to the corresponding outbound IP address connection, or by matching incoming traffic to the corresponding IP address *and* port.
- ***Application-level gateway (ALG)*** supports address and port translation and checks if the type of application traffic is allowed. For example, your company might allow FTP traffic through the firewall, but may decide to disable Telnet traffic. The ALG checks each type of packet coming in and discards those that are Telnet packets. This adds a layer of security, but the cost is that it is resource intensive.
- ***Circuit-level gateway*** works at the Session layer of the OSI model, when a TCP or UDP connection is established. Once the connection has been made, packets can flow between the hosts without further checking. Circuit-level gateways hide information about the private network, but they do not filter individual packets.

Examples of network firewalls include:

- The D-Link DIR-655 SOHO router/firewall we used previously
- Cisco PIX/ASA firewalls
- Juniper NetScreens
- Microsoft Internet Security and Acceleration Server (ISA) and Forefront

CONFIGURE A SOHO FOUR-PORT FIREWALL

GET READY. To demonstrate a SOHO router, perform the following steps.

1. Access the D-Link DIR-655 router at the following link: http://support.dlink.com/emulators/dir655/133NA/login.html
2. Log on (no password is required).
3. On the main Device Information page, near the top of the window, click the **Advanced** link.
4. On the Advanced page, on the left side, click the **Firewall Settings** link. The Firewall Settings window opens.
5. Take note of the first setting: **Enable SPI**. This is stateful packet inspection. It should be selected by default, but if not, select it, and move on to the next step.
6. View the NAT Endpoint Filtering section directly under the Firewall Settings. Increase the security of UDP Endpoint Filtering by clicking the **Port and Address Restricted** radio button.
7. Next, enable anti-spoofing by selecting the **Enable anti-spoofing checking** check box.
8. Finally, scroll down and view the Application Level Gateway (ALG) Configuration. **PPTP**, **IPSec (VPN)**, **RTSP**, and **SIP** should all be selected.

In the following exercise, you will learn to scan a computer with Nmap. This vulnerability scanner is best known for its port scanning abilities. You will use this tool to scan for open ports on a computer.

SCAN HOSTS WITH NMAP

GET READY. To scan hosts with Nmap, perform the following steps.

1. Download and install the command-line version of the Nmap program. You will also be prompted to install the WinPCap program.
2. Extract the contents to a folder of your choice.
3. Write down the IP address of a Windows host on your network. For this example, you will use a host with the IP address 10.254.254.208.
4. Scan the ports of that host with the -sS parameter, for example `nmap -sS 10.254.254.208`.
5. If there are nonessential ports open, turn off their corresponding unnecessary services, such as FTP or HTTP. This can be done in a variety of places, including Computer Management. If there are no services that you want to turn off, enable one, then rescan the ports with Nmap (to show that the service is running), turn off the service, and move on to the next step.
6. Scan the ports of that host a second time, once again with the -sS parameter. This time, you are verifying that the services are turned off by identifying that the corresponding ports are closed.
7. If possible, scan the ports of a four-port SOHO router/firewall, or a computer with a firewall running. Use the -P0 parameter. For example: `nmap -P0 10.254.254.208`. This might take up to five minutes. It will verify whether the firewall is running properly, by displaying that all of the ports are filtered. The -sS option we used previously will not work on a fully firewalled device because the initial ICMP packets from the ping will not be accepted. -P0 does not use ICMP packets, but it takes longer to complete.

There are several online port scanners available. The following exercise requires an Internet connection in order to access one of them. This exercise will scan the ports of whatever device is facing the Internet. This could be the local computer if it connects directly to the Internet, or a four-port router, or a more advanced firewalling device. This will all depend on your network scenario.

SCAN THE INTERNET CONNECTION WITH SHIELDSUP!

GET READY. To scan the Internet connection with ShieldsUP!, perform the following steps.

1. With a web browser, connect to www.grc.com.
2. Click the **ShieldsUP!!** picture.
3. Scroll down and click the **ShieldsUP!** link.
4. Click the **Proceed** button.
5. Click the **Common Ports** scan. This initiates a scan of the computer or device that is being displayed to the Internet. If you access the Internet through a router/firewall, this will be the device that is scanned. If your computer connects directly to the Internet, the computer will be scanned.
6. Make note of the results. It should show the public IP that was scanned. Then, it will list the ports that were scanned and their status. The desired result for all ports listed is "Stealth," all the way down the line for each of the listed ports. If there are Open or Closed ports, you should check to make sure that the firewall is enabled and operating properly.
7. Try a few other scans, such as **All Service Ports** or **File Sharing**.

A ***proxy server*** acts as an intermediary between the LAN and the Internet. By definition, proxy means "go-between," acting as a mediator between a private and a public network. The proxy server evaluates requests from clients, and if they meet certain criteria, forwards them to the appropriate server. There are several types of proxies, including:

- ***Caching proxy*** attempts to serve client requests without contacting the remote server. Although there are FTP and SMTP proxies, among others, the most common caching proxy is the *HTTP proxy*, also known as a *web proxy*, which caches web pages from servers on the Internet for a set amount of time. This is done to save bandwidth on the company's Internet connection and to increase the speed at which client requests are carried out.
- ***IP proxy*** secures a network by keeping machines behind it anonymous; it does this using NAT. For example, a basic four-port router acts as an IP proxy for the clients on the LAN it protects.

Another example of a proxy in action is Internet content filtering. An ***Internet content filter***, or simply a content filter, is usually applied as software at the Application layer, and can filter out various types of Internet activities, such as websites accessed, email, instant messaging, and so on.

Although firewalls are often the device closest to the Internet, sometimes another device could be in front of the firewall, making it the closest to the Internet—a network intrusion detection system, or the more advanced network intrusion prevention system.

A ***network intrusion detection system (NIDS)*** is a type of IDS that attempts to detect malicious network activities, for example port scans and DoS attacks, by constantly monitoring network traffic. The NIDS then reports any issues that it finds to a network administrator as long as it is configured properly.

A ***network intrusion prevention system (NIPS)*** is designed to inspect traffic and based on the configuration or security policy, it can remove, detain, or redirect malicious traffic in addition to simply detecting it.

Redefining the DMZ

CERTIFICATION READY
How would you define a DMZ?
Objective 1.1

A perimeter network or demilitarized zone (DMZ) is a small network that is set up separately from a company's private local area network and the Internet. It is called a perimeter network because it is usually on the edge of the LAN, but DMZ has become a much more popular term. The DMZ allows users outside of the company LAN to access specific services located on the DMZ. However, when set up properly, those users are blocked from gaining access to the company LAN. Users on the LAN often connect to the DMZ as well, but without having to worry about outside attackers gaining access to their private LAN. The DMZ might house a switch with servers connected to it that offer web, email, and other services. Two common configurations of a DMZ include:

- ***Back-to-back configuration:*** This configuration has a DMZ situated in between two firewall devices, which could be black box appliances or Microsoft Internet Security and Acceleration (ISA) Servers.
- ***3-leg perimeter configuration:*** In this scenario, the DMZ is usually attached to a separate connection of the company firewall. So, the firewall would have three connections: one to the company LAN, one to the DMZ, and one to the Internet.

In the following exercise, you will learn how to enable the DMZ function of a typical four-port SOHO router.

SET UP A DMZ ON A SOHO ROUTER

GET READY. To enable the DMZ function of a typical four-port SOHO router, perform the following steps.

1. Access the D-Link DIR-655 router at the following link: http://support.dlink.com/emulators/dir655/133NA/login.html
2. Log on (no password is required).
3. At the top of the screen, click the **Advanced** link.
4. On the right side, click the **Firewall Settings** link.
5. Scroll down to the **DMZ Host** section.
6. Check the **Enable DMZ** option.
7. Type the IP address of the host that will be connected to the DMZ. At this point, you would also physically connect that host to a port on the router. Or you could connect an entire Layer 3 switch to the port, and enter that switch's IP address in this field. This would allow you to connect multiple hosts to the switch while only using one port on the router.

■ Putting It All Together

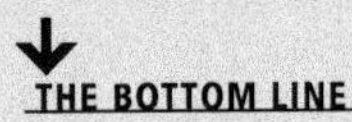

Building the entire network for an organization could take months or even years! The concepts covered in these lessons only scrape the surface of a gigantic networking world. However, what we covered up until now is still a lot of information. Let's try to complete the Proseware, Inc., scenario by combining the various technologies we learned about into one efficient, well-oiled network.

In this scenario, Proseware, Inc., desires just about every component and technology for their network. Let's list what they require and follow it up with some network documentation that will act as the starting point for our network plan. Here are the basic components that Proseware, Inc., requires for its network:

- A client/server local area network with the following:
  - Three hundred client computers some of which are laptops and tablet PCs
  - One master switch and four other secondary switches (one per department) set up in a hierarchical star fashion
- Five LAN Windows servers connected directly to master switch:
  - Two domain controllers
  - One DNS server
  - One DHCP server
  - One RRAS server
- Wired and wireless considerations:
  - Category 6 twisted-pair cable for the client desktop PCs
  - Wireless 802.11n connections for laptops and tablet PCs
  - 1000BASE-SX fiber-optic connections for the servers and switches
  - 10GBASE-SR fiber-optic connection for the master switch

- 3-leg perimeter DMZ with the following equipment and zones:
  - Switch with 1000BASE-SX fiber-optic connection
- Three DMZ Windows servers:
  - Web server
  - FTP server
  - Email server
- Intranet for remote users with authentication server
- Extranet for connection to partner company utilizing same authentication server as the intranet

Figure 8-8 shows an example of how this network documentation might start out.

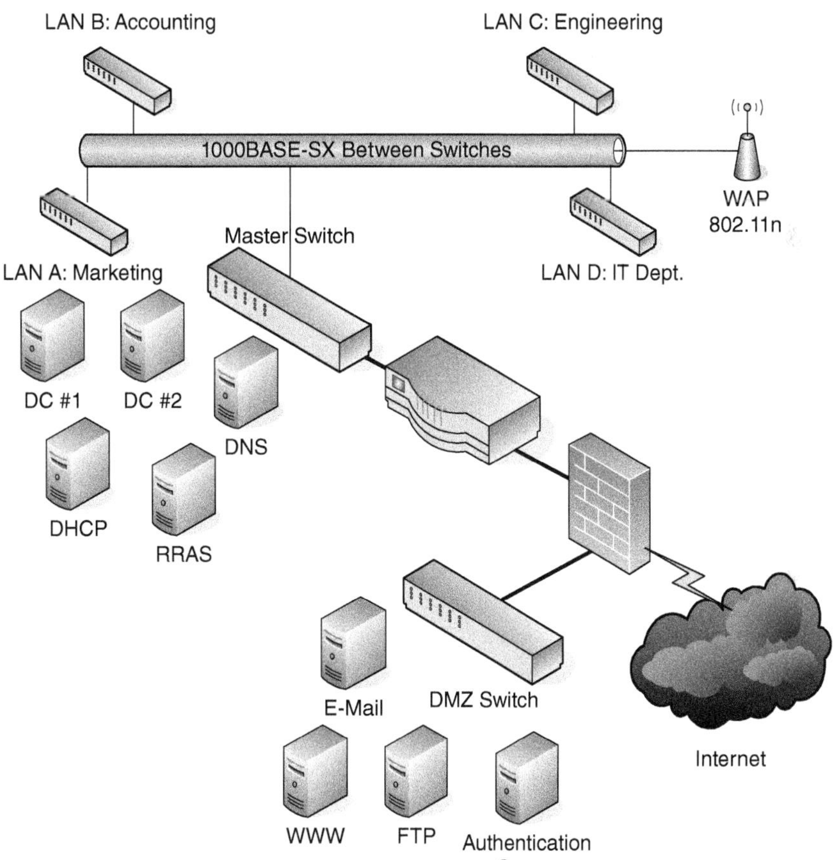

Figure 8-8
Network documentation

Take some time to think about exactly what would be entailed when installing this network. For example, determine which type of network adapters the LAN servers would require in order to take advantage of the 10-Gbps fiber connection that the master switch provides. Determine which type of firewall should be used in order to facilitate all the different connections necessary, such as intranet, extranet, LAN connectivity to the Internet, and so on.

This type of network documentation is just a starting point, of course. More documentation will be necessary to define how and where cables will be installed, to determine an IP addressing scheme and list of static IP addresses, and much more. However, this type of planning forms the basis for all the configurations and planning to come.

SKILL SUMMARY

IN THIS LESSON, YOU LEARNED:

- There are four types of VPN tunneling protocols that are available in Windows 10. They include Point-to-Point Tunneling Protocol (PPTP), Layer 2 Tunneling Protocol over IPsec (L2TP/IPsec), Secure Socket Tunneling Protocol (SSTP), and VPN Reconnect (or IKEv2).
- During a VPN connection, the user should be authenticated to prove who is logging on. Therefore, you need to choose the most secure form of authentication that can be deployed to your remote users.
- Security devices such as firewalls are the main defense for a company's networks, whether they are LANs, WANs, intranets, or extranets.
- Perimeter security zones such as demilitarized zones help to keep certain information open to specific users or to the public, while keeping the rest of an organization's data secure.
- A proxy server acts as an intermediary between the LAN and the Internet. By definition, proxy means "go-between," acting as a mediator between a private and a public network.
- A perimeter network or demilitarized zone (DMZ) is a small network that is set up separately from a company's private local area network and the Internet. It is called a perimeter network because it is usually on the edge of the LAN.

■ Knowledge Assessment

Multiple Choice

Select the correct answer for each of the following questions.

1. An authentication server is being set up on a DMZ that will allow only users from a partner company. Which type of network is being configured?
   a. Internet
   b. Intranet
   c. Extranet
   d. World Wide Web
2. When setting up a VPN that allows connections on inbound port 1723, which of the following tunneling protocols should be used?
   a. PPTP
   b. PPP
   c. L2TP
   d. TCP/IP
3. Proseware, Inc., wants to set up a VPN server. Which of the following services in Windows Server 2016 should be used?
   a. FTP
   b. DNS
   c. RRAS
   d. IIS

4. The IT director wants to install a firewall. Which of the following is *not* a type of firewall?
   a. NAT filtering
   b. DMZ
   c. ALG
   d. Stateful packet inspection
5. An issue with one of the ports on the firewall is suspected. Which of the following is the appropriate tool to use to scan the ports?
   a. PPTP
   b. Protocol analyzer
   c. NMAP
   d. NIDS
6. A client wants a server installed that can cache web pages in order to increase the speed of commonly accessed websites. Which type of server is required?
   a. Proxy
   b. DNS
   c. Firewall
   d. VPN
7. A customer desires a device that can detect network anomalies and report them to an administrator. Which type of device is necessary?
   a. Internet content filter
   b. Proxy server
   c. WINS server
   d. NIDS
8. A manager wants to set up an area that is not on the LAN but not quite on the Internet. This area will house servers that will serve requests to users connecting to the intranet. Which type of network area or zone should be set up?
   a. DMZ
   b. Extranet
   c. FTP
   d. VPN
9. A client wants to install a VPN server that can offer unencrypted tunnels by default or encrypted tunnels by using IPsec. Which of the following services should be used?
   a. DNS
   b. L2TP
   c. WINS
   d. IPsec
10. After setting up a default VPN in Windows Server 2016, the supervisor is not satisfied with the level of security. She would rather have L2TP combined with IPsec. Which tunneling protocol is used with the default VPN settings and is less secure than L2TP with IPsec?
   a. RRAS
   b. L2TP without IPsec
   c. PPTP
   d. VPNv2

11. To use VPN Reconnect, which VPN protocol should be used?
    a. PPTP
    b. L2TP
    c. IKEv2
    d. SSTP

12. A client wants to use a Windows Server 2016 server as a VPN server. However, the networking team allows only HTTPS through the firewall. Which VPN protocol should be used?
    a. PPTP
    b. L2TP
    c. IKEv2
    d. SSTP

13. A client wants to use smart cards with the VPN. Which authentication protocol should be used?
    a. PAP
    b. CHAP
    c. MS-CHAPv2
    d. EAP

14. Which authentication protocol should *not* be used because it is the least secure?
    a. PAP
    b. CHAP
    c. MS-CHAPv2
    d. EAP

15. Which of the following describes the easiest way to set up a VPN client on a computer for a user who is not technically savvy?
    a. Using a PAP
    b. Providing the user with step-by-step instructions and screen shots
    c. Using a group policy to configure the settings
    d. Using CMAK to create an executable to install

Fill in the Blank

Fill in the correct answer in the blank space provided.

1. _____ allows users to interact with each other and contribute to websites.
2. The _____ defines DNS.
3. The _____ is an enormous system of interlinked hypertext documents.
4. A network zone that allows remote access for employees of a company is set up. This is known as an _____.
5. A VPN server that uses inbound port 1701 is installed. The server is utilizing the _____ protocol.
6. A VPN server is installed and a VPN adapter is configured on a client computer. However, the connection cannot be completed from the client to the server. This is because the _____ step was skipped.
7. The VPN server has been configured and is running properly. However, it has not been configured to hand out IP addresses to clients. When a VPN server is configured this way, the clients will obtain their IP addresses from a _____ server.

8. A firewall will normally have a private and a _____ IP address.
9. A firewall that accepts or rejects packets based on a set of rules is installed. This firewall keeps track of the state of the network connection. It is running a type of packet filtering known as _____.
10. As an administrator for a company, you have configured a firewall so that all ports are closed. Now you are attempting to scan a firewall's ports to verify that there are no open ones. You should use the _____ parameter within the Nmap port scanning program.

■ Business Case Scenarios

Scenario 8-1: Setting Up a DMZ

A client wants you to set up a DMZ with two servers. Each server will service a different set of users:

1. Server #1 is to service employees who work from home.
2. Server #2 is to service two partner companies.

Which two types of network zones will enable this functionality?

Scenario 8-2: Selecting the Appropriate Solution

The ABC Company wants you to install a solution that will allow the company to do the following:

1. Enable remote client computers to connect via tunneling.
2. Allow for a high level of security during remote connections.

Which solution and protocol will enable this functionality?

Scenario 8-3: Setting Up a PPTP Server

Proseware, Inc., requires that you set up a PPTP server on a D-Link DIR-655 router. Details for the IP configuration are as follows:

- **IP address:** 10.254.254.50 (Static)
- **Subnet mask:** 255.255.255.0
- **Gateway address:** 10.254.254.1
- **PPTP server IP address:** 10.254.254.199
- **User name:** administrator
- **Password:** 123PPTPABC##

Access the DIR-655 emulator at the following link and configure the DHCP server appropriately: http://support.dlink.com/emulators/dir655/133NA/login.html.

Capture a screen shot showing your solution.

Scenario 8-4: Creating a WAN with VPN

In this case scenario, you will connect two separate networks together over a simulated WAN and then implement a VPN between the two (see Table 8-1). Normally, a client on one IP

Table 8-1
IP Chart

City	LAN Networks	WAN IP (2ND NIC)
New York City	192.168.1.0	152.69.101.50
London	192.168.2.0	152.69.101.51

network cannot connect to or ping a client on a different IP network. The goal is to have the clients on both networks pinging each other through a routed connection. Each city is considered its own separate LAN. New York City and London will connect to make this WAN. You will need the following at your disposal:

- Two Windows Server 2016 computers with two network adapters (systems with two network connections are known as multihomed machines or computers)
- A minimum of two client computers
- A crossover cable

You will need to change the IP addresses on all machines.

Servers should be set up as IP host address x.x.x.1.

Client IP addresses should ascend from there. Make sure to also set the gateway address to the server's LAN IP address.

When all IP addresses are configured, make sure that all clients can ping the server on the LAN.

TAKE NOTE*

Remember that when you make a crossover cable, be sure to use the 568A wiring standard on one end, and the 568B standard on the other. Wiring was covered in Lesson 3.

1. Try to ping any host in the other city. You should not be able to. The results should say Destination Host Unreachable or Request Timed Out. You should, however, be able to ping all hosts, including the server, in your city.
2. Verify that your servers have the second NIC set up and functioning with the proper IP address. Label it WAN card.
3. Connect your crossover cable from the WAN card on the NYC server to the WAN card on the London server.

Now create the internetwork, and then set up the VPN connection from one city to the other so that clients in one city (your choice) can log on to the VPN server in the other city.

Workplace Ready

Examine Various Levels of Firewalls

Firewalls are extremely important in network security. Every network needs to have one or more of these in order to have any semblance of security.

Even if your network has a firewall, individual client computers should be protected by a software-based firewall as well. Most versions of Windows come with a built-in firewall program. Some versions, such as Windows 10, also include the Windows Firewall with Advanced Security. You can access this by going to Start > Control Panel > System and Security > Windows Firewall. Then, click the Advanced settings link. From here, you can implement custom inbound and outbound rules and monitor the firewall as well. Check it out!

When you are finished, access the Internet and research firewalls from the following companies:

- Check Point
- Cisco
- D-Link
- Linksys
- Microsoft (ISA)

Describe the pros and cons of each of these vendors' solutions. From your analysis, define which solution would be best for the following scenarios:

- Home office with 4 computers
- Small office with 25 computers
- Midsized company with 180 computers
- Enterprise-level company with 1,000 computers

In your argument, prove your point by showing devices that can support the appropriate number of users.

Appendix A
Networking Fundamentals: Exam 98-366

Exam Objective	Skill Number	Lesson Number
Understanding Network Infrastructures		
Understand the concepts of Internet, intranet, and extranet	1.1	8
Understand local area networks (LANs)	1.2	1, 3, 4
Understand wide area networks (WANs)	1.3	6, 7
Understand wireless networking	1.4	3
Understand network topologies and access methods	1.5	1
Understand Network Hardware		
Understand switches	2.1	1, 2
Understand routers	2.2	5, 7
Understand media types	2.3	3
Understand Protocols and Services		
Understand the Open Systems Interconnection (OSI) model	3.1	2
Understand IPv4	3.2	4
Understand IPv6	3.3	4
Understand names resolution	3.4	6
Understand networking services	3.5	6
Understand TCP/IP	3.5	5

Index

L

M

N